AMERICAN MADE

WHO KILLED BARRY SEAL? PABLO ESCOBAR OR GEORGE HW BUSH

WAR ON DRUGS BOOK 2

SHAUN ATTWOOD

First published in Great Britain by Gadfly Press (Shaun Attwood) in 2016

This book is a work of non-fiction based on research by the author

A catalogue record of this book is available from the British Library

ISBN: 9780993021534

Typeset and cover design by Jane Dixon-Smith

Cover art by Jeremy Arviso

For Selina

MY SOCIAL-MEDIA LINKS

Email: attwood.shaun@hotmail.co.uk
Blog: Jon's Jail Journal
Website: shaunattwood.com
Twitter: @shaunattwood
YouTube: Shaun Attwood
LinkedIn: Shaun Attwood
Goodreads: Shaun Attwood
Facebook pages: Shaun Attwood, Jon's Jail Journal, T-Bone Appreciation Society

I welcome feedback on any of my books.
Thank you for the Amazon reviews!

ACKNOWLEDGEMENTS

A big thank you to Barbara Attwood, Derick Attwood, Penny Kimber, Emma Bagnell, Jane Dixon-Smith

GET A FREE BOOK

Sign Up For My Newsletter At:

http://shaunattwood.com/newsletter-subscribe/

MY BOOKS

English Shaun Trilogy

Party Time
Hard Time
Prison Time

War on Drugs Trilogy

Pablo Escobar: Beyond Narcos
American Made: Who Killed Barry Seal? Pablo Escobar or George HW Bush
We Are Being Lied To: The War on Drugs (Expected 2017)

Life Lessons

Making a Murderer: The Framing of Avery and Dassey by Kratz and Other Parasites (Expected 2017)

Two Tonys (Expected 2017)
T-Bone (Expected 2020)

CONTENTS

PART 1

THE VICTIM BARRY SEAL

CHAPTER 1

Official Story of Barry's Death

While Barry Seal packed his briefcase at his home in Baton Rouge, three Colombian hitmen in a hotel room prepared to kill him.

"Debbie, I'm leaving," Barry said, stood in the living room under a grand chandelier, gazing upstairs for his wife.

With brown permed hair, Debbie appeared in a white floral top and blue pants. "OK. I'll meet you for breakfast if you want," she said, resting a hand on the banister, the other holding a hair brush.

"Right after my jog?"

"You started jogging!"

Barry smiled. "Every morning around my new home," he said, referring to the Salvation Army halfway house a judge had ordered him to stay at from 6 pm every night. "If I can't be rich, I might as well still be pretty," Barry said in a slow and pleasant Louisiana accent.

Resting her elbows on the banister, Debbie beamed. "Well, you're pretty to me, rich or poor."

"Whoo-whee!" Barry yelped, shimmying his hips and shoulders. "I'm way past poor, baby doll!" As he checked his watch, his smile evaporated. "Oh, I've got to go. It's quarter to six."

"I love you," Debbie said.

"I love you, too, Mrs Seal."

As her hefty husband with chunky sideburns walked out, Debbie yelled, "Be careful!"

In a hotel room, the Colombians disguised a machine gun by wrapping clothes around it. Walking briskly in light-coloured suits and clothes, they went downstairs and got in a car. The sun had almost disappeared from the skyline as they drove towards the Salvation Army halfway house.

Cruising along the streets of Baton Rouge in a white Cadillac, Barry was looking forward to the end of his six-month sentence at the halfway house. He'd been told that the Medellín Cartel – run by powerful Colombian drug lords, including Pablo Escobar – had put a $500,000 bounty on his head after his status as an informant had been leaked to the press by the Reagan-Bush administration.

It was dark when Barry arrived at the halfway house. He reversed his car towards a two-storey beige building. He was about to get out when a shadowy figure took him by surprise. Barry squinted at the man next to his Cadillac: a thin Colombian with a moustache and a hostile gaze. The man jumped forward and aimed a gun at Barry.

News Anchor Peter Jennings reported, "He used to smuggle drugs and he got caught and he became one of the government's most valuable informants in the war against cocaine. But last night in Louisiana, Barry Seal's enemies caught up with him and killed him. Tonight, three men are in custody. NBC's Brian Ross reports that Seal was about to testify for the government once again."

"Authorities believe that last night's machine-gun killing," Brian Ross said, "of top drug informant Barry Seal was ordered by drug bosses in Medellín, Colombia, who sent five men to Baton Rouge to kill Seal. Seal's son Barry Jr, one of five children, was restrained by police, who said the gunmen had waited in ambush for Seal at a Salvation Army shelter, where Seal had been sentenced by a federal judge on a drug charge to do community service. Seal was a tough-guy TWA pilot, who got caught smuggling cocaine and became one of the most important and daring undercover operatives, infiltrating the top Colombian drug operations. In a recent interview, Seal said he knew he was risking his life."

A clip of Barry's face was shown in a cockpit wearing sunglasses. "The old saying:" Barry said, "'If you can't stand the heat, don't work in the kitchen.' I can take the pressure."

"It was Seal who posed as a smuggler," Brian Ross said, "and flew into Nicaragua and took these pictures showing Colombian drug dealers and Sandinista officials loading cocaine on his plane."

The Reagan-Bush administration had claimed that Pablo Escobar was on one of the grainy pictures.

"Seal busted up the Colombian connection in the Caribbean country of Turks and Caicos, setting up a payoff meeting on videotape that led to the arrest and conviction of the country's prime minister. And Seal was scheduled to be the key witness against this man, Jorge Ochoa, the top Colombian drug boss now in jail in Spain, about to be extradited to the United States. Authorities say the Ochoa drug organisation was responsible for the bombing of the US embassy in Bogotá last year, the assassination of Colombia's attorney general and now the murder in Louisiana of the man who was perhaps the most important undercover drug informant ever."

The rest of the media followed suit by reporting that Barry had been a government witness against drug traffickers, including Jorge Ochoa and Pablo Escobar of the Medellín Cartel, who had sanctioned the hit. Having refused to go into the Federal Witness Protection Program, Barry had been ambushed outside a Louisiana halfway house and died in a hail of bullets. The media later reported that a three-man Colombian hit team had been caught, convicted and sentenced to life without parole. Case closed.

As I researched Barry's life for my War On Drugs trilogy, the official story fell apart. Barry was deeply involved with powerful people who specialised in assassinations and trafficked drugs and weapons on an international scale. The information that he'd amassed working for them as a pilot had rendered him a liability. He died with George HW Bush's telephone number in his possession. To understand why Barry was killed, it's necessary to examine his life beyond its portrayal in Hollywood and the relationships he forged while working for the CIA.

CHAPTER 2

A Young Pilot

Born on July 16, 1939, Barry became obsessed with flying at a young age. He'd bicycle over to a private airport near his one-storey home in Baton Rouge and gaze at the comings and goings of the small planes. By age fifteen, he was flying and making money from towing advertising banners. His earnings from his paper round went towards flying lessons, which cost $14 each.

His mother, Mary Lou, was a housewife. His alcoholic father, BC, was a candy wholesaler and a member of the Ku Klux Klan, a hate group whose members donned white hoods and robes and danced around burning crosses. They despised blacks, but also reserved plenty of hatred for Jews, immigrants, gays and lesbians. Across the US, some of their members were responsible for atrocities such as hanging people and bombing and setting fire to black churches.

Barry was the oldest of three children. The boys enjoyed playing ball and tinkering with old cars. When Barry's mother asked his flight instructor, Eddie Dufford, to not give him lessons, Eddie said, "Ma'am, that boy of yours is gonna find a way to learn to fly, no matter what. Somebody's got to be the one to teach him." Trusting Eddie, she relented.

While his schoolmates took lengthy bus rides to out-of-state football matches, Barry flew there. At one high-school game, he landed a helicopter on the field. He even took girls on dates in the sky.

While his skills as a pilot were apparent, so was a risk-taking nature that would land him in trouble. Barry took some friends up in a small plane, which he stalled on purpose just to give them a fright. The prank backfired when the plane refused to start. As the aircraft lost its propulsive power, Barry mustered all of his concentration in an attempt to land in a field. The descending plane sheared treetops and crash-landed. A passenger broke his arm. Barry broke his ankle, creating an injury that would trouble him throughout his life. While the owner of the plane appreciated the skills that Barry had demonstrated by managing to land, he banned Barry from his plane.

In 1955, Barry joined the Baton Rouge Civil Air Patrol. On a joint training exercise with the New Orleans unit, Barry met another trainee called Lee Harvey Oswald – who, eight years later, would be set up to take the fall for the assassination of President John F Kennedy. Oswald had joined the Civil Air Patrol in the mid-1950s, according to the few surviving records of the squadron – most of the records were stolen in late 1960. Oswald spoke Spanish and Russian and came across as intelligent.

David Ferrie was in charge of the New Orleans Civil Air Patrol. He was alleged by the New Orleans District Attorney Jim Garrison to have been involved in the conspiracy to assassinate JFK. Ferrie suffered from alopecia areata, a skin condition that rendered him increasingly hairless as he aged. With a reddish home-made wig and pasted-on eyebrows, he was a sight to behold. Watching Ferrie bark orders, Barry admired his discipline.

Formerly a priest who was unable to control his proclivities towards boys, Ferrie had been defrocked. He'd obtained a pilot's licence and taught aeronautics at Cleveland's Benedictine High School, but was fired for several infractions, including taking boys to a house of prostitution. In 1951, he moved to New Orleans and worked as a pilot for Eastern Air Lines, until losing his job in August 1961 after being arrested twice on morals charges.

Ferrie had been involved with the Civil Air Patrol since 1947. To get air cadets, he procured kids from troubled homes, some of whom he gave unauthorised physicals. He steered cadets such as Barry Seal and Lee Harvey Oswald into clandestine services. As well as being an ace pilot, Ferrie was a medical researcher, a linguist who spoke Italian, an armchair psychologist, a hypnotist and a CIA pilot and arms trafficker. Originally supportive of Fidel Castro in Cuba, Ferrie turned against him after Castro announced he'd become a Marxist. His flying missions to Cuba included bombing and sabotage raids, as well as extracting anti-Castro resistance fighters.

David Ferrie and Barry Seal had a few things in common, including photographic memories and flying for the CIA. Barry also had the ability to read upside down. When unwanted attention focused on Barry and Ferrie, they were labelled CIA contract pilots to give the impression that they were rogue agents operating on their own. After becoming liabilities to the interests they were serving, they were disposed of.

Ferrie and Oswald died after the media turned on them for their roles in the JFK assassination – Chapter 5's examination of which offers clues about Barry's killers.

Under Ferrie's tutelage, by 1958, teenage Barry was transporting weapons to Fidel Castro before Ferrie turned against Castro. Barry was provided a P-51 Mustang: an American long-range single-seat fighter and fighter-bomber used during World War II. With US weapons manufacturers profiting from both sides in the Cuban Civil War, Barry also flew munitions to the forces opposed to Castro.

Barry was establishing relationships with the military and intelligence services and getting a taste of the international arms trafficking that would lead to his demise. Consequences were far from his mind. As the cash from arms trafficking rolled in, Barry bought three planes: a Champ, an Arcana Chief and a Comanche.

CHAPTER 3

CIA

For decades, Barry worked for the CIA, right up to the time of his death. Examining the nature of his employer offers clues about his killers.

Established in 1947, the CIA specialised in propaganda, economic warfare, regime changes, assassinations and, in later years, trafficking weapons and drugs, which Barry assisted. By the early 1950s, the CIA controlled over twenty-five newspapers and wire agencies, and had over 3,000 employees engaged in propaganda. Journalists promoting their views included members of the *New York Times, Time Magazine, Newsweek, The Washington* Post and CBS television.

On Twitter, the CIA describes itself: "We are the Nation's first line of defense. We accomplish what others cannot accomplish and go where others cannot go." The CIA has definitely delivered on its latter claim over the years.

In 1954, the CIA was unhappy with President Arbenz of Guatemala, who had taken 240,000 acres of land from a company called United Fruit, which had the former CIA director, Allen Dulles, on its board of directors. The land was distributed to 100,000 peasants. The CIA armed right-wing army officers, but the uprising failed, so the CIA sent thirty airplanes that dropped leaflets and bombs and fired machine guns. This time, the uprising succeeded, and the CIA director, Walter Bedell, was rewarded by joining the board of United Fruit. The US gave the new government almost $1 billion in aid, but by 1957, the CIA was plotting regime change. In July, the president was shot and killed at his dinner table in the presidential palace. Violence in

Guatemala continued for forty years, with approximately 150,000 deaths.

In 1955, the CIA managed to get a bomb on-board a plane that was supposed to transport Chou Enlai, the Chinese Communist leader, who was scheduled to fly from Hong Kong to Indonesia. But Chou changed his mind at the last minute, avoiding a flight that blew up over the South China Sea, killing everyone on board.

Obtaining power through political manoeuvring, torture and murder, Rafael Trujillo had become the president of the Dominican Republic in 1930. He was an ally of the US until about 1960, when US foreign policy makers turned against him. In 1961, he was gunned down by assassins armed and trained by the CIA.

Despite employing their most creative methods, the CIA failed to assassinate Cuba's Fidel Castro numerous times over a period of twenty-five years. On February 2, 1959, an American contract killer, Allan Robert Nye, was arrested with a high-powered rifle in a Cuban hotel opposite the presidential palace. Undeterred, a CIA officer hosted a meeting a month later between American mobsters and a former Cuban death squad leader opposed to Castro. They discussed killing Castro outside the presidential palace.

The CIA drew up various plans to drug Castro. They wanted to saturate the radio studio where he broadcast his speeches with LSD delivered by aerosol. They put psychoactive drugs and lethal poisons in Castro's favourite types of cigars.

When Castro was scheduled to appear at the United Nations in New York in 1960, the CIA planned to put poisonous thallium salts in his shoes and on his night table to cause him paralysis or death.

In 1960, the CIA paid $150,000 to a mobster, Johnny Rosselli, to arrange the death of Castro. Rosselli consulted two Mafia dons: Sam Giancana and Santos Trafficante. The CIA had requested a dramatic mafia-style machine-gunning of Castro, but Giancana proposed putting poison pills in Castro's food or drink. A CIA lab produced six deadly botulinum pills that were transported inside a hollow pencil. Just to be on the safe side, the CIA also provided a box of cigars soaked in botulinum toxin that were so deadly that even touching them was fatal. Trafficante gave the pills and cigars to a Castro insider who owed the Mafia a gambling debt, but the insider chickened out. Another batch of botulinum pills ended up at a restaurant favoured by Castro, which he fortuitously ceased to visit before the pills arrived.

With Castro dodging various assassination methods, strengthening ties with Russia and committing the ultimate evil of expropriating land from the United Fruit Company, something more concrete was required. Barry and Ferrie would both play their parts as pilots.

In March 1960, President Eisenhower allocated $13.1 million to the CIA to overthrow Castro. President Kennedy had been in office for only twelve weeks when the invasion was due to happen. Members of the CIA with inside information bought shares in sugar companies, causing prices to surge. US Mafia figures were on standby to retake control of the casinos. United Fruit Company was ready to pounce on the banana plantations.

Using Guatemala as a springboard, over 1,400 paramilitaries assembled, divided into five infantry battalions and one paratrooper battalion, before setting out for Cuba by boat on April 13, 1961.

Two days later on April 15, eight CIA-supplied B-26 bombers attacked Cuban airfields. On the night of April 16, the main invasion landed at a beach named Playa Girón in the Bay of Pigs, where it overwhelmed a local militia.

The Cuban Army launched a counter-offensive with 25,000 soldiers. On a weapons delivery mission, David Ferrie ended up trapped. Legend has it that he managed to get his plane off the ground with one hand while using the other to fend off a soldier who had stabbed him in the belly – where Ferrie did have a huge scar. As a pilot, Barry didn't encounter any life and death situations in Cuba.

With the exile force stuck on the beachhead, things deteriorated rapidly. The CIA was banking on JFK following through with a full-scale invasion, but he wouldn't budge. On April 20, over 1,000 invaders surrendered. Just over a hundred had been killed. The majority of the captives were publicly interrogated and put into Cuban prisons.

President JFK described the Bay of Pigs as the worst experience of his life. Previously, Kennedy had said, "First, I want to say that there will not be, under any conditions, intervention in Cuba by United States armed forces. This government will do everything it possibly can, and I think it can meet its responsibilities to make sure that there are no Americans involved in any actions." Now he had no choice but to take responsibility for an unprovoked invasion of a sovereign nation that had failed. It was a violation of several treaties and US law. Having made overtures about world peace, this was a major embarrassment.

Kennedy decided to shatter the CIA into a thousand pieces. He started by firing the CIA leadership. He closed down camps in the US where Cuban exiles were trained by the likes of David Ferrie and where Lee Harvey Oswald hung out.

In June 1963, JFK pushed his luck too far by ordering the issuance of $4.2 billion in United States Notes as opposed to the usual Federal Reserve Notes. It was interest- and debt-free currency backed by silver reserves in the US Treasury. This challenged the Federal Reserve System owned by private banks, which printed money and profited from loaning it to the government. When the government needed more money, the banks in the Federal Reserve System used paper and ink that cost a few thousand dollars to print billions of dollars. They charged the billions to the government. The only other president to print interest- and debt-free currency was Lincoln. After issuing Greenbacks, Lincoln was shot in the head in public.

Associates of Barry, such as Ferrie, were calling for JFK to be shot. It wouldn't take long.

A CIA plot hatched against Castro in 1963 involved giving

him a gift of scuba diving gear lined with a deadly combination of Madura fungus and implanted tubercle bacilli. Attractive deep-sea clams in an area where Castro dived were to be rigged with high explosives. In November 1963, a ballpoint pen was produced that doubled as a syringe filled with lethal Blackleaf-40, an insecticide that was forty percent nicotine sulphate. As usual, none of these methods worked.

The CIA had more success hunting down another South American revolutionary: Che Guevara. The plot involved the Nazi war criminal Klaus Barbie and Felix Rodriguez – a friend of George HW Bush – from whom Barry Seal sometimes took orders at the CIA. Klaus Barbie's story is in the third instalment of this trilogy: *We Are Being Lied To: The War On Drugs.*

In many of the countries America invaded, drug production surged. The CIA formed alliances with opium lords in Burma, Thailand and Laos, which caused an alarming rate of addiction of US troops during the Vietnam War. A CIA front company, Air America, flew opium out of the mountains of Laos. According to the ex-CIA pilot Tosh Plumlee, Barry was with Air America in 1967-68 in South Vietnam and Laos, performing Search and Destroy and Special Ops. Plumlee saw Barry's name on cables going back to 1964.

Numerous South American countries received US weapons on CIA flights. The aircraft were packed with drugs for the return journey – documented by the journalist Gary Webb in his "Dark Alliance" series, and ex-DEA Agent Celerino Castillo in *Powderburns: Cocaine, Contras and the Drug War:* "The connections piled up quickly. Contra [Nicaraguan rebel group] planes flew north to the US, loaded with cocaine, then returned laden with cash. All under the protective umbrella of the United States Government. My informants were perfectly placed: one worked with the Contra pilots at their base, while another moved easily among the Salvadoran military officials who protected the resupply operation. They fed me the names of Contra pilots. Again and again, those names showed up in the DEA database as documented drug traffickers. When I pursued the case, my superiors quietly and firmly advised me to move on to other investigations."

Senator John F Kerry was put in charge of a committee to investigate the drugs for weapons business. His Senate Committee Report on Drugs, Law Enforcement and Foreign Policy found:

Involvement in narcotics trafficking by individuals associated with the Contra movement.

Participation of narcotics traffickers in Contra supply operations through business relationships with Contra organizations.

Provision of assistance to the Contras by narcotics traffickers, including cash, weapons, planes, pilots, air supply services and other materials, on a voluntary basis by the traffickers.

Payments to drug traffickers by the US State Department of funds authorized by the Congress for humanitarian assistance to the Contras, in some cases after the traffickers had been indicted by federal law enforcement agencies on drug charges, in others while traffickers were under active investigation by these same agencies.

Non-traceable drug cash was ideal to finance activity that was covert and illegal, such as assassination programs. It was used to bribe politicians and to pay mercenaries and death squads. For over forty years, the US government has pretended to fight a War on Drugs, while watching the flow of drugs increase into America by design. Gary Webb's research exposed how the CIA protected certain traffickers, while using drug laws to wipe out the competition with a goal of increasing the US's influence over South America.

The CIA's rise to power gave birth to the military-industrial complex – a network of individuals and institutions involved in the production of weapons and military technologies, who lobby for the lion's share of taxpayers' money.

From 1965 to 1972, the CIA ran the Phoenix Program, a

counterterrorism operation in rural South Vietnam. Between 1967 and 1971, participants in the program killed 20,587 Vietnamese National Liberation Front activists, according to CIA Director William Colby. The South Vietnamese claimed that the number was 41,000.

An intelligence officer in the Phoenix Program, Barton Osborn, stated, "Quite often it was a matter of expediency just to eliminate a person in the field rather than deal with the paperwork." On top of the murders, 29,000 suspects were interrogated. Survivors testifying before Congress in 1972 described parts of their bodies getting cut off, including fingers, ears and testicles. Some victims had wooden dowels shoved into their brains. Others received electric probes into their rectums. Electroshock was a favourite.

The CIA overthrows governments – including democratically elected ones – who are uncooperative with US corporate interests. When the bombs start to fall and the death squads fire machine guns, most of the people killed are civilians such as schoolteachers, students, miners and manual labourers. Their crime: demanding higher pay, freer elections and better living conditions than those provided by the dictators the US had often installed. Cutting the heads off village people and electro-shocking nipples and scrotums are done far more easily when the victims are branded as Communist sympathisers or activists who presented a threat to US national security.

Flying for the CIA fulfilled Barry's need for excitement, but he had surrounded himself with cutthroats and killers, many of whom viewed the people working below them as expendable. But no harm would come to Barry while he was still in their good graces.

Their influence prevented Barry from serving prison time following his earliest arrests. In Longview, Texas, Barry was busted with a plane full of weapons destined for Cuba, according to Reggie Griffith, a close friend of Barry. Not only did Barry avoid incarceration, but no record of the arrest exists. Other missing documents include Barry's flight logs for most of 1959 and 1960, a period of weapons smuggling to Cuba.

In 1972, US Customs in New Orleans arrested him for attempting to smuggle seven tons of C-4 explosives into Mexico, destined for a group of CIA-trained Cubans looking to usurp the Cuban president. In handcuffs, Barry said, "All I need is a bunch of Cubans after me." Getting escorted into the federal courthouse by armed guards, Barry grinned at the photographers.

Bailed out of jail, Barry went to buy some food from Plantation Chicken. He found himself smitten by the young woman on the cash register. When she gave him his change, he held her hand for a few extra moments. Debbie was impressed by his TWA captain's outfit. With the C-4 case making little progress in court month after month, Barry persisted in asking Debbie out. She eventually relented on Thanksgiving Day a year after they'd met. Barry offered to take her entire family on a joy ride in a plane. Having never travelled by aircraft before, Debbie said yes.

Barry wrote to the lawyer representing him in the C-4 case: "Don't forget that while in the employ of TWA I volunteered for hazardous duty without extra compensation to fly TWA's contract US Military flights into hot water zones in Vietnam, which I did with tons of explosives and war material. Youngest captain for TWA on Boeing 707's, too."

Despite his arrest, TWA didn't fire him until 1974, the year he finally came to trial.

Outside the courtroom, Barry and his wife approached an undercover agent whom he knew from two years earlier.

"Frank, was it hot when we were in Veracruz?"

"Very hot," Frank said.

"And I was wearing a suit and sweating a lot, wasn't I?" Barry said.

"Yes, you were."

"And the bus broke down on our way back into Veracruz, right?"

"I saw you standing beside it, yes, as we drove by on our way back into town."

"Well, tell my wife that. She thought I was out having a good time." Barry laughed.

The prosecutors introduced as evidence an automatic weapon that had nothing to do with the charges, and the judge declared a mistrial in June 1974. Such unusual events led congressional investigators to suspect that Barry had a special relationship with the US government. Indeed, it was CIA intervention. They'd told the US attorney's office to shut the trial down in the interest of national security.

By late 1974, Barry was flying full time for the CIA. The planes he used included a Lockheed Lodestar that reached 300 mph. By his early twenties, Barry was earning the equivalent of thousands of dollars a week and had several profitable businesses: Seal Sky Service, Aerial Advertising Associates, Helicopter Airways, Seal's Texaco.

CHAPTER 4

JFK Assassination

On November 22, 1963, John F Kennedy's presidential party arrived at Dallas Love Field Airport. Dressed in a dark grey suit, JFK greeted the crowd. Mrs Kennedy and JFK spent several minutes shaking hands. Dressed in pink, the First Lady received a bouquet of red roses, which she carried to a blue limo with two flags on the front.

In a dark suit, the Governor of Texas, John Connally, and his wife were in the open convertible as the Kennedys sat behind them. The plastic bubble top had been left off the limo. Vice President LBJ and his wife were in another car in the motorcade. The procession left the airport and started on a ten-mile route that wound through downtown Dallas on the way to the Trade Mart where JFK was due to speak at a luncheon. Crowds of excited people on the streets waved to the Kennedys and took photos.

The car turned off Main Street at Dealey Plaza around 12:30 pm. As it passed the Texas School Book Depository, gunfire erupted from various directions. JFK yanked the hand he had been waving towards his chin. His other hand rushed to his throat. Alarmed, Mrs Kennedy turned towards her husband and reached out her white-gloved hands. She held him as he lurched forward, shot in the back. The governor rotated his body towards JFK, who was sitting behind him.

As Mrs Kennedy leaned forward to examine her husband's throat, a bullet hit the front side of JFK's forehead, causing an explosion of blood, brains and skull. The governor and his wife ducked, getting their heads out of sight. As JFK slumped to the side, Mrs Kennedy climbed onto the back of the vehicle on all fours, raised herself with her left arm, reached out with her right hand and grabbed a piece of JFK's skull.

A Secret Service agent climbed onto the rear of the car and told Mrs Kennedy to get back in. She crawled back into the car still clutching the piece of skull. The governor had been hit in the chest, wrist and thigh. The limo sped through a triple underpass towards Parkland Memorial Hospital just a few minutes away.

Dozens of people rushed up a grassy knoll towards where gunshots and puffs of white smoke had been witnessed. The area was quickly crowded. Fifteen railroad workers said that shots had come from behind a fence on the grassy knoll. Muddy footprints and cigarette butts were found, indicating that the assassins had been there for a while.

The police encountered several men with Secret Service IDs, none of whom were supposed to have been stationed at Dealey Plaza.

At the hospital, Jackie Kennedy offered the piece of her husband's skull to the medical team. "Here, will this help?"

Little could be done. A Catholic priest was summoned to administer the last rites. At 1 pm, JFK was pronounced dead. Though seriously wounded, the governor recovered. The limo was cleaned right away, destroying all of the evidence on it.

JFK's body was brought to Love Field and placed on Air Force One. Before the plane took off, Vice President LBJ – putting on a grim face – stood in a crowded compartment and took the oath of office, which was administered by a judge. The brief ceremony took place at 2:38 pm.

Nobody pointed out that the shots had taken everyone by surprise that day except for LBJ. Upon reaching Dealey Plaza, LBJ had ducked, huddled down into his vehicle and got on a walkie-talkie before the first shot had been fired as if anticipating it. His car had been three cars behind JFK's limo.

Assuming the presidency, LBJ gained a lot from the death of JFK. At that time, he was facing political ruin and prosecution because Robert Kennedy – who wanted him out of office – had a dossier on the bribes LBJ had been taking. The US Senate was investigating him in the Bobby Baker Scandal. Baker was involved in taking millions in bribes for LBJ. The main suspects in the hit – the CIA, organised crime, big Texas oil and the military-industrial complex – all had special relationships with LBJ. He oversaw the budget for the CIA. He took bribes from the Mafia to protect their illegal gambling operations. He supported the Oil Depletion Allowance, worth millions to the oil companies, which JFK wanted to scrap. JFK longed to end the war in Vietnam, whereas LBJ was taking suitcases of money from military companies. LBJ had insisted that JFK visit Texas. LBJ had also stated that he had quit his powerful job as Senate Majority Leader for the vice presidency because he'd calculated that there was a one in four chance of JFK dying. Jackie Kennedy, who didn't like or trust LBJ, was told by French intelligence that LBJ was a driving force behind the assassination plot. The KGB reached the same conclusion.

Less than an hour earlier, the police – acting on a tip from US military intelligence – arrested Barry's former fellow air cadet, Lee Harvey Oswald, who'd been hired to work at the Texas School Book Depository just two weeks earlier. He was held for the assassination of JFK and the fatal shooting of a policeman on a Dallas street. In handcuffs, surrounded by police, Oswald, bewildered and sporting a black eye, was accosted by the media at around 7.55 pm.

"I'd like some legal representation," Oswald said. "These police officers have not allowed me to have any. In fact, I don't know what this is all about."

"Did you kill the president?" a reporter asked.

"No, sir, I didn't... I work in that building."

"Were you in the building at the time?"

"Naturally, if I work in that building, yes, sir."

"Did you kill the president?"

"No, they're taking me in because of the fact that I lived in the Soviet Union." Before disappearing behind a door, Oswald protested that he was a fall guy: "I'm just a patsy!"

Oswald had been working at the Texas School Book Depository building when JFK's limo had gone by at about 12:30 pm, so he couldn't possibly have shot JFK in the front side of the forehead. For a front shot, Oswald needed to have been in a building that the limo was approaching. From the sixth floor of the Texas School Book Depository, there was no clear line of sight to shoot JFK due to the trees. The police found no gunpowder on Oswald's hands or face. Although portrayed as an expert sniper, Oswald had flunked his first Marines' test because he'd failed to hit the target. On his second attempt, he only just qualified by two points, earning the lowest of the three shooting-range categories: marksman, which is below an expert and a sharpshooter. The rifle he'd allegedly used had cost roughly $2 and it had a $10 scope. It didn't even aim straight. The army's ballistic-test expert said that before they could test fire the rifle for accuracy they had to put three pieces of metal under the telescopic sight to align it with the barrel of the rifle. All of the evidence, including the rifle, was removed from the hands of the state police and sent to the FBI that night. Even though the FBI had arranged all of the evidence to implicate Oswald, they didn't find his prints on the gun.

On Sunday morning, November 24, Oswald was being transferred from the police headquarters to the county jail. Viewers across America watching live TV saw a man aim a pistol at Oswald and fire at point-blank range. The assailant was Jack Ruby, a local nightclub owner with Mafia ties. Oswald died two hours later at Parkland Hospital.

Ruby was filmed getting escorted from court. Asked by the media who was behind the assassination of JFK, he said, "When I mentioned about Adlai Stevenson, if he was vice president there would never have been an assassination of our beloved President Kennedy." Asked to clarify, he said, "Well the answer is the man in office now [LBJ]."

On Monday morning, Oswald's dead hand was placed on the rifle and the world was told that his prints had been found. The head of the FBI, J Edgar Hoover – LBJ's neighbour – put his stamp of approval on the Oswald story. Hoover had helped LBJ become vice president by handing LBJ a dossier on JFK's sex life, which LBJ had used as leverage over JFK. The FBI had commandeered all of the evidence, and, unaccountable to anyone, they had the power to lose evidence and create phoney documents. The rapid removal of evidence from the state police to the federal authorities is exactly what happened in the aftermath of Barry Seal's death.

With Oswald dead, all that remained was to discredit the witnesses who'd reported that up to ten shots had been fired from six different locations. This was achieved by the Warren Commission appointed by LBJ. He put Allen Dulles in charge, the former long-serving CIA director whom JFK had blamed for the Bay of Pigs and fired.

The Warren Report (1964) stated that three shots had been fired during the assassination from a lone gunman and there was no credible evidence that any shots had been fired from any location other than the Texas School Book Depository. The FBI and the Secret Service had announced that day that the first shot had hit JFK, the second had hit Texas governor John Connally in the back and the third had hit JFK in the back of the head, killing him. None of the testimony from the fifty-one witnesses who'd seen or heard evidence of shots fired from the grassy knoll made it into the Warren Report.

It later surfaced that a shot had actually missed JFK and injured a bystander. This posed a dilemma for those committed to the three-bullet theory. For months, the Warren Commission ignored the bystander. After being confronted with photographic evidence of the bullet mark, the official story was changed to include a magic bullet that defied the laws of physics and gravity by changing directions three times, while remaining pristine. It was claimed that the shot had actually hit the back of JFK's neck, exited his throat, causing a non-lethal wound, and entered the back of Connally, shattered Connally's fifth rib and right wrist bone and hit his left leg. Although anatomically impossible, it became the official account because otherwise the throat wound and the wounds to Connally would have implied other shots and shooters.

But JFK's clothes told a different story. The damage to his shirt and suit indicated that a bullet had entered between his shoulder blades, not the back of his neck. To get around that, an expert was procured to say that JFK had rotated his body, which had moved his clothes up the back of his neck.

The autopsy doctors claimed that the photos shown to the public were fakes and not the ones that they had taken.

Meticulous examination of the medical, ballistic and eyewitness testimony indicates that JFK was hit four times: once in the back (from behind); once in the throat (from in front); and twice in the head (once in the back of the head from behind and once in the right temple from the right/front). The shots don't appear to have been fired from the sixth floor of the Texas School Book Depository. Three appear to have come from the Dal-Tex Building, a seven-storey office building at 501 Elm Street in the West End Historic District of downtown Dallas. The Dal-Tex acoustics were such that the shots sounded as though they could have been fired from the Texas School Book Depository.

Many people were sceptical of the official story, including Jim Garrison, a New Orleans District Attorney, who began an investigation into the assassination in late 1966, after receiving several tips that Barry's former flight instructor, David Ferrie, had been a co-conspirator. With so many people linked to the assassination ending up dead – almost a hundred died mysteriously – Ferrie was under no illusions about the danger he was in. In Oliver Stone's film, *JFK*, Ferrie was played masterfully by Joe Pesci. After his name was leaked to the media, Ferrie protested that he couldn't go home because he was a dead man. In a hotel room, he met Garrison and his staff. Garrison asked him who he was afraid of.

"Me," Ferrie said, pacing around. "Everybody. The Agency [CIA], mob, Cubans. That's it. Follow the Cubans. Check them out. Here, Miami, Dallas..." Ferrie attempted to grab a notepad from one of the staff. "Hey, hey, don't be writing this down! I ain't cooperating here with no one! What's going on here? There's a death warrant for me! Don't you get it? Damn! Wait a minute!" Ferrie patted the staff down for listening devices and peeped out of a window. "Agency plays for keeps. I knew Oswald. He was in my Civil Air Patrol unit. I taught him everything. He was a wannabe. No one really liked him 'cause they thought he was a snitch. But I treated him good."

"Did you ever work for the CIA?" Garrison said.

"You make it sound like some remote fucking experience in ancient history. Man, you don't leave the Agency. Once you're in, they got you for life."

"And Shaw?" Garrison said, referring to another suspect in the JFK assassination.

"Shaw's an untouchable. Highest clearance. Shaw, Oswald, the Cubans: all Agency."

"What about Ruby?" Garrison said, referring to the man who shot Oswald.

"Jack was a pimp. A bagman for the Dallas mob. He used to run guns to Castro when he was still on our side. We almost had Castro with us, then we tried to whack him. Everybody's flipping sides all the time. Fun and games, man."

"How do the mob figure into this?"

"They're Agency, too. The CIA and the Mafia working together, trying to whack out the beard [Castro]. Mutual interest. They've been doing it for years. There's more to this than you could dream! Check out something called Operation Mongoose. Government Pentagon stuff. They're in charge. But who the fuck pulls whose chain? Who the fuck knows? Oh, what a deadly web we weave when we practise to deceive."

"Then who killed the President?"

"Why don't you fucking stop it?" Ferrie threw his hands up. "Shit! This is too fucking big for you, you know that? Who did the President? Fuck! It's a mystery. It's a mystery wrapped in a riddle inside an enigma! The fucking shooters don't even know!

Don't you get it? Fuck, man! I can't keep talking like this! They'll fucking kill me! I'll fucking die…"

"Just talk to us on the record. We'll protect you."

"They'll get to you, too. They'll destroy you. They're untouchable. I'm so fucking exhausted, I can't see straight."

Less than a week later on February 22, 1967, Ferrie was found dead in his apartment, accompanied by two unsigned undated typed suicide letters. The autopsy concluded that there was no evidence of suicide or murder and that Ferrie had died of a massive cerebral haemorrhage due to a congenital intracranial berry aneurysm that had ruptured at the base of his brain.

"I suppose it could just be a weird coincidence that the night Ferrie penned two suicide notes, he died of natural causes," Garrison said.

According to Debbie Seal, Barry flew a getaway plane as part of the JFK assassination. Ferrie and Oswald were not the last of Barry's associates to end up dead, either.

CHAPTER 5

Medellín Cartel

In 1977, a small twin-engine plane laden with marijuana was flying approximately fifteen feet above the Gulf of Mexico to avoid radar detection, almost skimming the waters off Louisiana's coast. As rain lashed the cockpit's windshield and the plane bobbed from the wind, the co-pilot turned a face drained of colour towards his partner and cursed Barry.

"Low and slow," Barry said, steering the plane, grinning confidently. "Relax, man. My boys had been flying grass in like this for the past four years and they've never ever been touched."

The plane flew over a cemetery, dropped its load onto a river and arced away from the scene. A barge manned by some good ol' boys in cowboy hats retrieved the bulky plastic-wrapped package and motored off through swampland. A mechanical whirring noise drew their attention skyward. A helicopter dropped a cable with a hook towards the barge. The drugs were attached. The helicopter flew to a remote rural area where a van was parked. The dropped drugs were packed into the van. On a bridge, the van's windows went down. Packages were ejected over the side to smugglers below in four cars. Each took a package and drove off.

The 1991 TV movie about Barry, *Doublecrossed*, included scenes of Barry's drug smuggling, while omitting his relationship and ongoing work for the CIA. But, as David Ferrie pointed out in *JFK*, working for the CIA is a lifelong commitment. Most Hollywood directors refuse to cross such lines.

Doublecrossed showed a scene in 1979 in which Barry was flying solo in his twin-engine plane over the green mountains of Honduras, crooning away to music. Flying in from Ecuador, he was landing to refuel. As his wheels touched down at the National Airport, Honduran soldiers in battle fatigues charged onto the runway. His plane came to a halt with a dozen guns aimed at the cockpit.

Barry put his hands above his head. "Is it my singing or you just don't like the song?" He cackled. Officials in Honduras had been paid to accommodate Barry's smuggling, but the government had recently been replaced, so the wrong people had been bribed. Barry was arrested for possessing an automatic weapon. The plane was seized.

What the movie didn't show was that Barry had previously landed at a deserted runway on one of Honduras' Bay Islands and dropped off a Moroccan Jewish passenger with a briefcase full of cocaine handcuffed to his wrist and two military duffel bags containing cocaine. For three days, the passenger had waited with forty kilos of cocaine for Barry to return, but was finally arrested in a hotel room by three soldiers.

The authorities stole twenty-three kilos and announced to the media that they'd busted seventeen kilos worth $25 million. The US didn't have a problem with the Hondurans trafficking cocaine because they were supporting US interests in the area. Despite Honduras being awash with drugs, the DEA closed its office there in 1983, citing budgetary reasons and a lack of productivity.

Barry's passenger made a statement on TV: "I arrived from Ecuador on business as an assistant producer for American television. A man I didn't know invited me to a drink at the bar and we conversed about many things. I confided that in two days, I would be leaving to go to Miami where my wife would be waiting. He said he would introduce me to two friends who could take me as far as Honduras, thus saving on my fare. In the following days, Mr Stefan was introduced to me. A few minutes later, an American, Adler Barryman Seal, arrived and we left for Honduras." The passenger added that Barry had informed him of problems entering Honduran territory and had insisted on dropping him off with an assurance that Barry would pick him up the next day. "At the island... they forced me to leave the plane. To show that they would be coming back for me they left their baggage. I accepted. I had no alternative." The passenger claimed to have no knowledge of the cocaine.

The movie *Doublecrossed* showed Barry getting strip-searched. Naked, other than a blanket wrapped around him, he was led into a dark tunnel that soldiers manoeuvred through with flashlights.

"Have you guys ever seen a movie called *Midnight Express*?" Barry said.

They threw him into a dungeon-like cell and clanked an iron-bar door shut.

"Fuck!" Barry turned to face his cellmates: a dozen locals, gazing suspiciously and angrily. The door opened. A guard threw his belongings on the floor. The cellmates scrambled to steal his clothes. "Get your hands off my shit, you Bayou swamp-rats!" he yelled, attempting to wrestle his belongings from them.

Stepping out of the shadows, a cellmate in a white vest towered over five-foot-seven Barry. He picked up an item of Barry's clothing and stood in front of Barry, chest to face, with an expression that said, *What are you gonna do about it?*

Barry opened his blanket, revealing his naked body, and urinated on the giant's leg.

The giant walked away with Barry's clothes, until everybody started laughing. The giant gazed at the stain on his leg, threw the clothes down, turned around and charged at Barry. Just as he was about to throttle Barry, an American wearing a blue baseball cap emerged from the darkness and struck the giant in the head with a work boot, knocking the giant out.

"Handy weapon you've got there," Barry said.

"Pretty handy weapon you've got there, too." Chewing gum, the American pointed at Barry's penis. He had dark eyes, a square face and big sideburns.

"Well, thanks for your help," Barry said, smiling.

"Hey, you know, I can't let some Louisiana boy get whooped."

"How'd you know I'm from Louisiana," Barry said, frowning. "Where are you from?"

"Slidell."

"Slidell! That only eighty miles from my home: Baton Rouge," Barry said.

"I just wanna ask you one thing. What did you plan to do when that big monster had figured out he'd been pissed on?"

"Sometimes, I just play things as they come along. Make 'em up," Barry said, getting dressed.

"Well, you'd better be damn glad that I was there."

"If you don't take the chance, you don't get the fun. I had a damn good time pissing on him. What are you doing in this hole?"

"I'm smuggling drugs, just like you."

"What. You think I'm a drug smuggler?" Barry said quietly.

"You kidding?"

Barry laughed. "My name is Barry Seal," he said, shaking the American's hand.

"No, it's not," the American said, smiling. "But I'll call you that if you want me to." Pointing at himself, he said, "Emile Camp." On the same day as Barry's arrest, Emile had been arrested with a group of smugglers.

"It's my real name. There's no sense lying in here. Hell, they're gonna be telling me that I can go home for supper anytime now." Barry peered out of the door.

"What you flying?" Emile said.

"A Cessna 310. You?"

"Whatever I can get a job flying. Whatever God gives me with wings, I fly."

Barry sat next to Emile on a stone ledge. "Who do you work for, Camp?" he said quietly.

"Anybody that'll give me a job."

"How about me? I've got five pilots flying for me now. I'll hire you."

Emile looked down. "No, sorry."

"Why not? I pay one-hundred-and-fifty thou a run."

"Nope," Emile said, getting off the ledge.

"Why in the hell not?"

"It appears to me you tend to get caught." They laughed.

In prison, Barry and Emile grew close. Barry made other smuggling contacts, which came in useful later on, including Roger Reeves, a New Orleans smuggler. Roger told Barry that he'd been doing business with the Colombians.

"What's this ol' boy down there in Miami's name?" Barry said, hoping that Roger would connect him with the Colombians.

"Lito. And this guy works directly for the man himself: Jorge Ochoa [a business partner of Pablo Escobar]. I mean, you know who he is, don't you?"

"Oh, yeah. He plays third base for the Cubs right?" Barry said.

"Listen to me, Barry," Roger said. "These ol' boys down there, they have no sense of humour. You know what I mean. None."

"But, I'm a very funny guy." They laughed.

Debbie Seal – who'd given birth to three children in quick succession, who were now six-months old, two and three – received a call stating that Barry had been arrested. Eventually, Barry managed to call. He guaranteed that he'd be home in a few days. Six months later, he was still making the same assurances.

Trying to bribe the right person in Honduras was difficult. Barry had paid plenty to officials, but an election had brought in new people. Starting from scratch was frustrating. Barry formulated an escape plan that included outside help and a helicopter, but it was abandoned.

While bribery negotiations continued, Barry used his money to live luxuriously. In the La Ceiba prison, he commissioned the building of an air-conditioned house with a movie screen and a projector. His food came from the best restaurants in the port.

On the weekends, Debbie flew to visit without the kids. As Barry was spreading so much money around, she received celebrity status from the guards. She wasn't searched for contraband. Freshly showered, Barry would embrace her at the prison gate. They spent the night in a room with a cot and candles and bananas hanging out to dry. Country and western music filtered in from a bar across the street. Gazing at Debbie, Barry reassured her that he was still the man she had married.

After nine months and for a bribe of $500,000, Barry was released. In Baton Rouge, he celebrated his freedom by taking Debbie to a jazz and blues club.

In *Doublecrossed*, Barry flew to Miami to meet Carlos "Lito" Bustamante, a Colombian with a handlebar moustache and a ponytail who oversaw US cocaine distribution for the Medellín Cartel. Barry introduced himself as Mr Ellis MacKenzie.

"We give one run," Lito said, walking along a crowded beach with children squealing in the water. "Do good. Maybe we give more. Do you want that?"

"How do I know who you are?" Barry said.

"You don't. I don't know you either. Look, we pay $3,000 a kilo. With that much money, you take the chance."

"What happens if I lose a load?"

Lito glowered. "We kill you."

Barry laughed. "When do we start, man?"

Lito gave Barry three pager numbers to contact him.

To avoid getting arrested, Barry studied drug cases in the federal court system and attended trials. With their lights off, his planes flew in and out of Louisiana at night. His pilots had $5,000 night-vision goggles and top-of-the-line equipment. The Colombian military in charge of monitoring airspace had been bribed. Returning to the US, his pilots reduced their speed to 120 knots, so that they would appear as oil-rig helicopters on radar. Over Louisiana marshland, duffel bags of cocaine parachuted from the planes. Helicopters transported the cocaine to men in vehicles, who drove it to the main hubs: Miami, Los Angeles and New York.

Barry invested in two condominiums – one on top of the other – and drilled a hole through the floor of the top one. Money from Lito was passed up through the hole and cocaine downwards.

Sometimes Barry ran into problems with honest law-enforcement agents not privy to his CIA protection. To smooth things over, Barry kept up to $4 million in a cottage in Fort Lauderdale.

That amount enabled him to stay out of jail during his early years working with the Medellín Cartel.

Barry ran the drug operation like a mini intelligence agency. They had the highest-tech CIA electronics and communications devices with digital scramblers. To keep their communication secret, Barry sometimes rented a whole floor of a hotel. Other times, people would fly to Mississippi and climb down into the engine room of a barge to attend a meeting where the machinery noise was so loud that eavesdropping was impossible.

The trips for the Colombians helped Barry buy a bigger house and cars for his family. When he wasn't flying cocaine, he was attending Little League baseball games with his kids, taking Debbie out dancing and eating at fancy restaurants. When Debbie asked about the money, Barry said that his company, Seal Aviation, was excelling at buying and selling planes in North and South America.

In *Doublecrossed*, Barry was shown driving a blue Mercedes convertible with Emile in the passenger seat. They saw an undercover car parked outside Barry's house.

"Oh, look at those idiots," Barry said, pulling up next to the police. "Hello, lieutenant. Hey, you know I'm going over to my office. Then I'm gonna go over to RJ's for lunch. And then maybe I'll go over to Ascension. I'm telling you just in case you get lost."

"Go to hell, Seal!" said a burly lieutenant with a thick moustache.

"Don't you get mad, lieutenant," Barry said, pointing at him. "I just hate to see Louisiana state police wasting tax payers' gasoline following me. You know what I mean?" Barry drove away.

"I'm telling you," Emile said. "Maybe you shouldn't bait them like that."

"What right do they have following me around? They got nothing on me and they never will."

"You are the biggest baddest most-suspected bad guy in Louisiana and every cop in the state wants to know where you got all that money."

"Yeah, well, if that's the case, why don't they follow Jimmy Swaggart around?" Barry said, referring to a wealthy televangelist. "He lives in that big house right over there. Hell, he's got more money than I'll ever have."

CHAPTER 6

Mena

In 1982, with the authorities breathing down his neck in New Orleans, Barry moved his operation to Mena, a picturesque town surrounded by thick forest nestled into the Ouachita Mountains of Western Arkansas. Settled in 1896 and incorporated on September 18, 1896, Mena was named by the Dutch who financed its railroad. Almost 3,500 people lived there in 1900, rising to over 5,000 when Barry arrived. Early industry included timber, agriculture and mineral extraction. Over the years, the surrounding wilderness provided a sanctuary for outcasts, ranging from bandits and Civil War guerrillas to smugglers of liquor and marijuana.

Despite being in the backwoods, Mena's Intermountain Regional Airport was high-tech. It was renowned for rapid aircraft rehabilitation and maintenance and for hosting planes for customers who required secrecy. Agencies such as the military used its facilities, which included a long runway and numerous vast hangars.

One of the reasons that the CIA wanted Barry there was because the airport had a reputation as being a place where anything could be achieved even if it were illegal, especially aircraft alterations, which required Form 337 to be filed with the Federal Aviation Administration (FAA). Mechanics who failed to file Form 337 could be imprisoned or lose their licence. Modifications were strictly regulated due to aircraft safety considerations. From Form 337, the Drug Enforcement Agency (DEA) learned to identify traffickers by homing in on suspicious modifications. Mechanics who wouldn't file Form 337 were in high demand. The

CIA hired these mechanics to modify aircraft involved in black ops, so there was no paper trail. Some of the planes Barry used had cargo doors designed for drug drops and additional fuel bladders. The CIA provided his planes with advanced aviation electronics. Barry had a Learjet, helicopters and cargo planes, many of which he purchased from entities covertly owned by the CIA such as Air America and Southern Air Transport. Eventually, the DEA got in on the Mena action as they didn't want a paper trail to disclose the modifications to Barry's aircraft, which were being used in their missions. The US government paid to have Barry's aircraft illegally modified to avoid its own laws.

In *Partners in Power*, Dr. Roger Morris and Sally Denton cite coded records of the Pentagon's Defense Intelligence Agency (DIA) that show Barry Seal on the payroll beginning in 1982. Around this time, he was part of Operation Seaspray. Selected as one of the best of the top pilots, Barry flew four miles above the borders of El Salvador, Honduras and Nicaragua, intercepting communications from political groups.

The favourable political climate in Arkansas at that time was thanks in part to Arkansas Governor Bill Clinton. According to Larry Nichols, who worked for Clinton back then, Barry and the CIA chose Arkansas because the Clintons were amenable to the guns-for-drugs smuggling. Assisted by Hillary Clinton's law firm, the Clintons profited from the money laundering side of it and were paid handsomely by the CIA for the right to operate in Arkansas.

According to Russell Welch, the Arkansas State Police Investigator in charge of the Mena investigation, "[Barry Seal] said 1983 was his most profitable cocaine smuggling period ever. The airplanes that he had placed at the Mena airport… were purchased solely for the purpose of cocaine smuggling."

In addition to using Mena, small clearings were made across Arkansas to be used as drop points. Making several weekly flights, each of Barry's planes fetched anywhere from 200 to 500 kilos of cocaine. Duffel bags full of cocaine parachuted down at odd hours of the night. Men in trucks took the drugs to hubs in Miami, New Orleans and New York. The distribution network included the Mafia, South American suppliers, corrupt officials reaching to the highest offices in the US government and opportunists out to make fast cash. It was all done so blatantly that the locals knew about it and criminal investigations were ongoing, yet no indictments were ever returned because Governor Bill Clinton had integrated key people as judges, high-level police and other law enforcement.

As insurance against prosecution, Barry maximised his value to the CIA. A priority of the Reagan-Bush administration was to get weapons and supplies to the rebels fighting a war in Nicaragua, but this had to be done covertly because it didn't have congressional approval. Barry's fleet of planes in Mena was ideal. Weapons were flown out of America and cocaine in. With CIA approval, drug money was used to finance the Nicaraguan rebels. In return, the CIA prevented Barry's flights from being intercepted by the DEA or US Customs. With the complicity of the US government, the Nicaraguan rebels were using the proceeds from cocaine to finance their war and to buy arms from US weapons manufacturers. The cocaine was sold on the streets of America at the exact same time as the Reagan-Bush administration was claiming to be fighting a War on Drugs.

The benefits of the CIA alliance were immediate. An investigation into one of his pilots by US Customs was stymied. An agent wrote a note to his bosses, "[name redacted] works for Seal and cannot be touched because Seal works for the CIA." A federal agent said, "Look, we're told not to touch anything that has Barry Seal's name on it, just to let it go."

The majority of the revenue from the cocaine smuggling – hundreds of millions per month – was funnelled by the CIA. Barry was making so much money that he imported two Rolls-Royces from the UK. After deciding they were too ostentatious, he donated them to the Fort Lauderdale Christmas Parade.

CHAPTER 7

Terry Reed

On August 23, 1983, Colonel Oliver North – a frontman for Vice President George HW Bush – called Terry Reed, a CIA asset with expertise in machinery. Using a fake name, John Cathey, North said that he knew about Terry moving to Arkansas. "I really can't talk about it on an unsecure line, but we've got an exciting project in the works down there and I think there may be a slot for you. If you're interested, it's best I just put you into play with the guy that's going to be running the operation for me. I'll make the introduction and have him look you up. I'll tell him you're a good guy."

"How do I know who he is and where to find him?" Terry said.

"He'll find you. His name is Barry Seal."

A few months later in Arkansas, Terry was at the company he co-owned – Command-Aire Manufacturing – working in its ultralight factory, when some men arrived in a limo.

"I'm Dan Lasater," said a multimillionaire bond trader with a handsome square face and predatory eyes, wearing a three-piece suit and Gucci shoes. "This is my driver, Roger Clinton." Lasater held an arm out towards Roger, a man with thick dark hair, broad features and a nose red and swollen from cocaine abuse. "He's the governor's brother." Lasater was a personal friend of Bill Clinton and one of his largest political contributors.

"Oh, yeah," Lasater said to Terry. "I guess I should introduce a client of mine. This is Mr Barry Seal."

Barry studied Terry: a man with sincere eyes, dark hair parted at one side, thick eyebrows and a moustache. When they were on their own, Barry told Terry, "We have a common friend who says you have some talent that I need."

"Does this common friend have a name?" Terry said.

"John Cathey," Barry said, referring to Oliver North. "I'm a contractor. I specialise in transportation. Whatever there is to transport, I transport. I have certain connections within the government. I presently have a contract that you may have an interest in. I'll talk to you later privately."

Barry was periodically in Little Rock depositing money at Lasater's company. Laundering cash in such a small area was problematic. Years later with numerous investigations underway, a secretary told the IRS that after some of Barry's flights, "there would be stacks of cash to be taken to the bank and laundered." To avoid any reporting to the federal government, launderers were instructed to buy cashier's checks totalling just under $10,000. One witness said, "The bank officer went down the teller lines, handing out the stacks of $1,000 bills and got the cashier's checks." And that was only the small change from Barry's operation.

At a restaurant, Barry and Terry discussed their military flight tours in south-east Asia. "So, besides being a flight instructor, you speak Spanish and you know how to coordinate air crews in order to put the shit on target?" Barry said.

Terry nodded.

"You're hired," Barry said. "But I got a more pressing problem right now. When can you go with me to Mena?"

To assess Terry's skills, Barry arranged a flight in December 1983. They took off in a Learjet, with Barry sitting on the right with his arm around the back of Terry's seat. "Now release the fucking brakes and let's have some fun," Barry said, increasing the pressure on Terry. "Relax, you're gonna like this."

Accelerating the jet, Terry was enjoying the exercise and bonding with Barry, who kept mocking his government handlers by calling them, "Fucking GS suits," meaning General Salary Schedule. "They've got no balls and very little brains."

"Maybe we can trade services," Terry said. "I'll teach you about manufacturing if you'll train me to handle these GS bean counters, so I can have a plane like this."

"It's a deal." Barry cancelled the flight plan and handed the controls to Terry. "It's your airplane. Wring this bitch out and show me what you're made of."

Grinning, Terry pulled a fighter-pilot manoeuvre. He headed north and dived towards an airstrip on a mountain. He skimmed the runway and shot up like a rocket.

"Watch out for the compressor stall!" Barry yelled. "Push it over the top and recover this thing. I'm overweight and these G's are getting to me." After Terry had stabilised the jet at 17,500 feet, Barry said, "Guess I'm too old for this shit. OK, hot dog, let's take it back to base. You've got the right stuff."

On the ground, Barry said, "It's time I let you know the truth about what we want you to do. Let's have some coffee." Over coffee, Barry said that the mission involved providing weapons for the Contra rebels in Nicaragua. Mena was going to be a hub for weapons and a training base for Nicaraguan rebels. Perhaps sensing that Terry was a straight shooter and due to the compartmentalisation of various aspects of the operation, Barry left out the most secret part: he was bringing drugs back on the return flights. "I'll have to talk to our friend [Oliver North] on this, but I need you in on this project. It's more difficult to make weapons parts than they led me to believe."

Barry said that the CIA was moving a weapons company, Iver Johnson's Arms, from New Jersey to Arkansas because Congress had banned the Defense Department from obtaining weapons for the war in Nicaragua through the usual vendors. So what if the war was unpopular, the CIA would find a way around it and a tidy profit would be made by everybody involved, including the arms suppliers. Publicly, Arkansas Governor Bill Clinton took credit for Iver Johnson's Arms – a company dating back to the American Revolution – coming to Arkansas by claiming that he'd campaigned to get it moved there to create jobs for the locals. But Barry knew better: the decision had been made by the shadow government, which included murky organisations such as the CIA operating outside of the law.

The military parts going to Nicaragua needed to be untraceable otherwise there was a risk that the US public would find out. In Jacksonville, Arkansas, Iver Johnson's Arms was producing sniper rifles as part of a classified contract with the US Navy, which was subject to inspection. To avoid the detection of the manufacture of untraceable parts, a plant at Mena had been selected. Iver Johnson's Arms provided ideal cover for the Mena plant.

"So now that you know what we're up to," Barry said, "what will it take in the way of machinery to cast and machine the lower receiver housing of the M-16?" The lower receiver housing makes an M-16 fully automatic.

"I'll need blueprints, and I'll need to know quantities," Terry said.

CHAPTER 8

DEA Trouble

In *Doublecrossed*, an airport scene showed a line of men in suits with badges and guns, flanked by police in uniform, marching down a runway towards Barry's cockpit – part of Operation Screamer – just after he had landed with 200,000 sedatives called Quaaludes.

An agent in the middle raised a DEA badge. "We have reason to believe you are transporting a controlled substance aboard this plane!" the agent yelled over the noise of the propellers. "Will you please step out!"

Pointing at them, Barry cursed. He was arrested and transported to Broward County jail in Florida. After the strip-search, he dressed in orange prison attire.

The movie scene was spectacular, but it never happened. Barry had been tipped off. He sent one of his pilots in a helicopter to his suburban home. The helicopter landed in the backyard, picked up his wife and kids and flew them to a secret airfield, where Barry was waiting in a Learjet. Barry flew them all to Las Vegas, where they spent an Easter vacation gambling. After six weeks, Barry turned himself in.

The Operation Screamer arrests were the culmination of an eighteen-month investigation into southern Florida's drug trade. DEA agents had recorded conversations in the high-end hangouts of drug traffickers, such as the Mutiny Hotel. Eighty-five people were indicted, including pilots, smugglers and money launderers. In early 1983, arrests were made in Florida, Colorado, California, Louisiana, Texas, Virginia and North Carolina. When the police tried to arrest one smuggler, he opened his door brandishing a handgun, a candle and a five-gallon can of kerosene. After barricading himself in his home for five hours, he set fire to the place.

After his stint in Las Vegas, Barry surrendered. *Doublecrossed* showed him in a cement-block-wall visitation cubicle, receiving a visit from Emile Camp and a lawyer. Speaking to them on a phone from the other side of a Plexiglas window, Barry asked Emile if Debbie knew he was in jail.

"Not yet," Emile said. "Debbie thinks you're in Mexico – you know – buying and selling planes like usual."

Barry turned to his lawyer. "So who fingered me?"

"They caught some guy up in Lauderdale," said the lawyer, a heavyset man with silver hair, wearing a business suit and a tie. "He gave up everybody he'd ever heard of to cut a deal."

Barry was indicted due to an informant who worked for the DEA agent in charge of Operation Screamer. Upon receiving information about Barry, the agent had contacted the DEA in Baton Rouge. "Hey, I got a guy. He's a pilot. He's from Baton Rouge. They call him El Gordo: the Fat One."

"We know who you've got and if you've got him, we're going to come down and kiss you. We've been working him for ten years and we've never been able to get him."

The evidence against Barry was the informant's testimony and wire-tapped phone calls. A federal grand jury indicted him in March 1983, for smuggling 200,000 Quaaludes. Even though this was a matter of public record and his name was in the media, he was insulated from suspicion by the Medellín Cartel because they knew him as Ellis Mackenzie.

In *Doublecrossed*, Barry said, "So, you're my lawyer. Get me out." Barry smirked at Emile.

"It's not that easy. It's bad, Barry. You're looking at sixty years."

Barry's face crimpled. "Sixty!"

"And that's not the worst of it. As soon as Baton Rouge heard you'd been arrested, they jumped on the bandwagon. There's a US attorney over there. His name's Thornton something."

"Thornton Biggs."

"That's him," the lawyer said. "Says he's gonna file his own indictment against you, too."

"I went to high school with him," Barry said. "Can't you talk to him?"

"Dammit, Barry," the lawyer said, frowning. "You know you're not too popular with Louisiana cops. You've been sticking their noses in it for years. Now this is their chance."

For a few seconds, Barry smiled, but his face returned to stone.

"What about Lito?" Emile said.

Barry shook his head. "Lito don't know about this. This flight was on the side."

"Barry you've been flying for Lito for five years now. Maybe he'll help."

"Lito can't know about this. If his organisation finds out that I've been arrested, they'll drop me like a rock."

They paused.

"The only way out of this I can see," the lawyer said, "is for you to turn informant."

"Bullshit!" Barry said.

The lawyer hung up the phone and leaned towards the Plexiglas. "We'll talk strategy after I post your bond. You'll be out of here in a couple of hours."

"I'll keep you out of this," Barry said to Emile.

"I doubt if you can," Emile said.

"I'll never give you up."

"I don't care. You know, I've been thinking about retiring for quite a while now. Yeah, buy me a farm. Costa Rica maybe."

"Ha! The only way you're ever gonna buy the farm is in an airplane, you old faker."

Briefly, they cackled. With their eyes misting over, they hung up their phones.

Posting a $250,000 bond secured Barry's release. In the hope of making a deal, Barry went behind his lawyer's back and directly approached the DEA agent in charge of Operation Screamer. Promising to deliver more cocaine than the DEA had ever seen, he wanted to travel overseas with minimal DEA supervision and charges to be dropped for two of his men indicted in Operation Screamer. The DEA agent was put off by Barry's attempt to broker a deal without a lawyer, not to mention Barry's ego and demanding nature. The offer was refused.

Doublecrossed showed Barry in a sky-blue three-piece suit, storming out of the office of Stanford Bardwell, his former classmate who had become the US attorney in Baton Rouge.

Waiting outside, Emile threw down a newspaper and jumped up. "No dice, huh?"

"I went to high school with that bozo and he won't even see me," Barry said, marching away. Aware that Barry was under investigation by a state and federal task force in Baton Rouge and New Orleans, Bardwell had considered Barry's offer to turn informant, and decided it was too cryptic. Barry had paid an intermediary $25,000 cash to broker the deal with Bardwell. The intermediary kept the money and went on to become a judge.

"High school ain't exactly a lifelong bond you know," Emile said.

"He ought to give me ten minutes in the office with him, don't you think?" Barry snarled.

"Well, what now?"

"I'm going to Washington DC," Barry said.

"Washington DC! Oh hell yes, that makes a lot of sense. Why don't you go talk to the governor first?"

"I don't know the governor," Barry said, throwing his hands up.

"Well, who the hell do you know in Washington DC?"

"Nobody," Barry said, not disclosing his connections. "But I bet they're dying to meet me." He put on reflective aviator sunglasses and swaggered out of the building. His contacts at the CIA advised him to call Vice President George HW Bush's Drug Task Force, who promptly made an appointment to see him.

CHAPTER 9

Mena

In January 1984, Barry met Terry at a restaurant they frequented called SOB's (Shrimp, Oysters, Beer). The food was Cajun and the band's loud music obstructed eavesdropping. Barry wanted to scout for a remote part of Mena, where they could secretly train Nicaraguan pilots.

"Christ, Cathey [Oliver North] didn't tell me we gotta teach those fuckers to fly, too!" Barry said. "It was my initial understanding these guys would all be skilled pilots and all we had to do was teach them how to hit the fucking target with a palletised load of supplies. I guess the truth of the matter is the fucking Nicaraguans don't have any pilots. Some fucking freedom fighters!"

To prevent the detection of illegal war supplies to Nicaragua, the Reagan-Bush administration wanted Nicaraguans to fly the cargo planes in case any were shot down. If a US pilot ended up dead or captured on Nicaraguan soil, the covert op would be exposed.

"Tell me about this airport you started in Oklahoma City," Barry said, grabbing some salad. "Especially the part about FAA [Federal Aviation Administration] licensing if you're near a vector airway." With Terry's information, Barry was figuring out how to stay in compliance with FAA rules to avoid any unwanted scrutiny of the pilot training. "Better yet, why don't I just put you on-board officially as an aviation consultant while I figure out exactly how you fit into all this."

"Sounds good to me," Terry said.

Later on in a Learjet, they circled a remote part of Western Arkansas to get a view of a field.

"Bank tighter to the left," Barry said. "More! More! There it is, off my left-wing. What do you think?"

"OK. I got it now," Terry said. "It's definitely remote. I like the surrounding terrain. But does the topography look similar to Nicaragua?" They were over Nella, twelve miles north of Mena.

"Yeah," Barry said. "The Nicaraguans will love it. They'll think they're home. Let's go land at Mena and drive back up here to see how it looks from the ground."

At Mena, they met the president of a metal-casting company. In the foundry, they discussed the computerised machine tools required to produce weapon parts.

They drove from Mena, but couldn't find Nella – a difficulty that provided a security benefit. Eventually, they arrived at dirt roads in Nella that only four-wheel-drive vehicles could go down. The mountains would add realism and danger for the trainee pilots.

Barry wanted Terry to return to Nella on another day to do a more thorough survey and to ensure that the selected location did not impinge upon any commercial flights, which could bring FAA scrutiny.

"As I survey these sites," Terry said, flying back to Little Rock, "I should take into consideration the proficiency level of the pilots who'll be using the field. That surrounding terrain could be pretty dangerous, especially in bad weather. They still peel about half a dozen flatlander pilots off Rich Mountain every year."

Barry laughed. "I got some good news and some bad news. The good news is Cathey says the Nicaraguans know how to fly single-engine planes. The bad news: barely."

They arrived at Barry's headquarters at Rich Mountain Aviation in a new building at the south-west end of Mena's Inter-Mountain Regional Airport. Over the following month, Terry met some of Barry's associates, including Emile Camp.

By February 1984, pressure was coming down from the Reagan-Bush administration for Barry to have Nella ready for the pilot training. Barry convened a meeting with Terry at SOB's. After devouring three dozen oysters, he grabbed a napkin to make notes on. "OK, you're the high-powered aviation consultant. Where the hell are we gonna build this goddam airstrip? It's time for a decision. Our friend [Oliver North] says we gotta come online sooner than planned. So what's your decision? Adjacent to the federal land to the west or under the Hog-2 MOA?"

The Nella site was ideal due to its MOA (protected airspace) and because it could easily be pinpointed from a cockpit with a long-range navigation receiver. "Our main considerations," Terry said, "should be security, a real-time training environment and the logistics of bivouac. I vote for Nella."

Surrounded by thick forest, Operation Jade Bridge began at Nella. The call sign for aircraft was designated as Boomerang. For camouflage, prefabricated chicken houses were installed as a barracks for the Nicaraguans. An old farmhouse served as the headquarters. Construction started to enhance a grass landing strip that would become a landing field and a drop zone. The covert weapons transfer program was codenamed Operation Centaur Rose. Its aircraft call sign was Dodger.

A few months later, Barry visited Terry in hospital. An engine had seized mid-flight, so Terry had tried to glide back to an open field but had crashed into giant pine trees. His crushed right foot had required eight hours of surgery and was at risk of amputation unless circulation normalised. As a nondrug user, Terry had refused painkillers, so he was in bed, sweating in agony.

"Hey, partner," Barry said, "you almost bought the fucking farm, huh. Your wife tells me your heart's bruised and almost dislodged. Did you go down making decisions or did you freeze?"

"I got an opportunity to sort of prove myself to myself, Barry," Terry said, enthused to retell his story. "Yeah, I was thinking all the way down all right. But most important to me was that I was flying all the way to the ground instead of freezing or praying to God. I was analysing my options and acting on them all the fucking way to impact. I think my old instructor would be proud if he knew. Don't laugh, but I like to think I performed as if I had the right stuff."

With Barry sitting next to the bed, they talked for hours about human mortality. They learned that they each shared the same birthday: July 16.

"Barry, I've come to a decision,"Terry said. "I want in full-time. This may sound stupid, but if I die, I want to die for something important and I think the Contra cause is important." In his compartmentalised role, Terry thought he was doing the patriotic thing by supporting the rebels in Nicaragua. He'd bought into the media manipulation by the Reagan-Bush administration, the very people who were using him and who considered him and Barry expendable.

"You're hired," Barry said. "Again."

After a few months of recovery, Terry resumed work at Nella. Concerned about drainage, Terry limped across a field with Barry to make an inspection.

"You want to be an instructor," Barry said, taking photos. "I've hired a guy from Tulsa, and another's coming down from Nebraska. Between them and Camp that'll make four if you're on board. But I shit you not, this is gonna to be dangerous. You told me that you love to fly at night. I could easily work you into the night schedule if you're interested. You want it?"

"Does the Pope shit in the woods?" Terry said. "Is a bear Catholic?"

On the flight back to Mena, Barry said, "We'll find you a plane and part of our deal is you can keep it over in Little Rock. Consider it a company car. Evans will perform all your maintenance at Rich Mountain. He'll have a secret source of bulk fuel for you to use, so that you won't be running up traceable fuel bills. The guy from Tulsa will be in charge of scheduling. He's created a perfect cover, which all the instructors are to use. If anyone asks you who you're training, just tell them you're a contract instructor with Ross Aviation and working in their foreign-student department." Based 100 miles away in Oklahoma, Ross Aviation was a real company that trained foreign students. "Have I left anything out?"

"What about communications?" Terry said. "Surely I don't use my home phone for scheduling, do I?"

"Oh, I forgot. As soon as we land, I'll take you by OSI and introduce you to Aki."

In Little Rock, Barry took Terry to Aki's company, Oversees International, which specialised in helping American corporations do business in Japan, while providing a cover for Aki's CIA activity. After Barry and Terry entered a mundane building next to a pizzeria, Aki, in a smart business suit, quickly shut the door. Aki handed Terry an OSI business card. In the intelligence community, OSI means Office of Special Investigations, a unit equivalent to the CIA within the Criminal Division of the United States Department of Justice. To avoid eavesdropping from Aki's employees, they went for food.

At Fu Lin's Chinese restaurant, Aki explained that his company mostly shipped raw materials to Japan and ships returned with pulpwood, bauxite and rice from Arkansas. Then they got down to CIA business.

"Now this is a little sensitive," Barry said, "since CIA agents aren't supposed to be operating in the US. But Aki here is the agency's resident guy. All three of us have a common friend [Oliver North]. From your point of view, Terry, Aki's your secure communications link. He has all the radio gear at his office. We'll all communicate through him. That way, since he's local, you won't have any long-distance charges on your phone over to Mena. While we're talking about phones, do not ever ever ever use any of the payphones in Mena. They're all bugged."

"How'd you know?" Terry said.

"I had Aki bug them for security reasons. Let's just say we're hunting for a mole. Get it." Not only was Barry recording all of his phone conversations, he was bugging payphones in the hope of identifying a double agent.

"What kind of communications capability do you have?" Terry asked Aki. "I mean, is it secure? And can you talk on aircraft frequencies?"

"Aki can communicate with God and the devil can't even jam him," Barry said.

"From an operational point of view, Terry," Aki said, "I'll be your primary contact from this point on. Mr Seal is out of state a lot, so from now on just consider me your boss. I'm glad to have you with us. You come highly recommended by Mr Cathey."

After dropping off Aki, Barry told Terry, "Hey, I know you're all gung-ho on this. But if I were you, I'd go slow. There is no guarantee here on how long this may last. For all we know, Cathey could get his way and the fucking Marines could invade Nicaragua tomorrow. This whole Mena thing could come to an end before it even gets started. In other words, I wouldn't want to see you and your wife hurt economically."

The next time he spoke to Aki, Terry requested to work nights at Mena as he preferred flying in the dark. As it was the most dangerous time to fly, the other instructors were fine with that. Working with machinery enabled him to hide what he was doing at night. Aki also asked Terry to keep an eye on Barry. He said they should meet once a week for lunch to communicate verbally rather than writing anything down.

CHAPTER 10

DEA Informant

On February 17, 1984, Barry was convicted of conspiracy and possession with intent to distribute Quaaludes, which carried ten years in prison. He was assigned the toughest sentencing judge in the Southern District of Florida. Also dangling over his head was the prospect of a second trial for more charges related to Operation Screamer with a maximum sentence of forty-seven years.

Despite his troubles, Barry still piloted for the Medellín Cartel. He hoped to parlay that relationship into a get-out-of-jail-free card if he could become an informant. Performing top-secret work for the CIA, he figured intervention from the federal government would eventually occur on his behalf otherwise the Mena operation would be jeopardised.

Since bonding out of jail on the Quaaludes charges, Barry had flown three cocaine loads for the Colombians. But the closer he had got to his February 1984 court date, the less trafficking he had done. A disappointed Lito told Barry that Lito's brother had transported 3,000 kilos for the Medellín Cartel. He wanted Barry to do the same.

"I'll just have to find a plane," Barry told Lito.

On his Learjet, Barry flew to Washington DC, where he presented himself at Vice President George HW Bush's Commission on Organized Crime Drugs Task Force. Sitting on a sofa in a plush office, facing Jim Howell – a Bush staffer and former US Customs drug agent – and Kenneth Kennedy – a high-ranking DEA agent – both in dark suits with clean-shaven faces, Barry complained that his offer to be an informant had been declined by the Fort Lauderdale DEA for personal reasons. Attempting to capitalise on the political priority of the moment, Barry said he could obtain proof that the Sandinista government of Nicaragua – the despised enemy of the Reagan-Bush administration – was involved in drug trafficking. According to Kennedy, when later testifying to a congressional committee, Barry's exact words were "Officials of the Nicaraguan government are involved in smuggling cocaine into the United States, specifically the Sandinistas."

Barry offered to get information on the Medellín Cartel, which he claimed was importing three quarters of the cocaine entering the US.

"Three quarters!" Kenneth said. "And how much would you say comes into the US each year, Mr Seal?"

"Oh, about a hundred ton. That surprise you, gentlemen?"

"Well, let's say this: if your estimate is correct, then we at the DEA aren't even touching the tip of the iceberg."

"That's right. You're not. That's why you need me. I can give you names, dates, landing strips, lab locations. Of course, we have to have a deal. Do we have a deal?"

"Er, well, I think the first thing we would like for you to do is to meet with some field officers of the DEA in Miami."

"Why?"

"Mr Seal, we're Washington bureaucrats. We need street experts to verify your claims. Men who know the territory."

"Well, just make sure they know what they're doing. Don't you waste my time now."

"I'll call and set it up right now. Bob Joura is the best there is."

Barry waited on a sidewalk by a shopping mall, wearing dark glasses and a hat, until Joura and his partner, Jake Jacobsen, arrived in their car. "Hey, Barry Seal!" yelled Jacobsen, a strapping man with a walrus moustache.

Dismayed by their lack of professionalism, Barry scanned the area and dived into the back of the car. "Drive out of here quick!"

The two DEA agents scrutinised him.

"Yes, sir," said Joura, a tall middle-aged man with a serious expression and dark circles under his eyes.

"Are you crazy or something shouting my name out like that?" Barry said, resting sideways on the back seat to keep his head below window level.

"Is someone watching you?" Jacobsen smiled.

"Oh, no, probably not, you know. We're just in Miami, the drug capital of North America." Barry started to sit up. "I'd rather not be seen getting into a four-door sedan with Blackwall tyres, if you know what I mean."

"I'm Bob Joura of the DEA." Joura displayed his badge. "This is Special Agent Jacobsen."

"You talked to Washington?"

"Yeah, they said you might help us out in our investigations of cocaine trafficking," Joura said.

"In exchange for what?"

"Well, they said you got a little problem in Lauderdale," Joura said. "But I'll tell you something: there's nothing we can do for you unless we get something real, Mr Seal."

In *Doublecrossed*, Barry gave up the name of Jorge Ochoa, a co-founder of the Medellín Cartel with Pablo Escobar.

"Do you want to tell us who you think Mr Ochoa is, Mr Seal?" Joura said.

"Huh, you don't know who Mr Ochoa is?" Barry smiled. "You're putting me on. Ochoa. Escobar. Gacha."

Raising himself in the passenger seat, Jacobsen turned his head and scowled. "Why don't you tell us, Mr Seal, who are they?"

Barry frowned. "Ochoa. Escobar. Gacha. Oh shit. Amateurs. They send me fucking amateurs! How the fuck am I supposed to make a deal with you people?" Barry spat out the words.

"Hey, man, cool it," Jacobsen said.

"You morons! I bring you the number one man in the whole fucking cocaine business! You assholes!"

"Hey!" Joura said. "Shut the fuck up!"

"And you..." Barry yelled.

Jacobsen pulled out his gun and pointed it at Barry. "You settle the fuck down."

"Get that fucking gun out of my face!" Barry yelled.

"Shut the fuck up!" Joura yelled.

"Fuck you!" Jacobsen yelled, thrusting the gun's barrel closer to Barry.

"You two are such stupid fucking assholes!"

"Shut up!"

"What the fuck am I doing? Stop this fucking car!"

The car pulled off the road and screeched to a halt. Barry jumped out. Following Barry, Jacobsen grabbed him by the back of the neck, pushed him up against a chain-link fence and put a gun to the rear of his skull. "You just stand right there. You move, I blow a hole in your head. You got that?"

Joura jumped out of the car. "Put the gun down, Jake! Cool down! Don't do something stupid!"

"OK. OK," Barry said. "Just put the gun away."

Jacobsen spun Barry around, grabbed him by the front of the neck and pushed the barrel of his gun into Barry's nose. "You don't tell me what to do and you don't call me an amateur just 'cause you know who Ochoa is and I don't," he said, mispronouncing Ochoa as okra.

Barry smiled. "It's Ochoa. It's Jorge Ochoa. He's the biggest supplier of cocaine to America. He's the head of the Medellín Cartel. If you're so goddam good at your job, why in the hell don't you know who he is?"

Jacobsen pointed at Barry. "'Cause I've heard plenty of crap from scumbags like you before, Seal. Maybe you're full of shit."

"And maybe you're a fucking amateur."

Jacobsen lunged at Barry. "Goddammit!"

Joura pulled Jacobsen back and stood in front of Barry. "Cool it, Jake. Cool it."

With Barry nodding and smirking behind Joura, Jacobsen promised to settle down.

Joura turned to Barry. "OK, you've made your point, Seal. Let's get back in the car, so we can talk."

"Talk about what? I came here to make a deal."

"Fine," Joura said. "Get in the car."

"I'll make some big busts for you," Barry said, "and then you go to bat for me in court. Deal?"

"The more you get us," Joura said, raising his voice, "the more we vouch for you. That's the only deal you get, Seal."

"I want an amnesty for all the people who work for me. I don't wanna see any of them hurt."

"You want a lot, don't you," Joura said.

"I'm gonna give you a lot," Barry said. "I'll make your fucking career."

"Huh!" Jacobsen laughed. "I can't fucking wait." Jacobsen started to walk towards the car.

"Why don't you grow up, asshole?" Barry said.

Jacobsen spun around.

Joura grabbed the chain-link fence either side of Barry and pushed his body down against Barry's chest. "You better play straight with me, Seal, or you'll be in for more trouble than you ever needed."

"This may come as a surprise to you," Barry said, "but I'm an honest man. How about I set it up so that I'm flying 3,000 kilos of cocaine out of Colombia for Ochoa? Is that big enough for you?" Barry said that he'd flown over one hundred trips, carrying at least 300 kilos of cocaine, earning $3,500 a kilo. Flying in over 30,000 kilos had earned him over $100 million.

The two Miami DEA agents and Steve LeClair, a US Justice Department attorney, agreed to use Barry as an informant. He was assigned the DEA number SGI-84-0028. His pay from the DEA would be $800,000 a year. His sentencing for the Quaaludes conviction would be postponed.

In *Doublecrossed*, the two DEA agents shadowed Barry as he met Lito in a booth at a dimly-lit diner.

"I need you to go to Colombia tonight," Lito said.

"Tonight?"

Lito scanned the room before dropping his boss's name. "Ochoa's plane's in Fort Lauderdale. He needs it."

"Why me?"

"It's what Ochoa wants."

"Ochoa wants to meet me?" Barry said incredulously. "Why?"

Lito looked around again. "Maybe you know."

"Me, hell, I don't know nothing," Barry said, wringing his hands.

"Vámonos," Lito said, meaning let's leave.

"Sure, let me take a piss, and then we're out of here."

Barry got on the payphone in the foyer and called the agents parked outside. He bragged that he was going to Colombia to meet Ochoa. "When I hand over Ochoa to you, you'll march down to that Fort Lauderdale judge and you'll tell him what a good boy I am."

CHAPTER 11

Medellín Cartel

Operating as a co-pilot, Barry struggled through heavy fog over the coast of Colombia, flying in predawn darkness to avoid the air force. The Honduran pilot was a friend of the Ochoa family. "We'll be going right over Jorge Ochoa's ranch and farm. Would you like to see it?"

"Certainly," Barry said.

The Cessna circled Hacienda Veracruz with its 5,400-foot airstrip. The pilots waved to someone on the ground. The Cessna headed south towards Medellín. Barry admired the thick green jungle and mountain range. The plane landed on a 5,000 foot grassy jungle airstrip. After the engine was turned off, workers climbed up ladders and painted over the plane's US registration number. The Ochoas had just lost a similar Cessna loaded with cocaine in the Bahamas. The Colombian registration number for the confiscated Cessna was about to be transplanted to the plane Barry had flown, so that the Ochoas could deny any knowledge of the seized plane.

Barry took note of the airstrip cut into the jungle. He was concerned about water from recent rain and the possibility of mud making things dangerous. A tractor emerged from the jungle towing duffel bags of cocaine, which were loaded onto a small plane that was getting refuelled for a trip to Andros Island in the Bahamas with 300 kilos.

In another small plane, Barry and the Honduran flew to Jorge Ochoa's aircraft base, a complex of hangers near Medellín, where a helicopter and jet were stored. They were driven into the mountains to a winding driveway at La Loma, the Ochoas' mansion, protected by guards with fully-automatic weapons. Giraffes, hippopotami and flamingos roamed freely on the grounds.

They waited in a sitting room until five mostly stocky Colombian cocaine traffickers entered, including three Ochoa brothers and Pablo Escobar. The Ochoas – Jorge, Juan David and Fabio – had grown up with money from cattle breeding and restaurants. Jorge was polite, strong on family values and didn't participate in drugs other than the occasional glass of wine. Pablo had a dark moustache, close-set eyes and short curly hair parted at the side. Although well-mannered, there was a dangerous aspect to him that the Ochoas lacked. Raised by a schoolteacher and a farmer, Pablo had spread terror across Colombia with bombing campaigns and by offering rewards to anyone who killed a member of the National Police. He didn't drink or smoke tobacco, but was partial to marijuana.

The men greeted Barry in Spanish, which the Honduran pilot translated.

"Yes," Barry said, "I am very glad to meet you after all this time."

"So, tell me, Mr MacKenzie, how is Miami?" Jorge Ochoa said. "I lived there for several years."

"Well, you ought to come back for a visit," Barry said.

Ochoa laughed. "Perhaps I will again someday." Ochoa asked about Barry's friend, William Roger Reeves.

Barry said he was glad to have been asked because Reeves had told Barry that he was owed $5 million by Ochoa.

"Oh, don't worry about that money for Roger," Ochoa said. "I gave it to a friend of Roger's. It's all taken care of." He told Barry that he could supply endless amounts of cocaine, but he had suffered some setbacks, including confiscations in the Bahamas and the loss of the Land of Tranquillity, a large cocaine processing lab in the jungle of Caquetá, Colombia, which had included nineteen labs, an independent water and electrical system and dormitories for its workers. Processing supplies had been flown in and processed cocaine was flown out via any eight airstrips. On March

10th, 1984, units of the Colombian National Police, assisted by the DEA, had raided the Land of Tranquillity, destroyed the complex and claimed to have disposed of 13.8 metric tons of cocaine valued at $1.2 billion. During the raid, documents had been found with the Ochoas' names.

"Things are real tight for us now," said Jorge Ochoa's brother-in-law. "People are investigating this large lab down in the Llanos Valley that Mr Lehder was running for us."

"Mr Carlos Lehder?" Barry said.

"Yes." While they were being forced to move their labs, Lehder had hidden their cocaine in underground bunkers throughout Colombia.

The next part of the conversation that Barry relayed back to the DEA may have been made up or at least exaggerated to entice the Reagan-Bush administration into helping him to remedy his legal problems. Barry claimed that the traffickers motioned him towards them and whispered that they had brokered a deal with Nicaraguan government ministers. The Reagan-Bush administration was desperate to link the Nicaraguan government with drug trafficking, so that they could drum up support to keep arming, financing and training the Nicaraguan rebels. The Reagan-Bush administration knew that the rebels were trafficking with the help of the CIA. Accusing the Nicaraguan government of involvement in trafficking would disguise their own complicity.

Barry later said that the agreement between the Medellín Cartel and the Nicaraguan government had been in its infancy. That he'd been sworn to blood secrecy never to mention the name Nicaragua again. "Even in the meetings from then on, it was going to be referred to as Costa Rica." Barry claimed that the Nicaraguans were making an airstrip for the refuelling of drug planes, so that planes could transport less fuel leaving Colombia and more cocaine.

At the meeting, Barry expressed surprise that the Medellín Cartel was in bed with the Communist government of Nicaragua. The traffickers protested that they were not Communists. "We don't particularly enjoy the same philosophy politically that they do, but they serve our means and we serve theirs."

"Well, I'm not real sure that an American would be welcome in Nicaragua smuggling cocaine," Barry said.

"You have nothing to worry about."

Jorge Ochoa said that he needed Barry to land and pick up 1,500 kilos of cocaine at a jungle airstrip north of Medellín and fly it to the USA, half destined for Miami, the rest for LA, where they were stockpiling cocaine in anticipation of high demand during the 1984 summer Olympic Games. After delivering the 1,500 kilos, Barry was to fly to an airstrip operated by the Nicaraguan government, while the Medellín Cartel prepared another 2,000 kilos. He wanted Barry to fly within ten days.

A week later in Miami, Barry met Lito at Auto World, a luxury car dealership that Lito co-owned with Pablo Escobar. Operated as a front company, Auto World moved 500 kilos of cocaine a week. Barry was informed that the Medellín Cartel had recently lost six planes in the Bahamas. The Miami distribution network was being overhauled by an ex-Venezuelan naval officer, Lizardo Marquez Perez, who was on the run from the authorities in his country for smuggling 667 kilos of cocaine and for calling for the overthrow of the government of Venezuela. He had earned an electrical-engineering degree from Georgia Tech in 1967. Like the Ochoas, he enjoyed horses.

In private, Lizardo told Barry that the Ochoas were concerned about Lito's laxity and complacency. Instead of using payphones, Lito had lazily used home phones. "I have to improve security," Lizardo said.

As well as investing in beepers with security codes, Lizardo showed Barry a draft of a security manual he had written, ten pages long, laying out the advantages and disadvantages of renting safe houses using false names. The document titled, "Notes to Meditate On (Ponder)," included, "The opportunity to obtain credit is lost... which makes it difficult in the future to obtain a new residence," but fake names allow, "the one who lives in the house" to "appear as the butler of the house. To any question [he can reply] 'the owners are travelling.'" He referred to cocaine as "the foods." "If something happens and the butlers are able to escape, no traces have been left of the foods, and so there wouldn't be any connection between: butler and food, between butler and the company and consequently, company and food. For this reason it is always necessary to use gloves."

Lizardo's criteria for houses included, "residential location, preferably in a low traffic street; lots of green space; garage for two cars; garage hopefully not within the neighbour's sight." The residents should be "preferably a couple with children," under instructions to "live a normal life... Try to imitate an American in all his habits, like mow the lawn, wash the car, etc. He must not have extravagant social events in the house, but may have an occasional barbecue, inviting trusted relatives."

As they both valued security highly, Barry and Lizardo bonded. Afterwards, Barry gave Lizardo's beeper number to the DEA. Barry transported Lizardo's daily reports to the Medellín Cartel, whose leaders were temporarily in Panama waiting for things to cool down in Colombia following the assassination of the justice minister.

With the pressure on to fly 1,500 kilos of cocaine, Barry told the cartel that he wanted to inspect the airstrip in Nicaragua first. In Miami, he bought a recreational vehicle for transporting the cocaine.

After Barry's Honduran co-pilot complained that Lito had stiffed him on $100,000 owed for a cocaine shipment he had flown to the Bahamas, Barry said, "If he owns half of Auto World, why don't you tell him that you'll take a brand-new automobile as part payment on your bill? Or two cars. One for you and one for your wife. And give me one while you're at it."

"Well, I never thought about it that way."

They went shopping at Auto World, where Barry picked out a four-door Mercedes 500 SEL priced at $63,585.

"If you want that one, you can have it." Lito gave it to Barry as a down payment.

Barry was due to fly 1,500 kilos of cocaine in two days, but during a test flight, his Learstar blew an engine. It cost $30,000 to fix and a week to repair.

In May 1984, Barry met the cartel in Panama. Pablo Escobar protested that they hadn't ordered the assassination of the justice minister. He claimed that it was a CIA plot designed to make the Colombian government want to extradite traffickers to America for trial. He said that their cocaine labs had been dismantled for relocation to Nicaragua. Cocaine supplies had been moved to the mountains. They wanted Barry to transport 1,500 kilos as soon as possible. They would instruct him from their new headquarters in Panama.

On May 20, 1984, Barry met them again in Panama in the basement of a white stucco house. The cartel introduced Barry to Federico Vaughan, who they claimed was a Nicaraguan government official. With slicked-back grey hair, Vaughan was sharply dressed in a silver business suit, tie, an expensive watch, sunglasses and cufflinks. Vaughan would accompany Barry to the Nicaraguan airfield, so he could inspect it. To avoid any harm in Nicaragua, Barry was to follow Vaughan's instructions. Vaughan introduced himself to Barry as the interior minister of the Nicaraguan Sandinista government, who were ready to process cocaine paste for the Medellín Cartel with ether from Germany.

The same day, Barry, his Honduran co-pilot and Vaughan took a commercial plane to Managua, Nicaragua, sitting separately, so as not to be associated with each other. At the airport, Vaughan got them through immigration without having their passports stamped. Vaughan's wife transported them to their house, where they stayed overnight.

Driving to the airfield the next day, Vaughan told them not to worry about the guards and checkpoints, which were a mere formality. In a rural setting five miles outside Managua, they stopped at a large oil refinery.

"This is the country's only refinery. Never fly near or over it." Vaughan pointed at anti-aircraft batteries on the perimeter. "Any aircraft that flies over the refinery, friend or foe, will be shot down immediately." He took them to a massive sunken lake, a volcano crater full of clear blue water. "This is the purest water in the country. The only unpolluted drinking water for Managua. In its own way, it's as vital as the oil refinery. If you fly near it, you will be shot down."

They travelled around a mountain, across a railroad track and onto an airfield called Los Brasiles with a lone paved runway. At roadblocks and checkpoints, Vaughan was waved through by guards wielding AK-47s. He took them to a hanger designated for their mission. Inside was a Piper Cheyenne owned by Pablo Escobar.

Barry asked about the length of the runway and its foundation and texture. Vaughan escorted them along the 3,500-foot runway.

When Barry and his co-pilot walked onto the grass to examine a drainage ditch, Vaughan yelled, "Stop! It's mined with landmines. If you have any problem landing your aircraft, don't veer to the western side or you'll be killed."

Afterwards, they ate at a steakhouse. Vaughan drew arrows on a map of Nicaragua to indicate the smuggling mission's entry and exit routes. "You need a code for entering Nicaraguan airspace. You are to call the Sandino tower on a certain VHF frequency and identify yourselves as Yankee November Whisky X-ray Yankee. Then the tower will reroute you to Los Brasiles. All approaches to the city of Managua are covered by anti-aircraft guns to protect against night attacks by the Contra rebels."

On the map, Barry drew circles around the gun emplacements, the oil refinery, Vaughan's house and the Sandinista People's Army headquarters.

Back in Panama City, Barry told the cartel that the runway was ideal, but the hangar was too small for the plane he had in mind.

Pablo said that Barry's mission had changed. Instead of

picking up a second shipment in Nicaragua of 2,000 kilos, Barry needed to go to Bolivia for 6,000 kilos of cocaine base for the new labs in Nicaragua.

After landing in Florida, Barry rushed to the Fort Lauderdale Federal Courthouse for his sentencing hearing.

In a black robe, grey-haired Judge Roettger entered the court room, sat on a leather chair next to the American flag and gazed down from his podium, unaware of Barry's role as a prized DEA informant. "Mr Seal, our purpose in this proceeding today is to hear my sentence for your conviction on one count of Possession With Intent To Sell An Unlawful Narcotic. The other charges against you before this court are yet to be tried, and they will be sentenced independently. Before I pass sentence, Mr Seal, I want you to know that I consider you an evil man. You deal in death and operate with no consideration for your fellow man. You don't care where the deadly substance that you smuggle goes or whom it hurts. Therefore, I impose upon you the maximum sentence available to me on this charge. That being ten years in federal prison. You will begin serving the sentence immediately." The gavel banged.

Barry stood and yelled, "Where is the goddam DEA?"

His lawyer grabbed him. "I don't know, Barry. They said they'd be here."

A guard handcuffed Barry and led him away. He was transported to the Broward County jail.

Two days later, the DEA agents visited Barry.

"Don't open that fucking door!" Barry yelled at a guard. "You let those assholes in here, I might kill them."

"I know how you feel, Barry," Joura said.

"How in the hell do you know how I feel?" Barry yelled from behind cell bars. "You been double-crossed lately?"

"I know we weren't there, but we're gonna take care of it," Jacobsen said.

"I know this won't help, but it was a screw-up," Joura said. "The judge didn't get the word on you."

"Ten years!" Barry yelled.

"We're trying to get a hearing right now," Joura said.

"We wanna stay in business with you, Barry," Jacobsen said.

"Why should I do shit for you? What does it get me? Go!"

Barry was incarcerated for two days until Jacobson and Joura convinced the judge in a closed hearing to release him on bond. Outside the jail, Barry got in the back of the agents' car. Joura apologised.

"The judge released you to us," Jacobsen said. "You can keep on working with us if you want. He's gonna re-examine your sentence in about five months."

"I owe you an apology, Bob, Jake," Barry said, his expression forlorn. "I'm sorry I blew up in there. I've had a chance to think about it a lot. I don't know whether you guys know this: I don't do drugs. When I first started out in the business, everybody was doing them. It was called recreational. Nobody was hooked. Nobody was dying. Bad guys weren't killing bad guys. It was all peace and love and that kind of thing. But now. So I thought about it. Well, I was on the wrong side. I'd even fooled myself into believing that working with you guys I was making up for the bad that I did, but I was wrong. The judge was right. I hadn't paid. I hadn't made up for it. But I'm gonna do it now. And I'm gonna prove myself to you. Anyway, I want you guys to know how I feel. Now I'm gonna go call Lito. He's gonna be wondering where I've been. And I'm gonna make up some kind of story, so we can get back into business and we can go out and we can burn some bad guys. All right."

CHAPTER 12

Carlos Lehder

Fresh out of jail, Barry called his Honduran co-pilot, who asked where Barry had been. Barry said he had been busy. With the 1,500 kilos scheduled to be transported the next day, they had no time to waste.

"I think my wife might have turned government informant," the co-pilot said, paranoid after free-basing cocaine. "She was busted for coke while we were in Panama, but when I got home, she'd been released. She had come with me on trips to Panama. She may have talked. Unless she comes with us, I'm not going. I need to keep an eye on her."

Barry tried to talk him out of bringing his wife, but it was no use, so he relented. For two days in Louisiana, Barry waited for the co-pilot, who kept promising to get on the next flight, but never showed up. In the end, Barry asked Emile Camp to step in.

On May 28, 1984, they flew a Learstar from Arkansas to Medellín over the Colombian jungle.

"That strip looks mighty wet!" Barry yelled.

"So," Emile said. "You gonna try it?"

"I didn't fly all this way to turn around."

"That mountain's awful close and that river's pretty high. Do not enter that banana grove. It'll take the wings off. That grass is too wet. You're gonna play hell getting out of there, I'll tell you that."

"Anything else?" Barry said.

"It's a piece of cake."

With its propellers roaring, the plane swerved to land. Water and mud splashed off the wheels as it skidded on the landing strip.

Barry was talking to the ground crew when a long-haired man with a mischievous boyish face galloped towards the plane on a white Arabian stallion, brandishing a machine gun and barking orders.

"Who the hell are you?" Barry said.

"Carlos Lehder!" he yelled. Barry had heard stories about Lehder, a co-founder of the Medellín Cartel who worshipped Adolf Hitler and John Lennon, and was notorious for militaristic behaviour. Of German and Colombian descent, he had managed to take over a Bahamian Island by buying the neighbours out and terrifying the rest by unleashing squadrons of neo-Nazis armed with automatic weapons and Dobermans. From 1978 to 1982, his island, Norman's Cay, was the Caribbean's hub for drug smuggling.

"Now you will do what I say. Immediately. Before someone sees your plane from the air!"

A tractor appeared, pulling over a ton of cocaine.

"Holy shit!" Emile said. "They expect us to fly out of this swamp with all of that shit."

"No, of course not," Barry said.

"We can't get up with that much weight."

"Don't you worry. I'm gonna reason with the man." Barry laughed. "Hey, lifting off this muddy strip with all of that weight is impossible."

Barry's attempt at reasoning ended up with him pinned against the tractor and Lehder shoving a gun in his chin. "I don't care what you say. You will fly every last gram of it out of here just like you contracted to do. And if you refuse, I'll kill you right now and your co-pilot will do it. We're going to load this plane and you're going to get out of here. You start loading fuel."

With a defeated expression, Barry complied. In fifteen minutes, 1,500 kilos of cocaine in duffel bags and burlap sacks were loaded.

Barry manned the plane. "You ready?"

"No," Emile said.

"I knew I could count on you."

As it picked up speed on the muddy runway, the plane rumbled and bounced, but failed to rise.

"C'mon, baby," Emile said.

Lehder galloped alongside, shooting at the earth, his workers lined up at the periphery of the jungle, cheering for the plane to lift. It elevated to a crescendo of cheering, but dropped and skidded. The right wheel sank into the mud and was ripped from its undercarriage. Barry lost control. The plane crashed with a mechanical crunch.

"Get out, man! The fuel's gonna blow!" Barry said, scrambling to exit.

Lehder appeared, bursting off more gunfire. "Gringos! Maricones!"

Anticipating an explosion, Barry and Emile dived into the jungle.

Lehder ordered his workers to rescue the cocaine from the burning plane.

"That crazy bastard's making them go to the plane," Emile said, clutching a tree. "They'll be barbecued."

Barry and Emile leapt from the jungle and tried to stop the two dozen workers charging towards the plane. They had no success.

"Help them now!" Lehder yelled, shooting his gun at the dirt around their feet.

Barry and Emile joined the men grabbing huge packages of cocaine from the plane. As they charged away, the plane exploded, knocking the men over. Flames shot dozens of feet in all directions. Two workers were burnt.

Eventually, the tractor transported the cocaine back to its storage facility, where it was inventoried.

"Cabrones, we have another plane!" Lehder yelled.

"I don't give a damn what kind of plane you've got," Barry said, his face muddy. "We can't take off with that load. We've gotta wait for this field to dry."

Barry and Emile were flown to Medellín. After showering in the mansion of a cartel member, they were shown around the grounds. They admired a waterfall, a tropical garden, a swimming pool and an Olympic-sized cycling track.

A replacement plane was found: a Titan 404. "Certainly you're not going to be able to carry the full 1,500 kilos that you tried to carry with the larger plane. Can you carry half of it?"

"No, sir," Barry said, worried about the plane going down over the Gulf of Mexico. "Because then I wouldn't be able to add any fuel."

"And with a stop in Nicaragua? How much can you take?"

"Well, with a stop in Nicaragua, we can probably take 700 to 750 kilos." The crash had played into Barry's hands because the sooner he could get into Nicaragua, the more the Reagan-Bush administration would be satisfied by the drugs link and the more predisposed it would be to helping his legal situation.

At the Hotel Intercontinental in Medellín, Barry called Joura in Gulfport to appraise him about the new flight schedule. In Gulfport, Joura and Jacobsen were with the recreational vehicle, awaiting the 1,500 kilos.

The next day, Barry and Emile returned to the jungle airstrip. Each got on top of the burned remains of the Learstar, while the other snapped photos. In the jungle, they spent three days with Lehder, who was guarding the cocaine. Showing them 3,000 kilos, he claimed that 6,000 kilos of cocaine base in Bolivia were waiting to be shipped to Nicaragua.

On June 2, 1984, Barry told the DEA that he was flying to Nicaragua the next day. On June 3, at 10:30 pm, Jacobsen received a call in Miami from one of Barry's associates, stating that a radio transmission had been received and Barry was returning to Nicaragua after experiencing engine trouble. Three hours later, Jacobsen heard that Barry had landed in Nicaragua and might have legal problems. No more contact was received.

Three days later, Barry appeared in the US without any cocaine. At a debriefing, he told the DEA that on June 3, he'd flown the Titan 404 from Colombia with 700 kilos. Stopping for fuel in Los Brasiles, Nicaragua, had taken longer than expected. After taking off in the darkness, Barry had flown without any lights over a mountainous region. North of Managua, the plane was illuminated by anti-aircraft tracers. His left engine was hit and the plane started to descend fast. To avoid crashing, Barry had returned to Los Brasiles. Unable to land at the dark airfield, he scrambled to radio Vaughan, but he had gone home.

With no options left, Barry radioed an emergency broadcast to Sandino International Airport in Managua, using a code provided by Vaughan. Upon landing, the plane was surrounded by soldiers. Barry insisted on talking to Vaughan. He was granted a phone call, but Vaughan was still absent.

A sergeant who knew Vaughan had the cocaine unloaded from Barry's plane. He told Barry and Emile to keep quiet and to play along with whatever happened. "Everything will be fine."

Barry and Emile were incarcerated overnight in The Bunker, a military compound in downtown Managua. The next day, they were released to Vaughan and transported to a large landed estate. Pablo Escobar greeted them. He'd moved there to supervise the cocaine-processing operation.

A few days later, Vaughan showed up with a newspaper: *El Nuevo Diario*. "This is the reason we wanted you to keep your mouth shut at the airport, because we had to keep this entire incident very quiet in the newspapers. We don't control all the newspapers here." He showed Barry a two-paragraph article that stated anti-aircraft gunners at Sandino Airport had shot at an Agrarian Reform Air Transport Company plane because the plane was unable to signal its location:

"The DAA [Anti-Aircraft Defense] had to signal and fire warning shots to induce it to land at the airport – which happened without untoward consequences."

Vaughan said the accident had happened because he hadn't prepared for a smuggling flight in darkness. The gunners hadn't seen Barry. They had heard him and shot at the noise. Better communication was required next time. Upset that he hadn't been able to reach Vaughan from the plane, Barry said they should buy walkie-talkies.

Pablo said that the new cocaine lab was at a ranch south of Managua. It would be ready for full production in two weeks. Lehder had almost fifteen tons of cocaine base, which would produce approximately one fifth of the cocaine consumed in America annually.

"Well, that's going to take a real large plane," Barry said. "You should buy a military cargo plane like what I've seen advertised in the aviation-trade magazine."

Pablo wanted Barry to obtain such a plane and pick up the first 700 kilos.

"Is that cocaine safe?" Barry said.

"We haven't lost one single gram," Vaughan said.

Pablo's Piper Cheyenne required maintenance in America, so Barry and Emile flew home in it.

Barry gave Lito Escobar's shopping list, which included night-vision goggles and a dozen high-frequency radios that cost $12,000 each.

CHAPTER 13

The Fat Lady

Through his CIA connections, Barry obtained a Fairchild C-123K Provider, a massive camouflage-green twin-engine military cargo plane used in the Vietnam War. He nicknamed it the Fat Lady. On June 18, 1984, Barry flew the Fat Lady to Rickenbacker Air Force Base near Columbus, Ohio. Repairing and retrofitting the plane, Air Force employees worked around the clock. The military made repairs worth $40,000 at the taxpayers' expense.

Barry was instructed to take pictures of Nicaraguan officials associated with cocaine. He told the CIA, "Let me explain something to you, mister. There's gonna be a lot of men with guns down there. Nervous men, who aren't gonna exactly say cheese to some gringo pilot with a camera."

Five days later, the plane landed at Homestead Air Force Base near Miami. A transponder was installed to allow the DEA to track its flight. The CIA added a hidden 35-mm camera in the nosecone and another was put inside a fake electronics box in the rear cargo hold, facing the doors. A pinhole lens in the box would allow the camera to film the cocaine getting loaded into the back of the plane. Barry was given a radio-controlled trigger for the cameras, with a long wire antenna attached to it.

"What! Where in the hell do you expect me to hide that? Stick it up my ass?" Barry said, scowling at the antenna.

"You can put it in your pocket."

"All five feet of it?"

"Put it in your pocket and let the antenna slide down your leg."

Barry did so and pressed the remote control. Enraged by the loud clicking noise the camera made, he cursed the CIA men in suits. "I'm tired of wasting my time with you assholes. I'll get your fucking photographs. Autographed! But what are you gonna do for me?"

"We have a deal, Mr Seal."

"The judge. Say it, dammit!"

"We'll speak to the judge on your behalf."

In a Miami hotel room, Barry called Vaughan. He recorded the conversation for the DEA. "I was going to see my grandmother at noon on Saturday," Barry said, using code for the cocaine shipment. Referring to the Fat Lady and worried about getting shot down again, Barry said, "It's a big Cadillac... Very big, big car... I just wanted to make sure that my grandmother was going to tell the landlord that the car was very big, so that the landlord wouldn't be excited when they saw it."

"No, no, no," Vaughan said. "Everything is OK about that."

On June 24, 1984, Barry told Vaughan about a party tomorrow at his grandmother's, meaning that the cocaine was coming the next day. "I mean, everybody is coming to the party and you've notified those boys in green." He was still concerned about getting shot down.

"Right," Vaughan said.

"They're all – everybody is notified?" Barry said.

"Yes," Vaughan said.

"Excellent. OK. I just want to make sure. I don't want any problems."

"Yes, everybody is going to be there."

"OK, good. And is Pedro coming? Because I have that liquor for him," Barry said, referring to Pablo and his shopping list.

"Yes, yes, he's coming," Vaughan said.

"I'm leaving for the party at midnight. Has it been raining on the yard where we park the cars at the party?" Barry said.

"It's dry and hard and only a little bit muddy in one small area."

"I can't stay at the party long. I have to try to leave as soon as possible," Barry said, hoping to refuel fast.

"Yeah, we're going to be ready for that."

"OK. Now remember this motorhome is very big and it's a funny, funny colour, so don't let anybody get excited."

Vaughan laughed. "No, that's perfect."

At 1 pm on June 25, 1984, Barry landed at Los Brasiles near Managua and dropped open the back of the plane. He delivered $454,000 to Pablo from Lito. He later claimed that on the ground were Vaughan, Pablo, another cartel leader called Gacha and a group of soldiers. "How do you like the plane?" Barry yelled over the engine noise. "I call her the Fat Lady."

Soldiers started loading duffel bags of cocaine into the cargo hold. Every time Barry pressed his remote control to take a picture, the camera clicked so loudly that it could be heard outside the Fat Lady. To drown out the noise, Barry switched on the plane's generators. Overhead, an American spy plane took high-resolution pictures.

"Shut down your engines!" Pablo yelled.

"I can't. We gotta keep them hot," Barry said, maintaining the sound to disguise the camera noise.

An overweight bodyguard with a gun entered the plane and started to nosy around as if he could hear the camera noise. Emile revved the propellers to camouflage the sound. The bodyguard checked around and finally left. After being loaded with 700 kilos of cocaine and 2,000 gallons of fuel – which took about an hour – the plane took off.

The following morning, the Fat Lady landed at Homestead Air Force Base. The DEA seized 700 kilos of cocaine and the CIA took the camera film. The mission had been a success. The photos showed Barry, Pablo, Vaughan and Gacha loading twenty-five-kilo duffel bags.

The same night of his return, Barry arranged a meeting with Lito at Dadeland Mall. Lito parked and Barry joined him in his car just before 10 pm.

"Where's the load?" Lito said.

"It's sitting right there in the Winnebago," Barry said.

Lito was unhappy. The cars in the parking lot were dwindling, leaving the Winnebago exposed. Barry left the Winnebago with Lito.

The DEA watched a man in a white T-shirt get out of a Chevy truck, get inside the Winnebago and drive off. It was followed by several cars and a helicopter. It was also followed by cartel workers in a Chevy truck and a grey Mercedes-Benz.

At a designated moment, a DEA agent in an old car crashed into the Winnebago. The Florida Highway Patrol arrived next. The accident had been staged to protect Barry's cover. The trooper had been instructed to allow the driver of the Winnebago to escape.

"Licence and registration, please," the trooper said.

The young Colombian produced his licence, but no registration. "Can I go across the street and make a telephone call?"

"Yes," the trooper said, allowing him to escape.

The Colombian walked across the street to a Wendy's restaurant, rushed behind the building and sprinted away. After witnessing the accident, a pedestrian saw the Colombian fleeing. He chased the Colombian and grabbed him. They were fighting when the police pulled up, leaving the trooper no choice but to arrest the Colombian.

At 2 am, Barry's phone rang. "Have you heard the news?" said an employee of Lito. "The load got busted."

Barry was summoned to meet Lito. Anticipating danger, he asked Jacobsen to organise surveillance.

At Tony Roma's restaurant, Lito told Barry that Jota – the Spanish word for the letter J – the highest-ranking member of the Medellín Cartel in Miami, wanted to see everybody right away. "One of our people was following the Winnebago. He said he saw a car ram into the side purposely. He's trying to say it was a setup."

Lito transported Barry to a luxury condominium in South Miami. A group of Colombians were inside. Jota said he was investigating the seizure. The young Colombian who had followed the Winnebago said he had seen a driver instigate the accident.

"He doesn't know what he's talking about," said Lito, whose role in the deal meant that he would be held accountable if it wasn't an accident. Lito asked for Barry's thoughts.

"If Jota thinks something's wrong," Barry said, "we should immediately shut everything down."

The Colombians conferred in Spanish. Jota asked to see Barry's driver's licence and said he would get back to him. Everyone had to remain in the condominium until Jota left to avoid him from being followed.

The next day, Lito called in a good mood. Everything was settled. He asked Barry to pick up more cocaine in Nicaragua. Barry agreed and called Vaughan in Managua.

"My friend told me that everything was OK," Vaughan said.

"Yeah, only one person in the hospital and he seems to be OK," Barry said, referring to one person arrested who wasn't talking to the police. Barry complained about the arrest and demanded that someone senior make some changes.

Vaughan said the cartel would listen to Barry. "They have a very, very good and special consideration for you. Our common friend [Pablo] wants a favour. Sometimes my English is not so good. Small water vehicle for, uh, to have fun... It's some kind of boat. Water boat."

Barry deciphered that Pablo wanted a rubber raft with an outboard motor. He added it to the shopping list, which included plane parts, video recorders, ten-speed bicycles, Marlboro cigarettes and Johnnie Walker Black Label Scotch. Pablo also wanted $1.5 million in cash to pay the Nicaraguan government for landing rights.

Lito prevaricated over getting the money.

In Miami's Omni International Hotel, Barry called Pablo. He had a translator with him. Without the translator noticing, he attached a small suction cup from a Sony Walkman to the receiver to record the call for the DEA.

"It's MacKenzie calling Pedro," the translator said in Spanish to the man who had answered.

"Tell him that they're jacking me around," Barry told the translator. "That you and MacKenzie are preparing to leave tomorrow night and we have all of the plane parts and everything, that the bill is about $150,000 and they won't give us that money."

"The gentleman with whom he works didn't deliver anything to him?" Pablo said.

"No."

Pablo said he would call the Friends. After being told that the $1.5 million hadn't arrived, Pablo said, "Oh, I see. I'm going to get in contact with them to see what the problem is."

Shortly thereafter, an enraged Lito called Barry. "I am down in the Keys vacationing. I just got notified that you need this million and a half dollars. And I got it from Pablo Escobar and his people. I don't work for Pablo Escobar and his people. I work for Jorge and I don't appreciate getting called out at this time of the night to bring you this million dollars."

The next day, Lito delivered $1.5 million in three suitcases and a cardboard box. The DEA sent a photographer to document the cash.

On July 7, 1984, Barry flew the Fat Lady to Las Brasiles, where he told Vaughan that he had received a radio message from one of his guys in Mississippi that the offloading site was under police surveillance. Unknown to Vaughan, Barry wanted to leave the cocaine on Nicaraguan soil because if he brought it back, the DEA would have to seize it. Two loads confiscated in a row would have put too much suspicion on Barry and perhaps ended the biggest investigation in DEA history.

Barry was taken to Pablo, who thanked him for his caution and suggested that Barry arrange for underground hiding places to be dug near his landing strips, as had been done in Colombia. Nine-hundred kilos would remain in Nicaragua.

The DEA wanted Barry to fly the cocaine base from South America, so that they could identify the locations of the labs in

Nicaragua and map out the cartel's supply network in Bolivia. The cartel authorised Barry to set up a radio communications base in Managua to guide the coca paste flights from the Andes to Los Brasiles. This massive opportunity would enable the DEA to trace the drugs back to their source. The DEA also wanted Barry to entice Jorge Ochoa and Pablo into a country that had an extradition treaty with America, so they could be deported and have to stand trial in the US.

Before Barry left Nicaragua, Pablo raised the matter of the cocaine base. He wanted the Fat Lady to transport the finished product from Nicaragua to an airstrip in northern Mexico acquired by Gacha, who was running the cartel's West Coast distribution. Small planes would transport the cocaine to the US, including to Georgia. Pablo wanted Barry to examine the airstrips in Mexico and Georgia. Barry agreed. The DEA planned to have the cartel leaders arrested in Mexico.

CHAPTER 14

Oliver North

On June 26, 1984, one day after Barry had transported 700 kilos to Florida, Oliver North – George HW Bush's frontman – wrote in his notebook: *nic drug operation C-123 acquired by DEA source installed two cameras Miami plane t/o landed Los Brasiles Freddie Vaughan works for Tomas Borge Photos show Vaughan + Nic Inf Troops 750 lbs of cocaine.*

With great urgency, the rolls of film containing the photos Barry had taken from the Fat Lady were flown to Washington.

On June 27, 1984, David Westrate, the DEA's deputy assistant administrator for operations, went to the White House to meet Oliver North and Duane "Dewey" Clarridge, a CIA agent. They discussed releasing Barry's photos in the hope of generating support for the Nicaraguan rebels.

Ron Caffery, the head of the DEA's cocaine desk in Washington DC, went to the Old Executive Office Building adjacent to the White House and showed Oliver North enlargements of the grainy photos of Vaughan and Pablo.

North was dressed in a military uniform with lots of medals and adornments. There was a large American flag on the wall behind him. "These pictures are already famous around here. The White House is very interested in anything that comes out of Nicaragua." Pointing at a picture, North said, "Now this is the guy that they call Federico Vaughan right?"

"He's a Sandinista official," said Dewey Clarridge, holding a dossier on Vaughan. "Assistant to Tomás Borge, Nicaragua Interior Minister," he said, referring to a co-founder of the Sandinista National Liberation Front in Nicaragua.

"Sandinista," Caffery said. "I wasn't told that."

"Oh. It's true." Pointing at a picture, Clarridge said, "And this is your undercover man. What's his name?"

"Seal. Barry Seal is his name," Caffery said.

They decided to send Barry back to Nicaragua with $1.5 million in DEA cash for more cocaine, as well as gifts for Pablo and Vaughan. North wanted the sting operation to go down outside Nicaragua, so that after Vaughan and Pablo were arrested, the $1.5 million could go to the Nicaraguan rebels to buy US arms. Caffery said the US Attorney's Office would never approve of such a plan.

"When will this information go public?" North gushed, referring to the photos.

"It won't," Caffery said.

"Why not?" North said.

"Well, it would end a vitally important investigation for one thing. And it'd seriously endanger Barry Seal's life for another."

"The public has a right to know the drug activities of Nicaragua, Mr Caffery," North said.

"Colonel North, Barry Seal is inside the biggest drug operation in the world. The leaders of the Medellín Cartel trust him, for God's sake. And we believe he might actually lure one of them to the US, so we can arrest him. And we can't throw that kind of opportunity away."

"Listen, Ron, there's an important vote coming up in Congress on an appropriations bill to fund the Contras," North said, referring to the Nicaraguan rebels. "Sandinista involvement in drugs will make a big difference."

"I'm sure the US Attorney's Office will make it public at the proper time," Caffery said.

"So tell us about this Seal. What sort of man is he?" Clarridge said.

"It depends on who you talk to. He's either a genius or he's scum of the earth."

Despite Caffery's warning about the dangers of releasing the information, it was immediately leaked out by the Reagan-Bush administration.

On June 27, 1984, a speech was made by General Paul Gorman, the head of the Pentagon's Southern Command, at the American Chamber of Commerce in El Salvador. The general said he had proof that the Sandinista government was involved in drug trafficking.

In light of the leaks, a meeting was held with Barry present among DEA and other officials to decide whether to send Barry back for more cocaine. An argument ensued over the source of the leaks. One official protested that his case against Jorge Ochoa would crumble if Barry were killed. The consensus was against sending Barry back.

Barry was stood in a navy suit, wearing his trademark gold-rimmed aviator sunglasses. "If I don't go, it's all blown."

"Yeah, but if you do, they might have made you," Jacobsen said.

"If I don't go, the whole investigation's over."

"But if you do, you might be dead," Jacobsen said.

"If you're feeling sorry for me, Jacobsen," Barry said, hand on heart.

"Jacobsen's right," Joura said. "The whole thing may fall down on top of you, Barry."

"Or may not. We've gotta play it out."

"It's enough," Joura said. "What we've got will get you a lighter sentence. Trust me."

"Wait a minute," Barry said. "It's not about a lighter sentence anymore. All right. It's about walking into that court one of these days with Ochoa, Escobar, Gacha. Every one of them in our pocket." Pointing at himself, Barry said, "I can do that. They haven't got me. Not me. I'm sure of it."

"There's no way you can be sure of that, man," Jacobsen said, throwing up his hands.

"In my guts. OK. And that's what this is all about," Barry said, shaking his fists. "I can do it. My guts tell me I can. I am the best. And don't you try and stop me now!"

"It's not worth the risk for one more run."

"One more run! They want me to haul 30,000 pounds of base from Colombia to Nicaragua. It can't all go to one place. Then I can find the labs and the new labs in Nicaragua. What is the Sandinista involvement? How much is that information worth to the DEA and the Justice Department?" With Barry laying it on thick about the Nicaraguan connection, the expressions in the room softened as the officials warmed up to sending him back. "I might even be able to bring Mr Ochoa himself right into the US here on the pretence that his organisation is falling apart here."

"Do you really think you could do that, Mr Seal?"

"I am the best." Barry approached an official and squatted down. "And it wouldn't hurt your career too much if I did, would it?"

The men laughed.

"What do you think about that, Joura?" Barry said.

"I think we just turned a corner in the War on Drugs, Barry," Joura said to more laughter.

"Alright then. I'll go just one more time. You've convinced me."

After the meeting, Barry told Emile Camp that he was flying solo. With a pained expression, Emile returned to Joura and Jacobsen at the hangar. Awaiting Barry's return, their stress rose during every hour that passed. The following morning, a radio signal came into the hangar: "Fat Lady. All is well. Do you read me? Jorge [Ochoa] would not come along. Not this trip."

On July 8, 1984, after Barry had left 900 kilos behind in Nicaragua, Joura discovered that the *Washington Times* was about to publish a story about Barry's undercover work. As the paper was a Reagan-Bush administration favourite, Joura figured that the White House was leaking information, probably via Oliver North with George HW Bush's approval. After the DEA contacted the paper, it agreed to postpone publishing the story for at least a week.

On July 17, 1984, the *Washington Times* ran the story just as

Barry was flying to a 40,000-acre ranch in Mexico to meet cartel members. After receiving a frantic radio transmission, Barry flew back to Miami.

Concerned that its cover would soon be blown in Florida thanks to the White House and the *Washington Times*, the DEA hurriedly obtained search warrants and indictments.

Barry lured Lito to the Skyways Motel in Miami, where he and an accomplice were arrested. Lito claimed that he was a simple car washer called Jorge Negrete and showed a driver's licence with that name. But the DEA knew that his real name was Carlos Bustamante.

All of the heads of the Medellín Cartel were out of the US, so they remained free. Denying any involvement in trafficking, the Nicaraguan government said that Vaughan had been a low-level trade official who had quit his job a long time before Barry's undercover work.

One of the DEA heads, Frank Monastero, lambasted Oliver North for the leak. North denied everything. He claimed that inaccuracies in the story proved that he had nothing to do with it. Monastero responded that he didn't believe North as planting inaccuracies in a story was a method used by a leaker to cover his tracks.

The story didn't even generate any support for the Nicaraguan rebels. Within months, Congress rejected providing the rebels with aid.

The leak had destroyed Barry's undercover work. After suffering a period of trouble, the heads of the Medellín Cartel returned to Colombia and it was business as usual. They were protected by armies of bodyguards and officials on their payroll. Pablo was living in Medellín and attending bullfights and soccer games. Cocaine production increased so much that the American wholesale price fell from $25,000 per kilo – its peak after the raid of the Land of Tranquillity – to $14,000.

CHAPTER 15

Mena

On a hot July 8, 1984, twenty Nicaraguans arrived in Mena aboard a black C-130 military cargo plane flown by an older pilot called Bill Cooper. Wearing Ray-Bans and a hodgepodge of civilian clothing, they carried their bags into a hangar. Spotting a Cessna, they dropped their belongings to check it out.

"Take those fucking sunglasses off, soldiers!" yelled a Panamanian called Diego, their temporary field commander. The trainees received Cessna 414 manuals. "You need to memorise them!"

Terry Reid and Emile Camp reckoned it would be hard work getting the Nicaraguans up to scratch – so they could fly missions over their country – within four months.

Barry flew in a new camp commander for the Nicaraguans. Ramon Medina – real name Luis Posada Cariles – was a Cuban mercenary and a terrorist who was supposed to be in a Venezuelan prison for bombing a Cuban airplane in 1976, killing everyone on-board. The CIA had helped him to escape.

Barry met Terry in Little Rock for dinner at the SOB's. "My plans have changed," Barry said, ruffled. "I won't be spending the night here. I need you to do me a favour in the morning. I've got a briefcase out in the car that's got some money in it to give to Dan Lasater. It's for a sure-fire investment deal he's turned me on to. I'm gonna need someone I can really trust and I mean really trust. I know Aki is having me watched. Ain't this a great business? Everybody's fucking watching everybody else. At some point, Terry, you're gonna have to decide who you really trust, too. So it's time to decide. Me or Aki? Who are you gonna go with?"

Terry paused to think.

"Look," Barry said, "you told me a long time ago, you wanted to learn how to handle the suits. Well, I'm ready to teach you, but I gotta know you're on my side. Play things Aki's way and he'll be using you forever while he gets promoted from one GS fucking level to the next."

"OK." Terry asked Barry about the information Barry had previously hinted that he possessed about Vice President George HW Bush.

"Oh, that's something I probably shouldn't have said. Let's just say I came into possession of certain sensitive information about the Bush family on my last trip to Central America."

"OK, but if this is a relationship built on trust, first, what have you been doing in Central America?"

"Lots of things. Some of which I can't tell you about. You really don't need to know, and I guarantee you don't want to know, so you don't become a liability, too. But the part I want to talk to you about tonight, if you're in, is guns and money. You sure you're in?"

"Barry, I'm not totally stupid. I've pretty much pieced together on my own that you're flying weapons down south. And I would assume that you're doing that with the blessing of the CIA and the White House. This operation is too large and too well-equipped to otherwise exist undetected. I would also assume that you're motivated for reasons other than patriotism. Barry, I fought a war in which I was paid nothing. It'd certainly be nice to fight and win one, not only to heal a bunch of old wounds, but to serve my country and get paid as well. Yeah, if that's what you're talking about, count me in."

Barry said he had been flying weapons from Mena to El Salvador and other countries. The size of the shipments had grown so big that he had been given the C-123 a.k.a. the Fat Lady. Barry had access to two identical C-123s, right down to having the same tail number. Barry said he had access to two of everything, including Navajo and Seneca aircraft as the CIA had planes hidden all over the place. Duplicates were required for various reasons, including human and mechanical error. Also, to move attention from a plane being used in covert activity, to send pursuers on a wild goose chase or to appear to be in two different places simultaneously.

Barry said that the US Army and National Guard had donated weapons parts for the Nicaraguan rebels and for Terry not to let Aki know that Barry had revealed that. Barry said the CIA was selling M16A1s – guns that had jammed when exposed to sand in Vietnam – to the Nicaraguan rebels. The CIA was keeping the profits and there was no paperwork to show that anything had transpired. To circumvent laws pertaining to the sale of fully automatic weapons, the guns were built out of parts from inventory and parts cast at the CIA's foundry.

He said key players, acting under the guise of patriotism, were making millions off the weapons transactions. Barry was flying so much cash to Arkansas for them that he didn't want to risk getting caught with it. "The Agency's having me move in large quantities of cash from foreign sources for investments here. Lasater's part of that operation. When we sell the weapons, I fly down there. The profits in cash are flown back here for depositing. Trouble is, the Agency doesn't want anyone to know about the profits. So, if I'm being followed out of Central America, and if someone knows I'm carrying the cash, I need a way to throw them off my tail."

To help avoid detection, he wanted Terry to fly a duplicate plane as part of a technique taught by the CIA, which was used to penetrate foreign airspace. On a napkin, Barry illustrated how two planes could piggyback: appear as one blip on radar, fooling air-traffic controllers. The main aircraft could then disappear on a covert mission, without air-traffic control realising it had been switched. Barry had two identical Senecas: November 8658 Echo and November 8049 Zulu. He would base one at Little Rock Air Center for Terry to rendezvous with above Texarkana. "You'll join in behind me on my tail, and I mean on my fucking tail! I want you to be able to count the rivets that mount the tail hook.

Use your night-vision system. Then after you become me, you just proceed up to Mena and land. It's that simple."

"Let's go out and practise in the daytime," Terry said.

"Sounds good to me. I'll bring Emile. He's in on this, too. And you know what's great? He and you look a lot alike. At a distance, with you sitting in the airplane, I've confused you for him."

Outside, Barry fetched a locked briefcase from his Mercedes. "Do me a favour, take this by Dan Lasater's place first thing in the morning and don't leave it unguarded. It's a sizeable deposit, courtesy of Uncle Sam."

"Can I ask where you're going? I thought you were gonna spend the night."

"So did I. Me and the Fat Lady have an appointment down south. See you later, piggyback."

With the White House and Oliver North leaking information to taint the Nicaraguan government, Barry's life was on the line from the Medellín Cartel, who now knew that the pilot of the Fat Lady was an informant. The *New York Times* announced, "US accuses Managua of Role in Cocaine Traffic."

Barry had brought the DEA their biggest drug case. The DEA in Florida had been protecting him, but now the DEA in Louisiana was going after him on drug charges. Aiming to take Barry down and gain glory and headlines, the Louisiana federal prosecutor was unaware of Barry's covert work for the CIA at Mena. Oliver North couldn't intervene with the Louisiana justice system because exposure of the covert work Barry was doing for him might have brought down the Reagan-Bush government, which was locking-up drug users from the poorest neighbourhoods at record levels while using the proceeds of cocaine smuggled into America to finance illegal wars.

Barry decided to fight back. With federal government agencies turning against him, it was time to go on the offensive with the knowledge he had about the extent of the Bush family's involvement in drugs.

In late September 1984, Barry appeared over Nella in a camouflaged Fairchild C-123. The Nicaraguan trainee pilots were spellbound as the massive plane skimmed a forest, almost cutting off treetops. Barry landed at Mena. Two privileged students each week were allowed to sit in the cockpit and daydream about flying a C-123. With a grim expression, Barry told his staff that the White House wanted the students flying missions as soon as possible.

Barry's problems were getting to him. Just when he needed them the most to testify in court, the DEA in Florida seemed to be abandoning him. Due to the Louisiana indictment, he planned to release some of the conversations he had secretly recorded during his work for the DEA, FBI, CIA and US Customs.

The day after Barry left Nella, bad weather rolled in from Oklahoma: a cold front with thunderstorms and tornadoes. The pilots' training ended early. In a one-ton gas truck, they were shuttled back to Mena, where Barry was stranded due to the storm. He came across as unusually apprehensive and preoccupied.

CHAPTER 16

Uncle Sam Wants You

In September 1984, realising that the government was double-crossing him, Barry abandoned his mode of secrecy to make a documentary about himself. Ostracised by the DEA and with the Louisiana justice system breathing down his neck, he aimed to televise proof of his relationship with the DEA that would prevent agents from denying their relationship with him.

He told John Camp, an investigative reporter at WBRZ-TV Channel 2 in Baton Rouge, about his work for the CIA and DEA. He backed his claims up with videotapes of news clips, which corroborated sections of his story. He allowed Camp to secretly record a meeting in Miami, during which one of his DEA handlers paid him $10,000 for his services. Camp's scepticism melted as Barry's claims proved to be true.

Barry provided documents that showed overzealousness on the part of his federal prosecutors. He griped about the US Attorney's office in Baton Rouge making a deal with a small-time criminal called Kenneth Webb, a former high-school classmate whom Barry had paid to do odd jobs. To entice Webb to inform on Barry, prosecutors had promised to get rid of his legal problems, including an auto-theft charge. Webb had a history of mental instability and minor arrests. He told a federal grand jury that he had delivered a shoe box filled with cocaine to Barry. John Camp interviewed Webb on camera. Webb admitted fabricating the cocaine story under pressure from drug agents. Webb's lawyer asked US Attorney Stanford Bardwell to allow the unstable witness to correct the perjured grand jury testimony. The request was denied.

In the meantime, prosecutors from Miami and Louisiana wrangled over making a deal for Barry.

A Justice Department prosecutor said, "Miami thinks the guy is the greatest thing since sliced bread, which is usual because he's helping them, and Baton Rouge thinks he is the worst drug dealer in the history of Louisiana, which he was."

Over breakfast at the Hyatt Regency Hotel in Miami, Barry got two of his lawyers together.

"We really shouldn't be sitting next to Barry at this public restaurant," Scalfani said.

"Why?" Unglesby said.

"What do you mean, why?" Scalfani said. "Don't you know there's a contract out on him."

"You're kidding," Unglesby said.

"Don't worry. He's sitting closer to me than he is to you."

Afterwards, they walked to the US Attorney's office by the Miami River. It took several hours to negotiate a plea-bargain. Barry would plead guilty to the charges in Baton Rouge and get the same sentence as in Florida on the Quaaludes case. Expecting Barry to have to serve at least three years, the prosecutors were happy. Barry and his lawyers left satisfied and in the mood for assassination jokes.

Walking towards a parking lot in downtown Miami, Scalfani turned to Unglesby. "Gee, Lewis, this is a great place for a hit."

On November 19, 1985, the plea-bargain was signed in the offices of the Organized Crime Strike Force in New Orleans. Barry had pleaded guilty to conspiring to possess with intent to distribute 462 kilos of cocaine and failing to file currency transaction reports for $51,006.04 deposited in four Baton Rouge banks. The sentence on the first count would equal the sentence received in Florida.

The second count carried no prison time, only that the judge would be allowed to set the conditions of probation. "As to count two of the instant indictment, the defendant will receive a period of probation to be determined by the court."

At home that night, Barry told investigative reporter John Camp about the plea bargain. On January 27, 2015, Camp posted an article at his website about the meeting. "In contrast to past braggadocio, he [Barry] was meek and apologetic in disclosing that he had agreed to plead guilty to a drug charge in Baton Rouge. I was given a copy of the agreement and asked to keep it quiet until an official announcement. He seemed confident that his Florida deal would keep him out of prison. 'As much cocaine as I've hauled into Louisiana, I don't know anything about this load,' Seal said. He claimed that mounting legal expenses caused him to accept the deal. The explanation was hard to believe. He seemed to be apologizing to me for the guilty plea, which was not particularly relevant to the issues raised in my documentary."

On November 20, 1985, Channel 2 in Baton Rouge broadcast Barry's one-hour documentary, *Uncle Sam Wants You*. It started with the meeting in a Miami hotel's parking lot that had been secretly filmed with Barry and the DEA agent, Jake Jacobsen.

"Barry Seal is an enigma," John Camp reported. "On one hand he has been working closely with federal drug agents in Miami and with the Central Intelligence Agency. He is a key witness in one of the most significant drug investigations ever conducted in South Florida. But at the same time here in his hometown of Baton Rouge, the veteran pilot has been a target of an intensive and what he describes as an unfair investigation."

"I'm not a drug smuggler," Barry said, wearing sunglasses and a combat flight suit. "I say prove it. Where is the proof?" Barry's smirk seemed like a challenge to his prosecutors.

"A gun smuggler?" Camp said.

"No. Where's the proof? Why am I not on the front page of the paper at Ryan Airport or any other airport with a load of dope, with a load of guns? If they're such good agents, and I'm so big, the biggest in the world, you know. The biggest in the world don't get away from the law and from justice, you know that." He accused Baton Rouge drug agents of setting him up. "The bottom line was, 'How about helping us make a bust? How about setting somebody up? Give us a load. We'll let you get away... If you don't help us, we're going to get you anyway.' I said, 'Well, it's real hard for you to knock on the door of my airplane at night when I'm doing 200 miles an hour and say, "You're under arrest." You're not going to involve me with anything.'"

John Camp insisted that the Baton Rouge investigators had gone to "extreme lengths" to prove that Barry was an international smuggler. Camp dissected the Louisiana investigation.

"I think that the investigation being headed up now by Mr [Stanford] Bardwell has floundered," Barry said. "I don't think that they, in fact, I'm positive they have no evidence of wrongdoing because they have threatened grand jury witnesses, they have threatened attorneys, local attorneys. These are things that just aren't done. I'm not caught up in a feud between two government agencies. I think what we're caught up in here, as I mentioned before, is now Mr Bardwell has found himself in the middle of a cover-up."

Barry accused the prosecutors of coercing witnesses to lie on the stand. The documentary showed Ken Webb claiming that the federal government had pressured him to do "whatever it takes" to nail Barry. Webb said that it was under such circumstances that he had lied to the grand jury about Barry.

"The federal authorities are," Barry said, "I think, for the most part good people. I think that there are bad eggs in every nest, but I think there's no real mystique about me. Most of what I do is out in the open. I don't hide anything I'm doing. When I'm employed by government agencies and they ask me to keep discreet what they tell me, I do. I try to move in the methods and the ways that they ask me to move, and maybe to some of the local authorities it may seem that sometimes it's on the board of criminalism, sometimes – sometimes not. But I think that the overzealousness of the local federal authorities in the Middle District of Louisiana has caused them to cross their fine line that they walk also between right and wrong."

After describing himself as "an aviation consultant," Barry said,

"The cost of living an exciting life is high. You can't sit in Baton Rouge and go to work from nine to five on Monday through Friday and go to the LSU football games on Saturday night and church on Sunday and have an exciting life. That maybe exciting to ninety-nine percent of the population, but to me it's not. And the exciting thing in life to me is to get into a life-threatening situation. Now, that's excitement... Whether you call it soldier of fortune or what, it's a way of life to me. I enjoy it and I'm going to keep doing it."

Camp asked about the contract on his life.

"John, there's a risk in all covert-operation work. There's risk in everything you do in this line of work. That's why the pay is so good... 'If you can't stand the heat, don't work in the kitchen.' I can take the pressure. I'm not worried about the contract. If it comes, it comes."

"Do you see yourself getting indicted?" Camp said.

"No. If they indict me, it means that I go to court. It means that then I get to tell my side of the story. All of this and much, much more that you're now hearing from me will be put out in the public eye. The Justice Department is not going to tolerate this. There's no way they can indict me."

Towards the end of the documentary, Camp said, "It is not the purpose of this report to suggest Barry Seal is innocent or for that matter guilty of anything other than those crimes which he has already been convicted. Certainly Seal had chosen a lifestyle that lends itself to suspicion. His association with Colombian cocaine suppliers and his involvement in exotic plots hatched by the CIA and DEA have given him a certain mystique. He claims it is this mystique that has made him a target of overzealous investigators.

"We have repeatedly sought comment from US Attorney Bardwell and other officials about the allegations of investigative and prosecutorial misconduct. They have refused to be interviewed and expressed considerable resentment that Seal was even given a forum to express his complaints. But Barry Seal and others have made allegations that go beyond their own personal problems with prosecutors. The targeting of individuals, the pressuring of witnesses and the abuse of the grand jury process raised questions about the integrity of our system of justice. And when such questions are raised, regardless who asks them, they deserve to be answered.

"I'm John Camp, Channel 2, *Eyewitness News.*"

The documentary embarrassed and incensed the Baton Rouge prosecutors. Barry's lawyer, Unglesby, said that it was "a declaration of war on the federal government here. You don't spit in the eye of a hurricane and then not plan to evacuate."

CHAPTER 17

Mena

By November 1984, during his meals at SOB's with Terry, Barry seemed to have emerged from a funk. He was satisfied with the plea bargain agreed to by the Baton Rouge prosecutor, which meant he would serve no prison time. He'd struck the deal without any CIA intervention, which had enabled him to protect his role in black ops. His problems seemed to be over.

At SOB's, Barry, Terry and Aki celebrated the plans for the graduation of the trainee pilots, scheduled for December.

Barry joked about giving them all a ride in the Fat Lady. "That ought to get their rocks off. We can have them kick a palette of cash out of the cargo door and see if they can hit the fucking lawn at the State Capitol." Barry laughed.

Aki was disturbed by Barry breaking protocol by implying that money from illegal weapons sales was being filtered back to members of the Arkansas government run by Bill Clinton at the State Capitol.

Remaining quiet, Terry had realised that the money Barry was laundering through Dan Lasater was a payoff to Clinton for allowing the CIA to run operations through Arkansas, including Mena. He knew that the only way their covert operation could have continued undetected was with the cooperation of the top levels of the Arkansas government and the state police.

"Are you asking me or telling me to graduate these four guys, Aki?" Terry said, referring to four students he felt were unsafe. "In my professional opinion as a flight instructor, they're dangerous and will probably get someone killed."

"That's the whole idea, Terry," Barry said, "to get someone

killed! Tell him, Aki. He does have a need to know. Aviation is serious business and I sympathise with him not wanting these four guys running around the skies of Central America being incompetent in an airplane. If you don't tell him, I'm going to."

Aki squirmed. He took a booklet from his briefcase – *Assassination Manual* – and pushed it across the table. "Terry, you were in a war. Many lives can be saved if the right people die. It's very important for the Agency to place some pilots in a position to be able to shorten the conflict. These four guys have been selected for a very special mission to eliminate key Sandinista leaders. It's important they graduate with proper credentials, so that they may penetrate the Nicaraguan aviation community and get near the targets."

Shocked by the level of detail, Terry said nothing for a few seconds. "I understand. Thanks for telling me. They'll be signed off. Tell Washington there'll be ten graduating pilots: four ground controllers, four transfers and two washouts. That's the graduation class of 1984."

After Aki left, Barry said he was going to make another deposit with Dan Lasater and he had something important to tell Terry in the evening.

After 7 pm, Barry tipped a waiter to get his favourite table in the corner.

"Do I keep the Company [CIA] airplane this winter while the school is in mothballs?" Terry said.

"Sure. All of this is on Uncle Sam. Rule number one: soak him for all you can get. But I do want you to trade out around the first of the year to a Seneca. I've got a special project of my own going on and you will need to be in a Seneca for security purposes."

"What's the project?"

"Right now, Emile and I are piggybacking the cash I told you about as it comes in from down south. We're using two Senecas that are identical to each other. I figure a third one would really confuse any overly curious air-traffic controller if the going gets tough." The CIA was providing Senecas under a scheme described to Terry by Oliver North, whereby the owners of the Senecas would give them to the CIA, report them stolen and claim the insurance money. Two of the Senecas described by Barry had disappeared from airfields in Florida and Dallas.

"Sure, that's fine. Do I talk to you or Emile about detailed instructions?"

"Talk to Emile. He'll give you the Seneca right around the first of the year."

"Why the first?"

"The tithing is gonna really go on the increase January 1."

"Tithing?"

"The money the state's working on for letting the Agency operation go on here. You don't think something this big could be going on without having to pay for it. Shit, you were in Southeast Asia. Didn't you tell me we had to pay some fucking prince in Laos every time the Air Force dropped a bomb there? You see, it's all the same. Just one fucking banana republic after another." Senior Arkansas state officials were charging the CIA ten percent to allow illegal airplane modifications, covert training of Nicaraguan rebels, arms and drugs shipments and the laundering of money through local financial institutions, including Bill Clinton's Arkansas Development Finance Authority.

CHAPTER 18

The Clinton Brothers

Over the years, numerous witnesses have described Bill Clinton getting high. An apartment manager told the *Sunday Telegraph* that in 1984 Roger Clinton had stayed there for two months. The newspaper reported that Bill had been "a frequent visitor… There was drug use at these gatherings… and she [the manager] could clearly distinguish Bill's voice as he chatted with his brother about the quality of the marijuana they were smoking. She said she could also hear them talking about the cocaine as they passed it back and forth."

Former 1958 Miss Arkansas, Sally Perdue, claimed that during her 1983 affair with Bill Clinton, she saw him use cocaine regularly. In her living room, he smoked joints that he kept in a cigarette case and he snorted lines of cocaine off a table. "He [Bill] had all of the [cocaine snorting] equipment laid out like a real pro," she said.

Grand jury witness Sharlene Wilson said, "I lived in Little Rock, Arkansas… I worked at a club called Le Bistros, and I met Roger Clinton there, Governor Bill Clinton, a couple of his state troopers that went with him wherever he went. Roger Clinton had come up to me and he had asked me could I give him some coke, you know, and asked for my one-hitter… a very small silver device, OK, that you stick up into your nose and you just squeeze it and a snort of cocaine will go up in there. And I watched Roger hand what I had given him to Governor Clinton, and he just kind of turned around and walked off."

The meeting led to her partying on cocaine with the Clinton brothers at Governor Clinton's mansion and attending toga parties. At the parties, which turned into cocaine-fuelled orgies, was the attorney general and members of the Arkansas State police.

"They began to dance around," Sharlene said, "do the cocaine in one room, have sex in another room, 'cause in the Coachman's Inn the rooms were adjoining, you know. And to be quite truthful, you end up with somebody in particular and you, nine times out of ten, end up having sex. And there was cocaine there I know. I'm the one that made sure it was there... I watched Bill Clinton lean up against a brick wall. He must have had an adenoid problem because he casually stuck my tooter up his nose... He was so messed up that night, he slid down the wall into a garbage can and just sat there like a complete idiot."

Sharlene admitted to having sex with Roger Clinton. She partied with the Clinton brothers until the early hours in the governor's mansion. "I thought it was the coolest thing in the world that we had a governor who got high."

After Sharlene testified at a grand jury, the investigation was shut down by the Republican-appointed US Attorney Charles Banks. Sharlene reported to Jean Duffy – a deputy prosecuting attorney and head of a drug task force – that her home was under surveillance and she was petrified of the "powers that be." She felt that she knew too much because she had worked "for three or four months unloading bags of cocaine at the Mena airport."

For speaking out, Sharlene was arrested at her home with less than $100 worth of methamphetamine and marijuana. Prosecuted by an ex-boyfriend involved in trafficking through Mena, she received a thirty-one year sentence, even though it was her first offence. Her prosecutor was eventually arrested for running his Seventh Judicial District prosecuting attorney's office as a criminal enterprise. In 1997, a jury found him guilty on five counts of racketeering, extortion and drug dealing. In comparison to Sharlene's punishment, he only received an eleven-year sentence.

Former model Gennifer Flowers had a twelve-year relationship with Clinton. After Bill denied the existence of such a relationship, Gennifer released smoochy phone conversations she'd secretly recorded. In January 1998, Bill Clinton admitted under oath that he'd had sex with Gennifer. She said that Bill had smoked pot in her presence. "I thought how foolish it was of him to carry marijuana around, but it was typical of his bullet-proof attitude."

Bill told Gennifer about the negative effects of his cocaine use. "He told me about the party he had been to, and said, 'I got so fucked up on cocaine at that party.' He said that it made his scalp itch and he felt conspicuous because he was talking with people who were not aware drugs were at the party, and all he wanted to do was scratch his head."

Bill's cocaine habit got to the point where he had to seek medical treatment, including multiple stays at a drug rehab according to Betsey Wright, Governor Clinton's chief of staff for seven years.

In a YouTube video, Dr Sam Houston, the former physician to Hillary Clinton's father, said, "A Dr. Suen, S-U-E-N, here at the medical centre in Little Rock has taken care of Bill Clinton for his sinus problems, which may indeed be drug-related to cocaine use as they destroy the sinus passages. Governor Bill Clinton was taken into the hospital – I believe it was the medical centre on at least one or two occasions – for cocaine abuse and over-dosage…"

Clinton was with a state trooper when he arrived at the University of Arkansas Medical Centre for emergency treatment for cocaine. Hillary was informed by phone. Unimpressed with the risks posed by Bill's affinity for cocaine, Hillary showed up.

"When Mrs Clinton arrived, she told both of the resident physicians on duty that night that they would never again practise medicine in the United States if word leaked out about Clinton's drug problem," said Christopher Ruddy, the CEO of Newsmax Media who wrote an article in 1999: *Did Bill Clinton overdose on cocaine?* "Reportedly, [Hillary] pinned one of the doctors up against a wall, both hands pressed against his shoulders, as she gave her dire warning."

In 1996, the columnist R. Emmett Tyrrell located and

telephoned one of the nurses who had been on duty the night that Bill had ended up in the emergency room. According to Tyrrell, the nurse didn't deny the story, but said that she couldn't run the risk of losing her job by talking about it.

Former Saline County criminal investigator John Brown said he'd interviewed a lot of people who had seen Bill Clinton take drugs, but they were too afraid to speak.

The extent of Bill's involvement in the cocaine flowing through Mena was exposed by someone who worked for the Clintons for ten years. Larry Nichols eventually became the Director of Marketing for the Arkansas Development Finance Authority (ADFA), which Clinton pitched to the public as a vehicle for creating jobs and assisting churches and schools.

"I'd been there about a month," Larry said, "and I realised that I was in the epicentre of what I'd always heard about all my life… I was literally working, sitting in the middle of Bill Clinton's political machine. It was where he made payoffs, where he repaid favours to people for campaign support." Millions of dollars were channelled into Clinton's election campaign, his inner circle of friends and to Hillary Clinton's law firm.

Two months into the job, Larry grew so suspicious that he started copying documents. "For about two months, I watched accounts accumulate money, and at the end of the month, they zero balanced. They were laundering drug money. There was a hundred million a month in cocaine coming in and out of Mena, Arkansas."

Larry Nichols said Clinton had contracted Lasater to launder cocaine proceeds: "Dan Lasater, who was a best friend of Bill Clinton… He didn't sell cocaine. Nope. They were giving it away. Huge piles of cocaine in his office. Ashtray upon ashtray full at the parties, and they'd give it to young girls."

As a state policeman assigned to bodyguard duty, Larry Douglas Brown a.k.a. LD was known as Bill Clinton's fair-haired boy. LD's fiancée was Chelsea Clinton's nanny. His future mother-in-law was the administrator of Governor Clinton's mansion. As well as protecting and driving Clinton around, LD was one of several troopers whom Clinton trusted to help him procure women for sex and to provide cover for his liaisons. LD was so close to the Clintons that he and Hillary shared their relationship problems.

"LD, I've always told you you'd make a good spy," Bill Clinton said on April Fools' Day, 1984, referring to an ad in the *New York Times* offering CIA employment.

With Clinton's help, LD wrote an application. "Governor Clinton has been an inspiration for me to further my career in government service and in particular to explore the possibilities of employment with your agency." Clinton told LD that studying Russian would help his application. LD set about doing so. He told the CIA about his understanding of the Cyrillic alphabet.

Calling the CIA to vouch for LD, Clinton didn't go through the official channels, but merely picked up a phone and chatted to someone at the CIA whom he knew personally, which impressed LD.

The application involved submitting an essay. "We decided that I would write a paper on Marxism in Central America. Governor Clinton and I," LD said.

At Governor Clinton's mansion, LD typed 800 words on the growing threat of Marxism in South America that was spreading towards the USA's border and the necessity of helping the rebels in Nicaragua. Clinton edited it.

After his application was approved, LD passed the entrance examination. Four months later in Dallas, towards the end of the summer of 1984, he met a CIA recruiter named Magruder, whom LD later identified as a member of Vice President George HW Bush's staff. Magruder asked if he was interested in working in narcotics, paramilitary and security. LD agreed to all of them. After signing a secrecy agreement, he was told that somebody would call him.

On September 5, 1984, he was officially notified of his nomination for employment. A month later, his home phone rang.

The caller, Barry Seal, had detailed knowledge about him. Barry arranged a meeting at Cajun's Wharf, a bar and restaurant in Little Rock.

LD later described meeting Barry: "Big guy. He had on one of those shirts that comes down… outside your pants, big-guy kind of thing… He knew about the essay and everything I had done, so absolutely there was no question in my mind… He'd been flying for the Agency. That's all I knew."

Over the following weeks, Barry spoke to LD as if he knew Bill Clinton personally. He referred to Clinton as "the guv." Barry asked LD to accompany him on an operation in Mena scheduled for before sunrise on October 23, 1984.

The only person LD told about the meetings with Barry was Bill Clinton. "[Barry] was kind of devil-may-care."

"Don't sweat it," Bill said. "You can handle it. You'll have fun."

Expecting to board a small plane, LD met Barry at Mena, where the Fat Lady was waiting. LD was stunned to see a huge plane painted dark charcoal with hardly any tail markings. Barry told LD to leave behind his ID, keys and jewellery. Inside the plane were three unidentified men: a co-pilot and two kickers. LD said that the engine made a thunderous noise. "[It] scared the shit out of me just taking off."

The Fat Lady stopped for fuel in New Orleans and headed for Central America, where it dipped below radar, climbed and dipped again to allow the two kickers to roll out tarp-covered pallets containing M-16 rifles, which were parachuted over a mountainous area to be picked up by Nicaraguan rebels. Returning to Mena, the Fat Lady stopped in Honduras, where the crew collected green canvas duffel bags.

In Mena, Barry gave LD a manila envelope containing $2,500 and said he'd be in touch about the next operation. LD accepted the cash without questioning. He later stated, "This guy [Barry] obviously knew what he was doing and had the blessing and was working for the Agency and knew everything about me, so I wasn't going to be too inquisitive."

When LD showed up for his next shift at the governor's mansion, Clinton patted LD's back. "You having any fun yet?"

LD smiled. "Yeah, but this is scary stuff." He described the mission in the Fat Lady.

"Oh, you can handle it. Don't sweat it."

Surprised by the governor's casual manner, LD later testified that Clinton knew everything about Mena and that the operation had been sanctioned and approved on behalf of the United States. "Well, he [Clinton] knew what I was doing. He was the one that furthered me along and shepherded me through this thing."

Barry called LD. "How's the guv?" Another mission was arranged for Christmas Eve, 1984.

Things went exactly as before, except Barry only picked up two duffel bags in Honduras. In Mena, LD was paid $2,500. In the parking lot, Barry brought a duffel bag to LD's car and extracted a kilo of cocaine, which LD later described as a brick-shaped "waxene-wrapped package."

In a panic, LD said, "I want no part of what's happening." Speeding back to Little Rock, he thought, *Well, this is an official operation. Clinton got me into this. It can't be as sinister as I think it is...* After telling his brother, LD decided to confront Clinton.

When LD showed up, Clinton was all smiles as usual until he noticed how angry LD was.

"Do you know what they're bringing back on that airplane?" LD said.

"Wait, whoa, whoa, what's going on?" Clinton said.

"Well, essentially they're bringing back coke."

Over a decade later, LD testified about Clinton's response. "And it wasn't like it was a surprise to him. It wasn't like – he didn't try to say, what? ... He was surprised that I was mad because he thought we were going to have a cordial conversation, but he didn't try to deny it. He didn't try to deny that it wasn't coming back, that I wasn't telling the truth or that he didn't know anything about it."

Startled by Clinton's complicity, LD said, "I'm not going to have anything else to do with it... I'm out of it. Stick a fork in me, I'm done."

"Settle down," Clinton said. "That's no problem." Attempting to downplay the CIA's role in the cocaine trafficking, Clinton said, "That's Lasater's deal."

Afterwards, LD withdrew his application for the CIA.

LD knew Lasater was one of Clinton's biggest donors and that Clinton had several meetings a month with Lasater either at Lasater's company or in the mansion, where Lasater had privileged access through the back door. Clinton also attended parties thrown by Lasater, where silver platters with piles of cocaine did the rounds. Wanting to protect Clinton, LD had urged the governor to leave one such party.

Roger Clinton has a long history of arrests and cover-ups. In 1981, Roger was arrested for ignoring speeding tickets. Governor Bill Clinton arranged for him to be released to the custody of a relative who chaired the state's Crime Commission. In March 1982, Roger was arrested for drunk driving and possession of narcotics. With Bill about to launch a re-election campaign, all of the charges were dropped.

"The sheriff's office and the prosecutor succumbed to political pressure," a journalist wrote.

"They leaned till they cracked," said a lawyer familiar with the case.

In the late 1970s, Roger got hooked on cocaine, according to his own statements to investigators. He snorted up to four grams a day. A therapist testified that he had been "close to a lethal dose." He paid for cocaine by dealing drugs. He had drug connections as far away as New York and Medellín. Upon learning that he was Bill Clinton's brother, his suppliers gave him drugs on credit. Through Little Rock's airport, he smuggled thousands of dollars' worth of cocaine hidden on himself. Roger took so many women to the governor's mansion to party on cocaine that a narcotics investigator said, "They used the home of the governor as a whore hotel."

"I can get you a quarter pound," Roger told a police informant in the early 1980s, while negotiating a $10,000 transaction. "I can get you what you want if you come up with the cash."

By 1984, Roger's addiction was spiralling out of control and ravaging him physically. A thief cut open the top of his convertible car and stole cocaine worth $8,000. He prevented his mother from reporting the incident to the police. Roger's drug creditors issued threats against him and his family.

According to an FBI report, Bill Clinton's solution was to have Dan Lasater house Roger at a thousand-acre thoroughbred farm in Florida. A summary of the FBI document stated, "Clinton asked him [Lasater] to give his ne'er-do-well half-brother Roger a job."

"Mr Lasater remarked at that point that he owed the governor a lot of favours," the farm's manager said.

Roger took the job from Lasater and $8,000 to pay off his drug debt.

"[Dealers were] putting the heat on him and something might happen to his brother and mother," Lasater told the FBI.

With drug money being laundered through Lasater's ranch and constant cocaine parties there, Roger continued his life of excess.

"You could tell Roger Clinton was really strung out the whole while he was at the farm," a senior farm employee said, according to the book *Partners in Power*. "I just remember he was always using, always saying he had been on the phone talking to his brother the governor, not worth a damn as hired help. I was told we were stashing him for some politician Mr Lasater was working."

During 1983-84, narcotics officers filmed Roger. A Hot Springs undercover policeman recorded him selling cocaine. Roger bragged to an informant, "I've got four or five guys in uniform who keep an eye on the guys who keep an eye on me." Roger had been dealing directly with a Colombian tied to the cartels.

As usual, Bill would have bailed Roger out of trouble. "Roger

Clinton was about to be swept under the rug," a federal prosecutor said, "by both the US attorney and the local boys, no question about it."

But brave state police publicised some of the evidence. "Some troopers put it [the evidence] out on the street where it couldn't be ignored," an investigator said. "They took a real risk."

By the spring of 1984, Roger was under investigation by a federal grand jury. As details leaked to the governor and his wife, Hillary told Bill that intervention in his brother's case would damage Bill politically. According to author Roger Morris in *Partners in Power*, Bill was ordered not to warn his brother or to prevent Roger's arrest as any such action would be used against him in his re-election campaign and later on.

"I don't think she [Hillary] ever knew how much coke Bill had snorted with Roger," said a state policeman, "or how many girls they'd done together, but we knew she'd tell him to feed ol' Roger to the feds for the sake of his career and that's what he ended up doing."

After Roger's federal indictment, Bill read a statement to the media: "My brother has apparently become involved with drugs, a curse which has reached epidemic proportions and has plagued the lives of millions of families in our nation, including many in our state." Clinton didn't take any questions. A reporter described Bill as "visibly shaken."

The head of the state police addressed the media. He claimed that when he'd notified the governor of his brother's arrest, Bill Clinton had told him to handle the case like any other. Bill Clinton used his brother's arrest to demonstrate that the Clintons were not above the law.

Formerly a military intelligence officer, Travis Bunn was an undercover policeman who filmed Roger in April, 1984. Roger told Bunn that he needed to "get some [cocaine] for my brother [Bill]. He's got a nose like a vacuum cleaner."

Suspecting that Roger was part of a larger criminal enterprise, Bunn wanted to "nab him, roll him over, and go on up the line" in order to arrest the bigger players. His plan was foiled after an Arkansas State Police officer working in Hot Springs told his superiors. State police took over the investigation. When Dunn found out – after being on the case for a year – he told a colleague who'd been investigating Roger, "We've been screwed."

Dunn said that the investigation turned into a damage-control operation. The state police handed the case over to the federal government. Even though he was familiar with Roger's crimes, Dunn was never asked to testify at the grand jury or Roger's trial. "The only reason this case got as far as it did is that they knew I had Roger already," Dunn said. "I had him before they ever got into it. And that was something they couldn't undo."

The original officers behind the case, who had developed the strongest evidence against Roger, were dropped from the investigation.

"We had a lot more than just Roger," said an officer close to the case, "like Lasater and who owned who in places like Springdale, and buys that included the state police. But Roger cops out, our narcs get taken out and the case stops there."

On August 14, 1984, Roger appeared before a federal judge who was partially deaf and renowned for sleeping during prolonged testimony. After pleading not guilty, Roger was released on $5,000 bail. So as not to disrupt Bill's re-election campaign, the judge scheduled Roger's trial for slightly after the general election.

After the hearing, a spokesman told the public that Governor Clinton "had no idea he [Roger] had even tried drugs, let alone that he had become addicted to cocaine."

Roger negotiated a plea bargain. For agreeing to plead guilty after the election and for offering to testify against low-level accomplices, he would receive a lesser sentence. To help mitigate the sentence, Roger and his family attended counselling sessions on drug addiction and co-dependency.

According to Hillary Clinton's biographer Judith Warner, in these sessions Hillary "took a leading role in the discussions and was quite astute at pointing out patterns and weaknesses to the assembled family." Warner added that "though he was grateful, her participation didn't always endear her at the time to her husband."

According to friends of Roger and Bill's mother, Virginia, some of Hillary's questions about denial and irresponsibility reduced Virginia to tears and pushed Bill into his next sex and drugs binge.

On November 9, 1984, three days after Bill won the election, Roger pleaded guilty to conspiracy and one count of drug distribution.

"[Roger was] one tentacle of cocaine distribution in Arkansas," said Republican US attorney Asa Hutchinson.

By design, none of the bigger players were investigated. Instead, Roger testified against a boyhood friend, Sam Anderson Jr.

"I guess I'm going to do Roger's time for him," Anderson said.

Right up to his sentencing, Roger partied on cocaine with women at the governor's mansion.

On January 28, 1985, Roger appeared in court, exceptionally alert. Also present were Bill, Hillary and Virginia. The judge suspended the distribution charge, and for the conspiracy charge he sentenced Roger to two years in federal prison. Roger's family watched him get handcuffed and escorted away by marshals.

The videotape of Roger describing Bill's drug use never surfaced.

Outside the courtroom, Bill announced, "I feel more deeply committed than ever before to do everything I can to fight illegal drugs in our state."

Roger served thirteen months in federal prison.

In 2001, Bill granted him a presidential pardon, which expunged his conviction from his record. Roger never had to suffer the problems of reintegration into society faced by hundreds of thousands of non-violent drug offenders sent to prison under Clinton's presidency as he escalated spending on the War on Drugs. Unlike Roger, those offenders were saddled with criminal records that precluded them from employment, education opportunities and housing.

The Secret Service gave Roger the code name Headache while his brother was in office.

A few years after Roger's arrest, his ex-boss, Dan Lasater, was also arrested. He pleaded guilty to federal drug charges of cocaine possession and distribution.

"I feel very sick about it," Bill Clinton said in response to Lasater's indictment, "and I'm sad about it because a person who supported me, who supported a lot of good causes in Arkansas and made a very great success in three careers has been devastated by getting involved in cocaine."

"Have you ever used cocaine?" a journalist said.

"No," Clinton said. "I'm not sure what it looked like if I saw it."

Doc DeLaughter, the police investigator in charge of Dan Lasater's cocaine case, said, "A fourteen-year-old cheerleader out of North Little Rock, she was a virgin and ultimately he [Lasater] ended up sending her to a physician of his. The physician put her on birth-control pills. He used cocaine... and ultimately she lost her virginity. She got addicted to cocaine, and the last I heard of her when we had her subpoenaed back to the federal grand jury, she was a hooker in Lake Tahoe... After Lasater was indicted, I started to receive quite a bit of harassment from my own department in the Arkansas State police. I knew the reason behind it was because of the affiliation with the state police and the governor's office with Dan Lasater and his business associates."

In December, 1986, Lasater was sentenced to 2½ years. In FBI documents, he admitted to federal investigators that he used cocaine and gave it away to his friends, employees and business associates.

Before being released on parole, Lasater served six months in prison, four months in a halfway house and two months under house arrest. Clinton gave him a state pardon in November, 1990.

"If you think he's [Bill Cinton's] tough on crime," Larry Nichols said, "think about a man who pardons a man who gives cocaine to kids." The rest of the people involved in the money laundering went to Washington with Clinton when he became president. The hot money had boosted his election campaign.

According to Larry, Barry Seal had chosen to relocate to Arkansas because Governor Clinton was sleazy and hooked on cocaine. In private, he had no qualms about using cocaine. As the president, he rejected a US Sentencing Commission recommendation to remove the disparity between crack and powder cocaine sentences – a tactic used to mass incarcerate black people for non-violent drug offences. He rejected ending the federal ban on funding for syringe access programs, which increased the spread of AIDS and other diseases. He gave more federal funds to states that built prisons and housed people for longer sentences. The federal three strikes law that was introduced under his tenure mandated lengthy sentences for repeat offenders. Under Clinton's presidency, the US prison population expanded by 487,000 – a rise fuelled by non-violent drug offenders. It was 235,000 more people imprisoned than under his predecessor, Ronald Reagan.

CHAPTER 19

Contract on Barry

On November 15, 1984, one of Barry's prime undercover targets, Jorge Ochoa, was arrested in Spain, which raised the DEA's hopes of getting him extradited to America for drug trafficking. As Barry would be the main witness against Ochoa, his value rose to the DEA.

In Baton Rouge, a private investigator who'd watched *Uncle Sam Wants You,* mailed a videotape of it to Fabio Ochoa in Medellín. Fabio dispatched an employee, Cano, to Miami with a copy of the documentary and instructions to straighten out the Ellis MacKenzie situation. A group of Colombians and an American watched the video in an office in a house north of Miami. They learned that MacKenzie's real name was Barry Seal.

Having flown with Barry on smuggling trips in Colombia, Cano described Barry's habits, while another Colombian, Rafa, took notes, including Barry's home address, the vehicles Barry, his wife and his secretary drove, his planes and their registration numbers, his preferred restaurants and hangouts.

They would get $1 million for capturing Barry alive, so Cano favoured kidnapping; however, if that was impossible, Barry should be killed, and they would still collect $500,000 from Pablo Escobar and Fabio Ochoa, who was running the Ochoa side of the business while Jorge was incarcerated in Spain.

As Colombians would stand out in Baton Rouge, Rafa told the American, Max, an overweight Jewish engineer, to silence MacKenzie one way or the other. If Barry had to be killed, they wanted it to look like a Mafia hit.

Having married a Colombian, Max had slipped into crime by

establishing a route for Colombians to be smuggled into America via the Bahamas. Eventually, he'd coordinated cocaine flights for Jorge Ochoa and managed Ochoa's accounting and distribution. His salary was $500,000 a year. Max feared that if he declined the contract on Barry, the Colombians would kill him on the spot. He was terrified of Rafa, who kept two hand grenades under the front seat of his car and constantly smoked cocaine while carrying a gun. Rafa also stored $1 million in cash in a suitcase for emergencies. When Max had previously attempted to retire from the Ochoa business, Rafa had responded, "There's only two real ways to get out: going to jail or getting killed."

A phone was handed to Max. Fabio Ochoa thanked him and wished him good luck. Fabio preferred a kidnapping. He put Pablo Escobar on the phone. Pablo thanked Max and gave the phone back to Fabio, who asked if he needed expense money. Yes, Max said and told them to use their discretion.

After the call, Cano said Barry had a wife and small kids. Max said he wouldn't kill women or children. Rafa said that if it were necessary to complete the contract, it would have to be done.

Rafa told Max that he wanted to bust Lito out of the federal Metropolitan Correctional Center in South Dade, Miami, by using a helicopter.

Having never killed anybody, Max called his friend Roberts, a trafficker who'd previously told Max that he could have people eliminated. After viewing Barry's documentary, Roberts agreed to handle the problem.

A young Colombian delivered a box to Max from Fabio Ochoa with $100,000 inside.

On January 5, 1985, four Colombians were extradited to America for the first time. One was linked to Jorge Ochoa. With the possibility of extradition looming, the Medellín Cartel wanted Barry dispensed with quickly.

In late January, Max and one of Roberts' associates flew to Louisiana to locate Barry. Max stayed in a hotel room in New Orleans and paid Roberts' associate $28,000 to find Barry. The associate located places Barry frequented, but not Barry, leaving Max no choice but to join the hunt for Barry in Baton Rouge. They found everywhere on Cano's list, except for Barry's helicopter business. The mission failed, so they returned to Miami.

Max requested that Cano return from Colombia to help them. In Max's Jaguar, they set off from Florida. Max asked if Jorge Ochoa was aware of the situation. Cano confirmed that while incarcerated in Spain, Jorge had sanctioned Barry's murder.

In New Orleans, they switched to a rental car to avoid driving around Baton Rouge with Florida licence plates. Over the course of the day, they located Barry's white Cadillac, his house, his offices, his preferred restaurants and even his helicopter business. But yet again, Barry was illusive. At a Holiday Inn, they relayed the bad news to Fabio Ochoa in Colombia and Rafa in Miami. Cano returned to Miami. In Baton Rouge, Max kept searching for Barry, but with no result, so he returned to Miami.

Rafa showed up at Max's place of business: an import shoe store at the Four Ambassadors Hotel. Accompanying Rafa was an infamous and peculiar-looking hitman called Cumbamba, who wore thick black-rimmed glasses and had curly black hair and a big chin. Max had known Cumbamba for nearly three years. Under pressure from Pablo Escobar and the Ochoas, Rafa wanted to know why the hit was taking so long. Stalling them, Max said it would take more time and they had to be patient.

Angry at not been given the hit, Cumbamba stayed in Miami. When he heard how much Max had been paid, he grew upset and scolded Max for his incompetence.

"Seal lives in a secluded area," Max said. "There is one way in and one way out. The road comes to a dead end. There is no way that it can be done unless everybody in the house is taken out and I'm not about to kill women and kids."

"That doesn't bother me at all," Cumbamba said.

"I have no authority to hand over the contract. You need to talk to Rafa, Fabio Ochoa and Pablo Escobar."

"I will."

Max returned to Baton Rouge. Seeing a blue Chevrolet exit Barry's driveway – which he knew from Cano's list to be Barry's secretary's car – he followed her. She turned into an industrial park, leaving him stuck at a traffic light. While attempting to catch up with her, she ended up behind him. He quit and returned home.

On June 5, 1985, Max was driving in a quiet suburban area twenty miles west of Fort Lauderdale, when his Jaguar was surrounded by agents in cars. Surrendering, he appeared relieved. They found a loaded gun in the car's glove compartment. At his ranch house, they found five more weapons, $73,000 in cash in a wall safe and $200,000 under his bed.

Having been snitched on by an informant and facing life without parole on charges of continuing criminal enterprise, Max cooperated. It took four weeks for the agents to get him to talk about the hit on Barry. Impressed with Max's insider knowledge about the workings of the Medellín Cartel and his photographic memory for names, places and dates, agents from numerous jurisdictions competed to get information from him. He detailed murders, kidnappings and how cocaine was transported.

CHAPTER 20

Legal Trouble

Early one morning, when he was asleep next to his wife, Barry received a phone call. After answering the call, he jumped out of bed, started gathering his clothes and told Debbie, "I've got to get down to Miami as quick as I can. A whole bunch of stuff is gonna be happening in the next few days."

"What stuff?"

"I can't explain now." He touched his wife's face. "You're just gonna have to stick by me, baby. I need that real bad now." Barry turned away to get the rest of his clothes.

Gazing sadly, his wife said, "Are they trying to kill you, Barry?"

Barry turned around. "Who?"

"The drug dealers. I'm not a fool, Barry."

"How much do you know?"

"Nothing, just what a wife knows. Tell me."

"I've been working for the government, Debbie," Barry said, nodding. "For the CIA."

Debbie leaped out of bed in a white negligee. "Don't treat me like an idiot, Barry!" She marched out of the room and slammed the door. Barry followed her and opened the door. "The CIA! The CIA! Jesus, Barry! It's one thing to fly drugs around and lie to your wife about that but don't–"

"It's the truth. The CIA. I've been working for them. I've been photographing some very important drug dealers down in Nicaragua." Debbie returned to the bedroom, with Barry following her. "I couldn't tell you."

"Oh, no! You can't tell the CIA's secrets. They hang you for that, don't they?" she said, standing at the end of the bed.

"I couldn't tell you," Barry said.

"Then why are you telling me now?"

"It may be all over now."

Unsteady on her feet, Debbie sat on the bed. "Oh, God, Barry, what have you done?" With glazed eyes, she looked at Barry. "What have you done?"

In an office with Joura and Jacobsen, Barry read from a newspaper: "Sandinistas linked to cocaine smuggling scheme involving three of Colombia's largest cocaine traffickers. Government officials cited photographs taken in Managua by the pilot, a DEA informant, showing a plane being loaded with cocaine." Barry slammed down the paper. "What do we do now?"

"Bringing Lito in is the only thing I can think of," Joura said.

"The Miami paper's gonna have that by the afternoon edition," Jacobsen said.

"Now Ochoa and Escobar," Barry said, throwing his hands up. "If I could just get them here to the US."

"Hey, man, that newspaper practically gives your name," Jacobsen said.

"Who did this to me?" Barry said on the verge of tears. "The bastards, man. I'll kill them."

Ron Caffery, the head of the DEA's cocaine desk in Washington DC, called Colonel Oliver North for an explanation about the leaked photos. "I'm mad as hell."

"What's your problem?" North said.

"The problem is your big mouth."

"Now wait a minute."

"You just couldn't wait to make your brownie points, could you? You decided that story should go out and you didn't give a damn who could get hurt, did you?"

"Back off, Ron. What are you talking about?"

"You know damn well what I'm talking about. You leaked that story to the *Washington Times* about our pilot in Nicaragua."

"Now wait a minute. I didn't do anything."

"The biggest drug investigation we've ever had. We were this close to getting the highest guys in the Medellín Cartel and now the investigation is dead."

"Well, there must have been a breakdown somewhere."

"Yeah, there was a breakdown all right, North. And all because of your precious Contras, wasn't it?"

"Now, Ron, you don't want to see Communism take over Central America any more than I do."

Cafferty slammed down the phone.

Barry's lawyer, Unglesby, suspected that Barry hadn't filled him in on the big picture. He told Barry that he could only defend him to the best of his ability if Barry brought him up to speed on all of his activity. Pushing a phone towards Unglesby, Barry told him to call a number and "Tell them you're me."

At the other end, the phone rang. "Vice President Bush's office. May I help you?" a female said.

"This is Barry Seal," Unglesby said.

"Please wait while I transfer the call."

The line was transferred to a man who said he was an admiral. "Barry, where you been?"

"I'm not Barry Seal. I'm his lawyer."

The admiral hung up.

Entering a courthouse, Barry's lawyer said, "This is just the hearing. It'll soon be over."

"Great," Barry said, strutting in a light-blue suit. "I can hardly wait to get back to my cement-block suite."

"The Witness Protection Program is saving your life, Barry," Joura said.

"Hey, listen, I'm a goddam prisoner in a windowless cage. That's funny, don't you think, Joura? I testify against the bad guys and I'm the first to go to jail."

"The Witness Protection Program is not jail," Joura said.

"Then what the hell do you call being locked up day and night?" Barry said.

"Barry." Barry's lawyer put his hand on Barry's shoulder. "There's something else that happened today that you need to know about. The State of Louisiana is going to a grand jury tomorrow to charge you with cocaine trafficking."

"What!" Barry opened the door to the men's' toilet. "Get your asses in here!" he yelled at the procession of agents accompanying him. "What in the hell are you talking about?" he shouted. "You told me they didn't have a case."

"I said we could beat their case," the lawyer said.

"I put my butt on the line here in Florida to reduce my time and I wind up doing twenty years in Louisiana!"

"I can make a deal with Louisiana," the lawyer said.

"What kind of deal?"

"You plead to one charge. There's no trial. Only a sentencing hearing."

Barry snatched his sunglasses off his face. "Why should I plead guilty in Louisiana?"

"Because that's the deal! Whatever you get in Florida, whatever the judge gives you there, you can't get any additional time in Louisiana."

"How much time am I getting in Florida?"

"You've got a very strong defence."

"No, no, no! How much time?"

"If we're lucky." The lawyer gazed down. "Five years."

"What!"

"I've got DEA agents lined up around the block to testify for you, Barry," Joura said.

"The fuck!" Barry said.

"It's going to take you at least a year to testify at the Miami trial," the lawyer said. "I think I can get that counted as time served."

"Four years ain't nothing, man," Jacobsen said.

"And then Louisiana can't touch you," the lawyer said.

"Then you're out of it, Barry. You're out of the game," Joura said.

"And rich," Jacobsen said.

"I want out of that fucking 10 x 10 room today."

"What do you want? A house?"

"I want my house and my family."

"It's five hundred thousand dead and a million alive," Joura said. "That's the bounty on you, Barry."

"Was I the best operative you ever had?"

"Bar none," Joura said.

"Then you put me back on the street," Barry said, thrusting a finger down.

"Barry, it's not safe," Joura said.

"I'm not gonna have fucking lawyers deciding my life for me! If I'm gonna go down, I wanna go down fighting."

"Barry," his lawyer said, shaking his head.

"Is the Witness Protection Program voluntary?" Barry asked his lawyer.

"Yes."

"All right. You put me back undercover today," Barry said, pointing at Joura.

"It's unsafe," Joura hissed.

"Don't put me in Colombia. Nothing to do with Ochoa. Other places in this country. Other organisations. You set them up. I'll knock them down. Or I'll walk right now." Barry strutted to the exit and turned around. "Is it a deal?"

"Deal," Joura said.

"All right!" Barry said. "Now I want everybody out of here. I've gotta piss. C'mon. Let's go." When he was finished, he turned to Emile who was standing by the door.

"They don't understand, Camp," Barry said.

"You don't want out," Emile said, leaning against the wall.

"That's right."

"You think you've gotta have your scare fix. You've gotta scare the shit out of yourself every so often."

Barry laughed. "That's right."

"Well, you've got to learn to live without that."

"Oh, yeah. How?"

"Settle down in Baton Rouge," Emile said. "Go to games on Saturday and church on Sunday. And you'll learn to like it."

"That's not me, Camp. That's not me. It's not over till I say it's over." Barry tried to open the door.

Emile pushed it shut. "My daddy used to say to me, 'Emile, boy, you've gotta change your ways.' Turns out the old man was right. It's time, Barry. Changing is what life's about and we all have to do it. Even you."

Putting his eyes close to Emile's face, Barry said, "Hey, Camp, we gave them a ride didn't we?"

"An eight-point barrel roll."

"In a rainstorm."

"Thunder and lightning."

They hugged.

CHAPTER 21

Mena

By 1985, locals had noticed the unusual aircraft activity at Rich Mountain Aviation, especially the bigger planes. With more hot money coming in than ever, the three pilots, Barry, Terry and Emile used lower profile Senecas. Barry was dropping duffel bags full of cash, which contained transmitters so that the people on the ground could find them.

At a January meeting in a hangar with Terry, Emile and Aki, Barry pulled out a pad of paper and a pencil. "The Agency has devised a way to make this almost idiot proof. I'll cover how we safely jettison and relocate the cargo from the green [cash] flights. Emile will talk about piggyback-flight procedures. Most smugglers are dumb shits and their own people can't be trusted. All it takes to bring down the whole operation is to have an internal leak and a tipoff about the location of a drop zone. With our method of operation there is no way the drop-zone location can be compromised."

"How so?" Terry said.

"'Cause I don't even know where the fuck it is until I jettison the load and note my location on the LORAN [Long-range Navigation Equipment]. The plane that is piggybacking sees the load go, denotes the same coordinates as a backup and never relays the coordinates by radio in the air."

"So how do you find the cash?"

"We have a homing beacon located with the cargo. Once we're sure the jettison was executed unobserved, there are several things we can do. Option one: we go back and get it, since we know the geographic coordinates within a few metres of the kick-out point. Option two: we verbally relay the coordinates to a pickup crew on a secure and scrambled frequency. Then they fly a helicopter into the drop area. Option three: we simply use the LORAN to navigate to a predetermined spot and jettison it near some friendly forces who just happen to have a receiver that will track the frequency of the transmitters in the bag. Combine that with the fact that the piggyback split gives anyone watching us two targets to follow – neither one of which is carrying anything at that point – and you got a pretty damn fool-proof system, courtesy of Uncle Sam."

"You just said transmitters. Is that plural?" Terry said.

"You're a flyer. You know a pilot needs at least two of everything just to be sure one works. You wouldn't want to lose three million in cash, would you, just because some fucking $2,000 radio didn't work?"

On Barry's pad, Emile began drawing the radio fixes in Western Arkansas. "I'll draw you a map of a typical mission. This won't be exact, but the concept's there." He drew two planes in piggyback formation, almost one on top of the other and with the one on top slightly in front of the other. A third plane, Terry's in this case, joins from below to become the bottom plane, slightly behind the middle one. To air-traffic control, they'd appear as one radar blip. The plane in the middle, Barry's plane, would be carrying the money. Emile's plane at the top would escort Barry's to the drop zone and continue to Mena on Barry's original flight plan. Staying together, Terry's and Barry's would head for Little Rock. Near Little Rock, Terry would inform air-traffic control that there are two planes. Meanwhile, Barry's plane would dive towards the trees, below radar detection and drop cash at a zone west of Little Rock. Terry would land at Little Rock. Still off radar, Barry would head south. Air traffic control would think that one plane had made one flight. If an additional plane were detected, it would be viewed as Terry's plane, which had landed at Little Rock. It was highly improbable that three planes would be detected.

"You left one thing out, Emile. Terry, when you rendezvous with us, before you come down to join us, take a real close look to see if Camp and I are being tailed. Those US Customs citations are painted black and are real hard to spot, so use your night-vision goggles and look real close. If you see anything, come up on our frequency and sing out."

"What happens if that's the case?" Terry said.

"You abort and just head on back to Little Rock," Emile said. "Barry and I will know we are being followed, so we got several options. We would probably just split up, giving him two targets to chase. But you don't worry about that. That's our problem."

"Aki, is this all legal?" Terry said. "Sounds like we're going to great lengths to avoid detection by other feds. Who do we consider our enemy here?"

"Terry, we are CIA! We are not law enforcement. We are not Justice Department. We are not Treasury Department. We are CIA! We answer to the director who answers to the president. You are dealing with the very top level. These other agencies are not in the loop. They are not cleared for major foreign-policy decisions. The CIA has to work this way all over the world. We are not breaking the law. We are above the law."

"I assume this will take some pretty good flying and coordination?" Terry said. "I'd like all three of us to go out and practise a little close formation work before we attempt this, especially at night. One thing that could blow our plan is to have three identical Senecas crash within a mile of each other."

"We'll do better than that," Barry said. "Tomorrow, weather permitting, we'll just go out and fly this whole mission in daylight, only difference being I won't be carrying any cash."

"Barry, of the three ways to do this," Terry said, "it appears to me that number three bears the greatest risk of discovery. Who is safeguarding the location of the drop zone you've set up in Little Rock?"

"I am," Aki said. "The Agency is. The drop is a safe field we have selected because people that own land there are under our control. So do not worry about that. Your job is just to be a shadow for Barry." Aki wanted them to start the test flights immediately. "There is major pressure for an increase in Agency deposits in Arkansas."

"Barry, maybe I'm just being nosy," Terry said, "but can't you just continue making deposits at Lasater's like you've been doing all along?"

"That was only tithing money," Barry said. "We're talking about much more than that now. It seems this has worked so well that Aki's people have decided to make a major investment here."

"Barry! You should not talk so freely about the Agency's investments. They are confidential."

"Aw, fuck, Aki," Barry said. "He's gonna figure all this shit out anyway now that he's part of it. Terry didn't fall off no turnip truck yesterday. And besides, I trust him a lot more than I trust those Little Rock fucks you're running around with. They're just a bunch of goddam politicians with their hands sticking out."

The next morning, Terry was flying at 10,500 feet, when he saw Barry and Emile's Senecas flying in piggyback formation.

"You got a visual on us yet?" Barry said.

"Roger, I've got a visual on you. You're in my 12 o'clock low, except you're tucked in so tight all I can see from here is one airplane."

"That's the way it's supposed to be," Barry said. "Get on down here with us. Convert your altitude to air speed and try to tuck in under me."

Terry dived to 4,500 feet. He approached Barry's plane below Emile's, inching into position. He didn't feel confident enough with the manoeuvre yet to get as close as Barry was to Emile.

"Now," Barry said, "I'm gonna have to jibber-jabber a lot since you're in my six [out of sight behind and below]. When we do this for real, we'll keep radio communications to a minimum. But right now, I'll talk you through it. Emile is on centre frequency and squawking. Just prior to the fix, Emile's gonna ask for ident. When he does, I'm gonna bank right in a standard-rate turn in order to pick up vector 573 to Hot Springs. Now, be careful there 'cause you gotta turn with me at the same angle and everything, or you'll get in my wake turbulence and it can get pretty hairy. So, when Emile says, 'Roger, ident,' ident will be the word we both execute the turn on, and be sure to use the standard rate. Any questions?"

As Barry's and Terry's transponders were turned off to avoid air-traffic control, Emile simulated radio conversation with air-traffic control in Memphis. As soon as he said ident, Barry banked to the right.

Turbulence rattled Terry's plane. Straining to remain tucked into Barry's plane, Terry concentrated hard. He wondered how difficult it would be to perform the manoeuvre at night.

"Remember what they taught you in flight school, Terry. My wake flows outward and downward. Try to stay exactly in my six and you'll have a smoother ride."

From his plane, Emile photographed Barry and Terry's piggyback formation. "From here you two look like you're either refuelling in mid-air or trying to fuck each other."

Now that it was necessary to descend together, Terry's anxiety surged.

"Terry, at the Hot Springs VOR, turn your transponder on to 1,200 and start talking to Little Rock approach. That'll make us about forty-five miles out of Adams Field. When they assign you a squawk code, the instant you say, 'Roger, ident,' I'm gonna dive directly in front of you in order to get down to the deck while your radar is still blossoming on their scope."

Terry radioed air-traffic control. "Little Rock approach, this is Seneca, eight-two-seven-five Tango, level three-thousand five-hundred, tracking the zero-seven-one degree radial of Hot Springs VOR, squawking twelve hundred, inbound Adams."

"Roger, Seneca seven-five Tango, squawk two-seven-four-three and ident."

"Roger, Little Rock, Seneca seven-five Tango is going to two-seven-four-three and squawking ident."

Barry dived so rapidly that the underbelly of his plane seemed to collapse onto Terry's cockpit. Terry's plane jolted. A clipboard fell from a mount. Terry struggled to keep control. Attempting to retrieve the clipboard, he heard Barry laughing.

"Oh, I forgot to tell you, Terry. When I split, it can get real rough back there. Ask Emile. He damn near wiped out the first time, too."

Emile laughed. Barry skimmed the treetops. All three turned and flew back to Mena. After another practice run, they were ready to do the real thing at night.

It was cold and dark but clear as Terry flew, straining to catch sight of Barry's and Emile's planes. His stress fell when he saw the red and green navigation lights on Emile's plane. "Dodger 1 and 2, this is Dodger 3," Terry said. "I've got a visual on you. Request identification." Emile flashed strobe lights, allowing Terry to find his target. Descending, Terry gained speed and managed to position himself under Barry's plane, while scanning for US Customs aircraft. Relieved they were up there alone, he awaited the code word "ident." His eyes latched onto Barry's tail hook in order to maintain a set distance from Barry's plane.

"Roger, ident," Emile said. "One nautical mile."

This time, Terry felt more confident as he and Barry turned towards Hot Springs, while Emile shot off to Mena. To his right, the lights of Hope, Arkansas were shining.

"You still with me, Dodger 3?" Barry asked.

"Roger, Dodger 2," Terry said. "On my mark, begin 500 fpm [feet per minute] descent to three-thousand five hundred. Five, four, three, two, one, mark."

Perfectly synchronised, both planes descended to 3,500 feet. As they approached Hot Springs, Emile got on the radio to air-traffic control, seeking permission to land at Mena.

Terry turned on his transponder and navigation lights. In order to land at Adams Field, he called air-traffic control and braced for Barry's plane to dive in front of him. Terry had adjusted so that he was directly behind Barry, which minimised the turbulence as

Barry dived. After a big jolt, Terry's plane stabilised.

With its lights off, Barry's plane paralleled an Interstate Highway. He pulled a steep left turn over a horses' stable and motorbikes winding across a field. Their headlights converged onto the cargo that had been dropped on the Triple-S Ranch, where an employee of Dan Lasater lived.

Terry calculated that $9 million a week was dropping from the sky into the hands of Bill Clinton and his cronies, courtesy of the CIA.

Dan Lasater's money-laundering scheme used customer accounts. An account in the name of Dennis Patrick had laundered $109 million. A Lasater employee whom Dennis had a relationship with had suggested that Dennis open a trading account with Lasater & Company. For the use of his social security number, Dennis had been promised a share in the profits. In 1985, he received $20,000.

Trouble started after he received a call from Patsy Thomasson – who went on to become Clinton's Director for Administration at the White House – asking him to sign over control of the account because of litigation. Dennis refused. The first attempt on his life was at his rural home in Kentucky, when a hit man arrived with fully-automatic weapons, $33,000 in cash and photos of Dennis, his family and car. Fortunately, the suspect was arrested and convicted. The cash had been a down payment on the hit. The next attempts involved his house being firebombed. Mystified as to why Dennis, a court clerk, would be targeted for professional assassination, the police said they were unable to protect him. Assuming a new identity, he fled with his family to Florida. Eventually, he found out about the $109 million in trades. "My account showed more government securities trades than Chase Manhattan that year," Dennis said years later. "There's certainly reason to kill a man for $100 million or knowledge of $100 million."

CHAPTER 22

Emile Camp

On February 20, 1985, Barry and Emile were to fly in a Learjet to Mena, but when they arrived at the Baton Rouge airport they found that Barry's jet had been stolen.

Barry received a call from Emile's wife at Disney World in Florida. Due to arguments with Emile, she'd gone there with their youngest child. She wanted Barry to send Emile away for a few days, so she could find some peace in her home when she got back. Barry assigned Emile to take flight records to Mena for review by an inspector. Emile flew in Barry's Seneca and Barry took a commercial flight to Miami.

Later the same day, Terry walked into his new house. Exhausted from resolving manufacturing issues for the CIA, he was looking forward to a drop of Scotch and soaking up a view of the golf course and a river.

Aki rang. "Emile's plane is missing. It's past due on a flight from Baton Rouge to Mena. I am telling you this because there is search activity going on. I am sure it will be on the news tonight. I do not want you over there drawing attention to yourself."

"How overdue is he?"

"Only several hours, but Barry and I fear the worst."

In a helicopter, Barry joined the search. His gut told him that he knew where Emile had crashed. On Feb 23, Barry located the wreckage. He was devastated. The plane had contained the original logs of the Fat Lady, which were missing from the crash site. Barry suspected foul play.

The official report stated that Emile had died when his Seneca had hit the North Face of Fourche Mountain, eight-and-a-half miles north of Mena Airport. The National Transportation Safety Board crash examiner reported that Emile had run out of fuel. This perplexed Terry and Barry. Emile was on a simple two-hour flight from Baton Rouge to Mena. His flight plan showed that he had three hours of fuel. After operating and maintaining the plane for two years, Emile knew it inside and out. It had state-of-the-art equipment. He was familiar with the approach he was making to land, which Barry said should have been "as easy as finding your dick in the dark."

Emile had taken off at 11:12 am. After being cleared for an approach at Mena, Emile had radioed at 12:55 pm that he would be landing within fifteen minutes, so the total flight time would have been approximately two hours. He went missing at 2:12 pm, when his fuel had supposedly expired. Barry and Terry calculated that Emile should have had an hour's worth of fuel, but there had been no fire at the crash site 200 feet below the mountain's crest. The cause of the crash was reported as pilot error. Terry and Barry found that unbelievable. They wondered why the Seneca had gone off course, why Emile hadn't radioed for help and why he had violated protocol by descending when he was off-course. Barry's examination of the wreckage led him to discover that the engine controls and switches had been adjusted to suggest that Emile was trying to restart his right engine. If that was the case and with there being no fire, where had the fuel gone?

Another pilot, Polk County Sheriff AL Hadaway, said, "He [Emile] could find this airport at night and land without lights. I've seen him do it."

The Mena airport manager, Rudy Furr, told reporters, "I've heard murder. That Camp had a bomb on board. That he had 500 pounds of cocaine and that he had $3 million in cash."

Russell Welch, an Arkansas State Police Investigator, wrote a report that included a quote from Fred Hampton, the owner/front person for Rich Mountain Aviation. Fred said the Seneca had been sabotaged to prevent Emile from testifying about Barry's undercover work in Nicaragua for the CIA and the DEA. Fred claimed Emile was in possession of documents in the Seneca pertaining to Barry's use of the Fat Lady in Nicaragua.

Knowing that he could easily have been on the plane that day frightened Barry.

While grieving over the loss of their friend, the reports and rumours worried Barry and Terry. If Emile had been set up, would they be next? Terry stayed awake at night, ruminating on scenarios. Had Emile been on a hot money flight without Barry piggybacking and deviated for an unknown reason? No, that didn't make sense. Was he trying to lose a US Customs plane? How had the person who tampered with Emile's plane infiltrated such a close-knit circle? What was his chance of survival if his own plane were tampered with? None. Examining his Seneca, Terry found nothing wrong, but that didn't reduce his anxiety.

The CIA employed a Puerto Rican to ensure that Barry and Terry's aircraft were not sabotaged.

With the loss of Emile weighing them down, Barry and Terry had dinner. Afterwards, Terry got in Barry's truck. Barry drove along the airport road to the end of a field. At an intersection, waiting to turn, Barry noticed a four-door sedan heading towards them. When Barry got on the highway, he flashed his lights at the sedan, exited the road and parked at a service station.

"Yep, it's time to slop the hogs," Barry said. "Reach under your seat and see if you find a paper bag." Terry pulled out a brown bag wrapped and sealed with masking tape. As the sedan drew near, Barry laughed. "Terry, meet my very own FBI Special Agent, and I do mean own. In fact, everybody should own one. They can come in handy. He's one of my inside guys and it's time to make my monthly instalment payment for intelligence. Hand me the sack, please."

The driver appeared apprehensive.

"You earned it this time." Barry tossed the bag to the agent.

"Who's that with you?" the agent asked.

"It's the guy out of Little Rock that flies around with Aki. Speaking of which, he just run off to Washington yesterday with his butt on fire due to an investigation he got wind of out of the Little Rock FBI office." Barry laughed. "Ain't that a hoot! Shit, you told me about that back in November."

The agent cut the conversation short and left.

"Ain't money great, Terry. With it you can buy damn near anything." Barry revved the truck and drove off.

CHAPTER 23

Undercover

In 1985, Barry participated in sting operations around the world. Despite an eight year investigation, the authorities had been unable to crack a case in Las Vegas. Within a month of Barry's arrival all of the heads of the conspiracy were arrested and cocaine worth $22 million was confiscated – the largest seizure ever in Nevada. Due to Barry's testimony, all of the co-defendants were convicted.

Another sting in February led to the arrest of Norman Saunders, the Chief Minister of the Turks and Caicos Islands or effectively the Prime Minister. Filmed by a hidden camera, Barry had paid Saunders $20,000 for the rights to allow trafficking on his British colony south of the Bahamas.

"I don't want you to feel as if I'm trying to push you into anything," Barry said. "You do exactly what you feel in your heart."

After a second meeting in Miami, Saunders and two other government officials were arrested. It was a landmark case for the DEA because it was the first time that a foreign head of state had been arrested for drug charges on US soil.

On June 28, 1985, Barry surrendered to US marshals. He had to start serving the sentence for smuggling the Quaaludes. As his life was in danger, he began the sentence in the federal Witness Protection Program. He spent fifty days underground in a windowless cubicle with only a bed, a TV and a bathroom. Allowed no visitors, he ate alone in the cubicle. Afterwards, at a permanent protection facility, he got an hour of exercise a day. His wife and kids flew 1,500 miles to see him, but were refused entry as they weren't on his list of approved visitors. When Barry found out they had been denied entry, he almost exploded.

Barry was extracted from witness protection for regular court appearances. In the summer of 1985, he was transported to Miami and Las Vegas.

A prosecutor issued a warning: "Barry, if you've held anything back, the slightest single thing, those defence attorneys will bring it out and crucify you. I want to know about everything. If you slept with some pygmy hippopotamus out in some bayou in Louisiana, I want to know about it. There better not be any pygmy hippopotamus out there."

"There's no pygmy hippopotamus," Barry said.

In the trial of the Chief Minister of the Turks and Caicos Islands, a videotape of the bribery was played in a courtroom crammed with lawyers eager to watch Barry in action.

"If you're sitting here conspiring, brother, it's called conspiracy," Barry said on the videotape to Norman Saunders. "You gotta be careful. You gotta know who you're dealing with."

"This guy [Barry] is really good," said Jay Hogan, a well-respected Miami lawyer.

The jury was equally impressed. Saunders was the first foreign head of government to be convicted on drug charges in the US.

Next up were Lito and three co-defendants, who were described as being part of "one of the largest cocaine organisations in the world." During his two days on the stand, Barry exposed the inner workings of what he described as "the Jorge Ochoa Cartel." His testimony was so damning that Lito and two co-defendants changed their pleas to guilty. The jury found the remaining co-defendant guilty. The convictions attracted little media attention.

Regardless of their convictions, Lito and his co-defendants were expecting their associates to land at the prison in a helicopter and wipe out the guards with machine guns and hand grenades. With Max's testimony, DEA agents located the helicopter: a sleek teardrop-shaped Hughes 500 Ranger that had been bought with $500,000 cash. The cartel had offered $300,000 for a pilot. In late October 1985, the authorities began surveying the helicopter at Tamiami Airport. The escape attempt was expected before November 1: the sentencing date for Lito and his co-defendants, after which they would be moved to another facility.

The DEA alerted the jail, a forty-two acre complex housing 700 inmates, ranging from minimum- to maximum-security. Housed in medium-security, Lito and his co-defendants had jobs which permitted them to move around the jail.

By November, details of the escape plan emerged. At 7 am on an unknown date, the helicopter would land when the prisoners were in the open yard preparing to go to their work assignments. Aboard the helicopter, they would fly at 160 mph to a local farmhouse. They were going to blow up the helicopter, drive to a small airstrip in the Everglades and fly to Colombia via the Bahamas. Agents watched the helicopter practise touch-and-go landings and take-offs. Some of the agents wanted to allow the helicopter into the prison to make arrests there, but others said it was too dangerous. Before any escape attempt was made, the DEA impounded the helicopter.

"Our fear was that there might have been a second helicopter that we didn't know about," an agent said. "We could have pursued the investigation, let it go on longer, but we were running out of time."

On November 1, 1985, Lito was sentenced to 40 years and his co-defendants to sentences ranging from 12 to 40 years. They were transferred to a maximum-security prison in Atlanta.

CHAPTER 24

Mena

By April 1985, Terry had been offered a position in Florida by the CIA and also an opportunity to set up a machine-tools business in Mexico. In a restaurant, Barry dissuaded him from the Florida opportunity by describing it as a shoddy operation with old aircraft and equipment and the pilots living in squalor in Honduras. Barry saw bigger opportunities available for anyone with business smarts and ideas because the CIA lacked creative people.

"Terry, the opportunity is right now if you want it," Barry said, over a plate of oysters. "You don't apply for the kind of job I have. You've gotta be aggressive and make your own slot. These guys claim to hate it, but they admire a level of aggressiveness that borders on insubordination. Understand? Between the CIA and their Nicaraguan operation, and the DEA and their objectives, there are bean-counters standing on street corners with sacks of cash and no ideas. You've obviously got some talent they need or they wouldn't be talking to you. I'd pursue it if I was you. For the most part, I'm just a pilot to them. I transport what they want transported and keep my mouth shut. You, on the other hand, have developed expertise that they need badly. If they're talking about an offshore operation controlled by Southern Air Transport or some other big proprietary, you'd better jump at the opportunity." Southern Air Transport was a Miami-based CIA front company with $50 million in assets and 8,000 employees. It ended up mired in allegations of drug trafficking. "And keep me posted on what it is they got in mind for you. I'd be real curious if there's some way I could work into that, too, if it's offshore."

The thought of Barry working in an offshore operation

surprised Terry as Barry had seemed so self-contained. He was unaware of the extent of Barry's problems with the government. "Why would you be interested in an offshore opportunity? Wouldn't it be difficult for you to get involved in another full-time operation?"

"It's like my daddy said: 'You don't catch fish unless you've got a baited hook in the water.' And I'm always trolling for something. Besides, with the problems Aki brought on, I'm sure they'll shut us down in Nella after the new students graduate." The next graduation was scheduled for August 1985.

With $40 million a month still being dropped from the sky, Terry was starting to suspect that there was more to the money than just bribing Arkansas powerbrokers. He was also concerned that a local businessman, Seth Ward, had learned too much about their operation and was trying to blackmail them. Terry had found out that the drop zone for Barry's money, the Triple-S Ranch, was actually owned by Seth Ward and his son-in-law. "Finis Shellnut is the gofer that lives there."

"I thought that was Dan Lasater's place all this time!" Barry said. "And I know this guy, Finis. He works for Dan as a bond salesman. Now ain't that interesting. How could Finis know about the weapons parts? Finis has nothing to do with that. I don't talk about anything except money when I'm at Dan's. Finis doesn't know who's flying the planes. And even if he did, how would he make the connection?" As the money and weapons operations were compartmentalised, Barry and Terry were concerned that people were becoming more aware of the big picture. "Well, maybe that explains some of the shortfall I've been accused of lately, concerning my nightly deposits. The books don't match. When I pick up the cash down south, it's all accounted for, supposedly. And I've been accused lately of having my hand in the till. Maybe this guy Finis is pocketing a little for the Ward family. Think I'll go talk to Dan about that. But you're saying there's another connection to Ward as well?"

"Yeah," Terry said. "He's got a pipeline right into the governor's office."

"Ooowheee! Tell me about that!" Barry moved closer to Terry.

"Ward's oldest daughter, Suzy, is married to Little Rock's ex-mayor, Webb Hubbell. Besides being a close personal friend of Bill Clinton's, Webb is a big wheel at the Rose Law Firm in Little Rock. Guess whose office is right next to Webb's?"

"With all this incestuous shit going on, I hate to take a guess."

"How about Hillary Clinton, the governor's wife."

"Bingo! There's your fucking leak. Somebody in state government had to inform the Ward family about the parts business through Webb Hubbell, and I'll bet you that somebody is Bill Clinton himself, if he's as close a friend to Hubbell as you say. You've got to expect these kind of problems in this business. It's nepotism. This is how it works in a banana republic." After pondering the situation, Barry said, "So Ward has basically threatened us, huh? Let him in or what? Let's call his bluff. It could get real interesting. This whole thing is turning out to be something very unprofessional. Let's bring it to a head right now! Tell him the Fat Man from the Agency said to go fuck himself."

Terry was concerned that Seth Ward might tell the media about their operation. He envisioned the FBI raiding the Mena weapons-manufacturing plant. "I really don't see what is to be gained from that approach, Barry."

"Hey, you're the one who said you wanted to live abroad and work for the Agency. Run a front company, you said. If you want to get out of here real fast, one way is to expose it, forcing the Agency to shut it down. That means they would have need of your Mexican operation sooner. You and I could run it together. That's all I was thinking." On a napkin, Barry drew a line from the Triple-S Ranch to Dan Lasater's bond company, through the Ward family, into the Rose Law Firm and ending up at the back door of the governor's mansion. Gazing up at Terry, Barry said, "This is turning into one big Chinese fire drill. Get ready to hook it and ride."

Barry's attitude disturbed Terry. Leaning towards moving to Mexico sooner rather than later, Terry calculated that the Mena operation would fall apart. With Barry about to go into the Witness Protection Program, Terry wondered if that was why Barry was being so reckless.

In May 1985, Terry was training the new batch of pilots with Emile's replacement Bill Cooper, a sharp sixty-year-old who was bald and plump. They were in a Cessna over mountainous terrain with rain spattering against the aircraft. In the dark cockpit, a confused Nicaraguan was trying to concentrate on the controls and the ground controller.

Bill whispered to Terry, "Shut down the left engine. Let's see what this fucker's made of."

Discreetly, Terry pulled a red knob. The Cessna leaned to the left. When the pilot didn't react appropriately, Terry yelled, "Rudder! Rudder! Right rudder! Now. Attitude. Bank angle. Airspeed. What the fuck are you doing? Why am I seeing trees in my windshield?" The pilot didn't know what to do as the plane rolled. "I'm gonna die with you. Did you go to mass today? I didn't. I'm not ready to die. If I can't talk you through this recovery, we're all gonna go down together. Now, believe your instruments! Push hard right rudder! Roll wings level, and lower the nose." The pilot slowly regained control. The Cessna climbed out of a valley.

In June 1985, Terry was performing more night training when he received a distress call from his command post. After blowing an engine, Barry had landed at Texarkana and needed someone to rescue his cargo. Terry found Barry sitting in a Rockwell Commander, a four-seater plane, its engine cover on the ground, an oil stain on its wing.

"I already checked her out," Barry said. "She's dead on arrival and I need to get out of here. I've got a duffel bag inside. You need to drop me off at Mena and then hightail it over to Russellville to deliver this." Barry handed Terry some boxes. "Don't drop these babies. They're real valuable electronics on loan from the Agency. I can't leave these lying around. They're not just for anyone's use. You might call these the key to the secret door."

After they got to Mena, Barry split. He was going to enter the

Witness Protection Program within two weeks.

The recipient of the duffel bag, Skeeter Ward, was surprised to see Terry delivering it. He told Terry, "I think Barry Seal's playing games with all of us."

On August 25, 1985, the Nicaraguan trainee pilots graduated at Nella. Oliver North was considering promoting Terry who was ready to move his entire family to Mexico. In September, when Terry asked Aki about Barry, he was told that Barry was working undercover on a special project.

Barry appeared at Mena in late November 1985. His face had aged and he'd gained weight. After depositing money with Dan Lasater, he arranged to meet Terry at SOB's.

"Where the hell you been?" Terry said. "I figured the Bermuda Triangle must have just swallowed you up. Or was it something I said?"

After apologising, Barry said his absence involved undercover work. "Let's not talk about old business. Let's discuss new business. I got some inside knowledge that not only affects you, but is gonna affect Arkansas in a big way. The good news is the Agency wants to do your Mexican venture. You've got Cathey [Oliver North] really excited. The bad news is I've been out of the loop for so long that you need to bring me up to speed, so I can get involved in this project in order to help you."

Terry said he'd taken his wife and three children down to Mexico. After scoping it out, he'd formulated a weapons-supply network.

Back on the subject of Arkansas, Barry said, "The Agency's getting real pissed at these guys here. Talk about outgrowing their britches, they're stealing fucking money from the Company. Terry, that's like robbing the mob. It's something you just don't fucking do. I guess Bill Clinton and his gang have been working on a lot more than their ten-percent cut. The decision has been made to pull the plug on the whole fucking deal."

"Operation Centaur Rose?"

"Yeah. This worked out real great up here and we all proved it could work. But the Agency's got much bigger plans for Mexico. Bigger plans than are included in your proposal. Terry, they want to build whole fucking guns from scratch, using your machine tools. Shit, man, you really opened their eyes on this manufacturing stuff. I even brought along some blueprints on the first weapon they want to build down there."

The Mexican operation would happen in two phases: the establishment of a front company in Mexico, followed by the importation of machine-tool equipment. Barry showed Terry a drawing of a weapon that fired plastic explosive cartridges. The CIA was marketing it to poor countries.

"And another thing, Governor Bill Clinton's gonna learn who's in charge – the hard way. He'll be lucky to get elected dog-catcher after they're through with him. What's important for both of us is for you to take them up on their deal, get your butt down to Mexico and be in a position to receive me once I help blow the lid on the whole Arkansas operation."

"How you gonna do that?"

Barry finished an oyster. "Let me worry about that. That's my job." Barry mentioned a secret meeting he'd arranged with his CIA handler. Endangered because of his undercover operations, Barry was putting special security into place for the meeting. "Remember how to piggyback? I think this is an appropriate time to use this procedure for something other than carrying cash." On a napkin, Barry drew a flight plan for a piggyback mission and wrote down codes they could use when he called Terry's house. "I'll refer to my handler as my brother. I'm trying to get this meeting set up to take place out of the country for security reasons. We won't be gone long. They'll miss me up here if I'm out of the country for more than a few days. Just be prepared for my call and don't say anything stupid over the phone. It's not secure."

"Can you give me an idea where we're going?"

Barry winked. "I'll take you for a trip on the dark side."

On December 13, 1985, Barry called Terry. "Glad I caught you, Santa Claus. It's time for the trip to my brother's place." Excitedly,

Barry continued a coded statement that instructed Terry where to rendezvous with Barry's plane.

They flew to Texas and filed a false flight plan to Mexico in Emile Camp's name and honour. They aimed to refuel in El Salvador and take off for Panama.

On-board, Barry had two GNS-500 navigational radios worth over $1 million. After typing in the coordinates of the flight plan, Barry said, "OK, I'll just hook up the ground-and-satellite communications equipment in this box and it'll be time for us to disappear."

Barry was setting everything in motion to prevent a Department of Defense satellite – designed to spot incoming missiles – from detecting his Learjet. He'd arranged for US Army intelligence personnel to emit energy bursts to jam US and Mexican radar. Terry was impressed by Barry's use of satellites for the flight plan versus getting instructions from the ground as was the case for most pilots. It showed that Barry was connected to the highest levels of the US government who could access the most sophisticated communications and weapons technology.

"You get ready to switch transponders to standby. I'll call our guys in Cuba on a secure frequency." Barry got on his radio. "Sea Spray, this is Lear one-three Sierra November. Thirty seconds from the window. How do you read?"

"Loud and clear. We've been expecting you."

Barry said to Terry, "When that clock reads thirty, switch both transponders to standby, hit the speed brakes and let's dive this bitch to the deck. Use your emergency decompression checklist." The transponder interrogation light went off. With its speed brakes extended, the Learjet shook and descended. Barry got on the radio to Mexican air traffic control, "Cancel our flight plan to your destination. We're going somewhere else." The Learjet was now off the radar, self-navigating towards El Salvador with a flight plan beamed in from outer space. It was a technique used to hide top-secret military flights, including Air Force One which transports the US president.

After landing in El Salvador, the Learjet was surrounded by soldiers, who guarded the area and provided lunch and Coca-Cola to Barry and Terry. The plane was refuelled with no exchange of money or any receipts created. As the plane taxied for take-off, Barry told Terry to hit the brakes. Barry got out and peeled some Mylar mask off the Learjet, which changed its serial number.

Flying to Panama, Barry said, "Now keep in mind, you got something these fuckers really want. It's your reputation and experience in the machine-tool industry. And that's what you have for sale. They want to build a front nobody will be looking at and you've got the creds to do that. So don't sell yourself short and don't talk money on this trip. View this as an operational discussion only. Don't forget, Leroy is just a fucking bean counter." Leroy was Barry's long-standing CIA contact. "Sometimes he acts like it's his money and not Uncle Sam's. I'll take care of the money discussions later."

"So what do you want out of this, Barry?"

"I wanna new life. They're gonna need major air-transportation capability for this program. I always wanted to own Air America. Maybe this is my chance to do something like that."

In Panama, they landed at Howard Air Force Base. A pickup truck transported them to the terminal.

"You guys are on time," said Leroy, a thin wrinkled man wearing sunglasses. "I love punctuality. This meeting's been moved to Chagres. A couple of the people who are attending don't want to be seen here."

In a Cessna 172, Barry flew them to a dirt airstrip on the banks of the Panama Canal, formerly part of a US Armed Forces Aeroclub with hangars and wooden outbuildings. The meeting was in a building overlooking ships.

Inside, waiting impatiently, was a man claiming to be Max Gomez – an alias of Felix Rodriguez – a friend of George HW Bush. He led Barry and Leroy into a corner, away from Terry.

After a brief chat with Felix, Barry returned to Terry. "This is a pretty sensitive area we need to talk about. There is another person present outside who represents another government that may wanna get involved in this operation. This other person would like to sit in on this meeting, but not be identified for security reasons. Got any problem with that?"

"What's his role?" Terry said.

"He just wants to leave this meeting fully informed and then file a report with his boss. He wants to be sure he hears everything straight from the horse's mouth. I got no problem with that, if you don't."

Terry shrugged. "Sure, we flew too far to fuck up the meeting now. I guess I can't be trusted yet with this guy's identity, huh?"

"Spook shit," Barry said, nodding. "Let them play their fucking games."

Felix brought in a clean-cut businessman with a glass eyeball who sat at the end of a long conference table.

"Terry," Leroy said, "I'm sorry about the security precautions taken to not divulge the identity of our guest. I'll show you my identification to allay your suspicions."

Seeing the CIA ID for Leroy Tracta on the table eased Terry's nerves. Barry and Terry sat next to each other, with Leroy opposite Terry, and Felix opposite Barry. At the end of the table, the stranger readied his pen over a yellow notepad. From his briefcase, Felix fished a file, which included a copy of Terry's business plan.

"Mr Reed," Felix said. "It appears you've been very busy. It's time to get beyond feasibility and into the reality of developing this front company. That is why we have requested this meeting. I want to thank you and Mr Seal for coming on such short notice. We felt it best to arrange a face-to-face meeting and have Mr Tracta interrogate – ask you – detailed questions. And he wanted to meet you in person."

Leroy nodded to the stranger with the glass eye, whom he introduced as a potential foreign investor who was filing a report for his people. Leroy handed everybody a copy of Terry's business plan stamped with TOP SECRET. There was a diagram of Mexico and a map of trade routes from Asia, the US and Europe entering directly into Mexico or from other countries, all ending at Mexico City. Export lines ran from Mexico to Latin American countries.

Terry detailed the plan and the companies out of Hungary, Germany and Japan interested in a machine-tool operation in Mexico. He expressed concern about Mexican licensing requirements and laws pertaining to foreign-owned firms. It was the kind of company that Mexico desperately needed to develop its export market through modern machine tools.

"This is something that is non-existent in Mexico," the stranger said in a non-descript accent. "And from what I've heard, this is the major attraction of Mr Reed's plan. When I file my report, I'm going to emphasise this point as well as expand upon the joint-venture concept." The stranger was impressed. Felix liked the Hungarian connection.

Terry said Mexico's poor road infrastructure made air transportation essential for the fragile electronics required for computerised machine tools. The air shipments would camouflage the weapons dealing.

"With all this air-cargo activity," Barry said, "we're gonna need a very specialised carrier that can operate freely worldwide, move sensitive cargo, and, most of all, keep its mouth shut. I propose the formation of a small elite air-cargo operation based out of Mexico that would be like a scaled-down version of Southern Air Transport. I can put all that together for you, and, considering the black ops capabilities in place from Operation Seaspray, we'll be able to move undetected throughout this region. The US army's anti-detection capabilities in the corridor around Panama and the Bahamas are excellently suited for this style of operation."

"What's this gonna cost me, Barry?" Leroy asked. "With you, that's a question I'm always afraid to ask."

"Leroy, haven't you always got your money's worth from me? I'm a professional, and you know it, and professionals cost money. I've instructed Terry to discuss no money figures today. He's sort of new at this. You come to me later, after Terry and I have had a chance to put a sharp pencil to it and then we'll discuss money."

"Oh, shit!" Leroy said. "Just what I need. Are you training him how to handle me, too, as you're always boasting?"

Everybody laughed.

"How did you know I said that?" Barry said. "You got my phones bugged again, Leroy?"

They laughed harder.

"This is Mr Cathey's project," Felix said to Terry, referring to Oliver North. "View him as the big boss. You need to be filing all of your reports with him as this progresses. I will be operations manager for this project, if it's a go."

After three hours, Barry and Terry were on a natural high as they flew back to Howard Air Force Base, where they were allocated rooms in the Bachelor Officer Quarters. It was dark out, but they were unable to sleep.

Seeing Barry's lights on, Terry knocked on his door. He found Barry on a bed, gazing at the ceiling fan as if contemplating the day. "Barry, tell me about this Max Gomez [Felix Rodriguez] guy. Back in the States you said he was a loose cannon and we had to play ball with him. From what I can see now, he's gonna be the guy in charge down here. I can't figure out if he's driven by ideals or greed. Does that bother you?"

"Terry," Barry said, "as a young man, I had ideals similar to yours. I was put into play early on with a group of guys wanting to liberate their country just as your Nicaraguan freedom fighters want to liberate theirs. Anyone whose ideals drive them has to be a little bit crazy. Gomez falls into that category. My Agency service has pivoted around a group of ragtag Cubans, and now, Panamanians. They just come with this business. They're always on the ragged edge between right and wrong and sometimes they'll pull you in there with them. You just gotta keep your head screwed on straight and remember why you got involved. Don't make their war your war or you can get into real trouble. But all I can tell you from an Agency point of view is they're the only game in town, at least on this side of the world. If you wanna play this game, you've gotta associate with guys like Gomez. They've turned fighting Communism into their own selfish full-time profession. You don't know what really motivates them: greed or ideals or hatred. But I agree with you: fucking Communism is a threat. I may be a wild-ass free enterpriser, but I'm also a patriot."

After a big breakfast in the Officers' Mess, Terry supervised the refuelling of the Learjet. Leroy requested a private meeting with Barry. As they walked away, Terry heard Barry say, "Well, I'm sorry, Leroy, if they feel like I'm blackmailing them. But this is business and I just gotta do what I gotta do."

Operating outside America would eradicate the problems that had arisen in Mena for the CIA. They included local law enforcement snooping around and the confusion some federal agencies harboured about Barry's role and who he was working for. Barry's drug trafficking was supposed to have allowed the FBI to become the controlling investigative body. By leading the investigation into Barry's trafficking, the FBI had hoped to keep state and local law enforcement away. Anyone who later tried to access the FBI's records pertaining to Mena would find a criminal investigation, when, in reality, the FBI was containing the cover-up or what Terry Reed described as "a shadow shadowing a black operation." As the FBI lost control, the CIA had used other resources including the Justice Department to prevent arrests and prosecutions. Barry's trafficking drew surveillance to Mena, which helped camouflage the activity twelve miles away at Nella. Barry hadn't only been transporting drugs for the Medellín Cartel. That was just cover for the CIA's facilitation of drugs entering the US that had been going on for decades.

On the flight back, Barry was on a natural high. "Yee-haw!" he yelled repeatedly, surprising Terry. "I'm gonna fucking make it! We're gonna do this, Terry. We've got these assholes eating out of our hands. Yee-haw! Give me the fucking plane." Barry grabbed the control column. The plane performed a series of sideways rolls, each a full 360° rotation.

Terry fought the urge to puke.

"OK, enough of that shit," Barry said. "You got the plane. I'll hook up the radios." Barry crouched under the electrical panel to make radio connections.

At the controls, Terry wondered why Barry was so euphoric.

Barry re-emerged and pounded the dashboard so forcefully that it almost detached. "There ain't nothing in this world more powerful than good old fucking blackmail, Terry. And don't let anybody ever tell you different. Jesus Christ, I got some good shit on some big people."

"Will you let me in on your party? Calm down, Barry! Tell me what's going on?"

"Terry, what's most important right now is for you to play ball with these guys and get your ass down to Mexico ASAP. I won't be able to come to Mexico right now. I've got a little matter to take care of. But you get on down there. Get in a position to receive me and I'll be joining you soon. Goddam, this'll be great. Won't it be fun working together and spending all their fucking money?"

"What's this blackmail you're talking about?"

"Ever heard the old expression, 'It's not what you know, it's who you know.'? Well, whoever said that just hadn't caught Vice President Bush's kids in the dope business. 'Cause I can tell you for sure what you know can definitely be more important than who you know."

"You gotta calm down and tell me what you're talking about, if you want me to know. What's this about the Vice President's kids and dope?"

"I don't wanna tell you too much 'cause truthfully you don't have a need to know. But, Terry, I've been working with several federal agencies for the past couple of years as you probably suspicioned. In the course of that business, a person can't help but run across some real sensitive information. It seems that some major players in the Medellín Cartel, whom I personally know, ran across some knowledge that is very valuable to both the Republicans and the Democrats. Real national-security stuff. It seems some of George

HW Bush's kids just can't say no to drugs." Barry laughed. "Well, you can imagine how valuable information like that would be, can't you? That could get you out of almost any kind of jam. You ever play Monopoly? The information I got is so good it's just like a get-out-of-jail-free card." Barry laughed. "Yee-haw!"

"Barry, are you telling me George HW Bush's kids are in the drug business?"

"Yup, that's what I'm telling you. A guy in Florida who flipped for the DEA has got the goods on the Bush boys. I heard this earlier from a reliable source in Colombia, but I just sat on it then, waiting to use it as a trump card if I ever needed it. Well, I need to use it now. I got names, dates, places. I even got some tape recordings. Fuck, I even got surveillance videos catching the Bush boys red-handed. I consider this stuff my insurance policy. It makes me and my mole on the inside that's feeding the stuff to me invincible. Now this is real sensitive shit inside of US Customs and DEA and those guys are pretty much under control. It's damage control as usual. But where it gets real interesting is what the Republicans will do to the Democrats in order to dirty up the people who might use this information against Bush."

"So you've got direct knowledge of the Republicans trying to neutralise some Democrats before they can nuke Bush with this?"

"Hell, yeah. I've been a part of it. Remember that meeting we had at SOB's when I told you you should play ball with these guys and get your butt down to Mexico and be prepared to receive me? Remember in that meeting, I told you I had a plan to blow the lid off the whole damn Mena deal and shut it down due to adverse publicity? Well, what I didn't tell you was that the project was already in effect and the Republicans were already trying to neutralise some important people in Arkansas: namely the Clinton family." Barry radioed to ground control. "Yeah, that day you explained to me the connection between the Ward family, the Rose Law Firm and the Governor's mansion, well, I about shit. You see, what you didn't know was I was on a secret mission by none other than the Agency to sort of dirty up some people real close to the governor. Now, I had been working on this through Dan Lasater. He's a good ol' boy and all that, but he's got a drug problem and he's got the balls to be stealing from the Agency, too. From what I hear, Dan's been doing a lot of questionable out-of-state investing. In fact, he's stashing a lot of cash in a resort in New Mexico. I was told to exploit that, which I was working on. But you come along with this new connection. When you told me that Finis Shellnut was the guy at the ranch, dollar signs started dancing in my head. I saw an immediate way to get some white stuff up some noses around Bill Clinton real fast. Now don't get mad, but that duffel bag I had you take over to Skeeter Ward wasn't really money."

"I'm afraid to ask what it was," Terry said, his eyes pinned to the flight director.

"Let's don't call it cocaine. Let's just call it neutralising powder. Least that's the way the Bush family saw it. This is just one family warring against another. Just like the mob."

"Goddam, Barry. This is heavy shit! Are you saying you were the source of the cocaine ending up around a lot of important people in Arkansas? Like the ones I've been reading about in the paper. There's a major scandal brewing there." They both fell silent. "Did you have anything to do with Roger Clinton and some of those guys in Lasater's firm getting investigated?"

"Terry, I told you when I met you, I'm in transportation and I transport what the government wants transported. In this case, the Republicans – the Bush family – wanted some stuff transported through Mena and into Arkansas that would end up in the noses of some very prominent Democrats. And yes, I must fess up, I've had a hand in that. Yee-haw! It's not who you know, it's what you know."

Shocked, Terry didn't know how to react. With the jet flying above the clouds, he contemplated in silence, disturbed by Barry's revelation and even more upset with Barry for having him unwittingly transport drugs. Terry thought of Roger Clinton, serving time for cocaine in a Texas federal prison. He'd heard that other players were nervous that the investigation into Roger had expanded and was going to lead to them. The local bond industry was at risk of being exposed for laundering cocaine proceeds. It would be a disaster for the Arkansas economy if business confidence was undermined. Dan Lasater had been targeted and other Clinton cronies. If Barry was right, Bill Clinton was George Bush Sr's real target. Terry didn't want to be involved with smearing the reputations of such powerful people. How could Barry be so happy blackmailing everyone? Barry was surely biting off too much by threatening to expose the drug-business dealings of Bush's sons. Terry wondered why the CIA would want its money-laundering operation investigated. That didn't make any sense. Maybe it was all Barry's doing to collapse the operation here, so he could escape his problems by evacuating to Mexico. Was Barry playing with everyone as Skeeter Ward had warned Terry? If he'd tricked Terry into transporting drugs, what else had he lied about?

Terry's shock turned into anger. "Barry, I gotta tell you. I'm sitting here pretty pissed off. This whole thing about putting cocaine up peoples' noses is not what I'm about. We got thrust together by a guy named John Cathey, and, up until today, I thought he'd made a great decision in putting the two of us together. But I gotta tell you, I'm having second thoughts about a lot of this. If we continue as friends, you've gotta promise me two things. I know the first one goes against the intelligence grain, but you've gotta start telling me everything, so I can make my own decisions. We're treading into some dangerous territory. Ours is getting way beyond a need-to-know relationship. Second, don't ever put cocaine near me again. If that's what you have to do for the Agency, then you go do it. I don't want to know about it."

"Terry, you're my friend, and, believe me, I need friends right now. I'm sorry if I upset you or if I compromised your values. It's hard to run across a person with values these days. They're scarce." A radio call interrupted the conversation. After landing at Little Rock, Barry said, "I'm sorry about the cocaine deal with Skeeter. I promise I'll never do it again. Captain, you and I have lots of good times ahead of us. I've taught you all I can teach you. It's time for you to solo."

"When will I see you next?" Terry said, concerned that the word solo was Barry's way of terminating their relationship.

"I don't know for sure. I've got to attend a legal orgy in Baton Rouge," Barry said, referring to a deposition being administered by the IRS, during which Barry would be required to answer questions about money being laundered through Arkansas banks. "Be careful with these guys and I'll see you down south soon."

Terry got out of the plane and turned to Barry in the cockpit. Barry smiled and gave a thumbs-up sign. Barry taxied onto the runway, still grinning.

CHAPTER 25

Sentencing

On October 24, 1985, Barry was back in a Miami court for a Rule 35 hearing, hoping that his work as an informant would mitigate his sentence – his reward for risking his life. The DEA praised Barry for being one of the most successful undercover operatives ever as well as for being a brilliant witness. He'd infiltrated the highest levels of the Medellín Cartel and exposed the sophisticated technology traffickers relied on, including Defense Department navigation and communication equipment designed to be used in nuclear war.

"The DEA considers the Ochoa investigation," Joura said, "or the Nicaraguan investigation, the most significant investigation that the DEA has been involved in since its inception. I have worked with a lot of informants over my career. I have never met someone who had as much potential and produced as much as Mr Seal did. I have known him for over a year and a half now and we have had almost daily contact during that time. He has been debriefed extensively. I have never caught him in a lie. I think once he decided to cooperate, he decided to cooperate wholly and completely. I think he has come to realise the effect that cocaine has on the fabric of society in the United States and I don't think it's something that he totally realised before his arrest when he flew drugs into the country. I think as a person who provided transportation, I don't think he ever considered the impact of what he was doing. I think now, through working with the DEA, he has come to have some realisation of this and wants to correct some of the things he has done in the past."

"If Mr Seal had done the things that he has done," Barry's

lawyer said to Joura on the stand, "and if instead of being a cooperating defendant, he was a DEA agent, can you tell us what kind of reward he would have gotten?"

"I suppose he would have been proposed for the Attorney General's Award, which, as far as I know, is the highest award available to somebody in the DEA."

When it was time for sentencing, the judge took his glasses off. "When I originally sentenced Mr Seal to ten years... I thought the evidence portrayed a defendant who was bright, cunning and, frankly, amoral. I would clearly have given Mr Seal more than the ten-year maximum at the time of sentencing because, from the evidence I saw, he struck me as being a man who, if I may describe in a word that most Americans shy away from these days because our language has become very bland: I thought he was evil.

"I think it's well known to all people in this district, promises of cooperation don't cut any ice with me at all, and the only time I let anybody out of jail entirely, rather than just a reduction of sentence, is when their cooperation rises to the level that they have put their life in peril. And when they do that, then I think they deserve to be suitably rewarded. Consequently, I'm going to reduce his sentence to time served. Enjoy your life, Mr Seal. You've earned it. You're a free man." The gavel fell.

Barry jumped up and hugged his lawyer and wife. He was now unconcerned about his Baton Rouge sentencing because the plea-bargain stipulated that he wouldn't have to serve any more time in Louisiana than he had for his Florida conviction, which was time served. The hearing would be a formality. He'd be out in no time.

In December 1995, Stanford Bardwell the Baton Rouge prosecutor held a press conference. He announced that Barry had agreed to plead guilty of two counts: cocaine conspiracy and money laundering. Attempting to save face in the wake of the documentary *Uncle Sam Wants You*, Stanford claimed to have scored a victory against Barry, and that a fifteen-month investigation had brought Barry down.

The investigative reporter behind the documentary, John Camp, stepped in with some penetrating questions:

"Is there a plea-bargain arrangement that has been made that will guarantee Mr Seal not receive any time excessive to what he's been sentenced to in Florida?"

"I'm not prepared to comment on that at this time," Bardwell said. He believed that Barry would have to serve at least a portion of the ten-year sentence for the Quaaludes smuggling. "It's my view that the sentence will not be reduced."

"How could you possibly make that judgement if you haven't talked with the judge?" Camp asked.

"Well, just based on prior experience. I just have a feeling that he's not in a position… he's got no reason to change it."

In court in Baton Rouge, Barry pleaded guilty to the two counts in Bardwell's indictment. Having watched *Uncle Sam Wants You*, Judge Polozola – a close friend of prosecutor Bardwell – grilled Barry about statements he'd made in the documentary, including whether Barry could specify any of the wrongdoing he'd alleged by federal officials in the Middle District. Barry stayed quiet.

In court on December 20, 1985, the DEA never showed up, but Barry believed that it was unimportant because the outcome had already been decided.

Sitting on the front row, leaning towards Barry, his lawyer said, "We've got a big problem. I just got some fascinating news from the CIA. I requested a letter testifying to your truthfulness and cooperation in your dealings with them."

"Yeah. Regent said he'd send that right over," Barry said.

"There is no Regent," the lawyer said.

"What!"

"Regent is a fake name. The CIA claims they've never heard of anybody with that name. They gave you a fake name."

"Bastards." Scanning the room, Barry frowned.

"Don't worry, Barry. This judge can only give you probation. Nothing more than Florida. That's the deal."

"Mr Seal, do you understand that you're here for sentencing today," Judge Polozola said.

"Yes, sir."

The judge scowled. "If I had the remotest idea, the slightest idea Mr Seal would not receive a jail sentence in Florida, under no circumstances, absolutely no circumstances, would I have accepted this plea agreement. As far as I'm concerned, drug dealers like Mr Seal are the lowest, most despicable type of people I can think of because they have no concern for the public... In my opinion, people like you, Mr Seal, ought to be in a federal penitentiary. You ought to be there working at hard labour. Working in the hottest sun or the coldest day wouldn't be good enough for drug dealers like you."

"Now, wait a minute, Your Honour," Barry's lawyer said. "Mr Seal is in a unique position. There's only one man in the United States who can testify against Jorge Ochoa, who is considered to be the biggest drug dealer in the world."

"Let me tell you what," the judge said. "I don't care who Mr Seal thinks he is. He's nothing special to me."

"Your Honour–" the lawyer said.

"In this particular case, somehow you got only probation in another court and this court has agreed not to extend your penalty. I don't like it, but there's nothing I can do about it now."

"Your Honour–" the lawyer said.

If Barry violated any of his conditions of probation, Polozola stated he would receive five years in prison. "You will not leave Louisiana, even to work for a government agency, without the court's approval. I don't care if it is in the Drug Enforcement Administration. I don't care if it is the CIA. I don't care if it is the State Department. I don't care if it is the US Attorney. I don't care who it is. You don't go anyplace – anyplace! – without getting my personal written approval in advance."

"Do you want me to refer all those agencies," Unglesby said with a hint of sarcasm, "since he talks to all of them, to you?"

"I don't care. I don't care who they are. The probation

department is going to see it. The US Attorney is here. He is the government's lawyer. We only have one government."

"I have found that, in this case, not to be entirely true," Unglesby said.

"It has come to my attention that there are certain people around you that carry guns," the judge said. "If the guns are in your houses, you're going to have a serious problem with revocation." The judge was referring to Barry's probation being revoked.

"I don't possess a gun," Barry said, "and I don't intend to. But I do intend to have bodyguards."

"Well, your bodyguards are going to have to be without guns."

"Well, why is that," Barry said, "if they have legal permits to carry them?"

"You take your chance, Mr Seal." The judge fined Barry $35,000. "And as a further condition of probation, the defendant shall reside at the Salvation Army Community Treatment Center, 7361 Airline Highway, Baton Rouge, Louisiana, for a period of six months."

Barry and his lawyer swung their heads towards each other and conferred in urgent whispers. Throughout the negotiations, no one had ever mentioned a halfway house. Stripped of the protection of guns and forced to reside at a designated location, it wouldn't take the Colombians long to find and kill him.

"Well, we want to talk about that, judge," Barry's lawyer said.

"There is nothing to talk about."

The lawyer banged the table. "This is a double-cross by the government!"

"In this court, I am the government," the judge said, pointing at himself. "This is not a double-cross by the government."

"Yes, sir, it is."

"Read the plea agreement on count two," the judge said.

"I've read it. I'm very familiar with it. I hammered it out. OK. It says no incarceration."

"This is not incarceration," the judge said, grimacing.

"Six months in the Salvation Army is incarceration!"

"He's free to work all he wants," the judge said dismissively. "He goes there at 6 pm but he can't leave until 8 am the next morning."

"This is not right!" the lawyer threw his hands down. "This is a death sentence. Mr Seal has a $1 million price on his head. With no protection, he's a dead man."

"Let me tell you what," the judge said. "I would love for this plea agreement to be broken right now!"

"Is that why you're doing this?" the lawyer shouted, approaching the judge.

"Mr Seal has one week before he must begin his Salvation Army stay. That's my sentence." The judge banged his gavel several times.

Barry's face was blank. His wife recoiled with shock.

"Do something! They'll kill him!" Debbie yelled at the lawyer. "They'll kill him! Do something!"

Stanford Bardwell was smiling.

Barry sat, shaking his head, gazing down despondently.

Still smiling, the prosecutor left the court room.

On the way out in the hall, Barry's lawyer said to one of the prosecutor's assistants, "Does the judge know the full extent of Barry's cooperation with the Miami DEA?"

"That's Florida and Las Vegas," the assistant said. "Barry hasn't done anything for us in Baton Rouge and until he does something for us, we're not that concerned about it."

Leaving the court, Barry was accosted by the media. "What are you going to do now? Go into hiding?"

"Oh, I don't hide," Barry said.

"Mr Seal, aren't you afraid for your life?"

"If it comes, it comes."

"What about the federal Witness Protection Program?"

"That's just another name for jail, you know. I'm not going to jail. I don't care what you call it."

"Aren't you afraid that the cartel will find you in Baton Rouge?"

"I can see a Colombian coming from a mile away in Baton Rouge."

What Barry and nobody else had noticed was an American private investigator in their midst, who'd been in the courtroom and was on the payroll of the Medellín Cartel.

After the sentencing hearing, Barry went to his lawyer's office and called Vice President George HW Bush. He told Bush that if he wouldn't help him, he'd expose the illegal weapons and drugs trafficking. Bush's response is unknown.

One morning, there was a loud knock on Barry's door. He jumped out of bed and peeped out of the window. More knocking woke up the entire family. His two teenage sons and little daughter entered the room. Barry went downstairs and opened the door.

A lady standing with a group of people in business suits identified herself as an IRS agent. "Mr Seal, this is a declaration of back taxes owed to the government. We are here to collect your assets in partial payment of that debt."

"Show me your warrant," Barry said.

They looked nonplussed.

"You're not coming in without warrant," Barry said.

"We'll be back with a warrant then."

Barry called Vice President George HW Bush. "If you don't get these IRS assholes off my back, I'm gonna blow the whistle on the Contra scheme [illegal drugs and arms trafficking]." Bush's response is unknown.

The IRS returned with a warrant. Barry tried to slam the door in their faces, but a large man in a boiler suit pushed it open. Removal men filed into the house and started taking the furniture.

"Mr Seal, you're on probation," the lady said. "Resisting an officer of the law would be a violation of that probation, resulting in your immediate incarceration."

"I have my rights." Barry examined the paperwork. "It says that I owe $29 million in back taxes." He shook his head.

"It was based on the earnings you reported in court for drug transportation."

"But you don't take Debbie's stuff, lady," Barry said. "You take my planes and my boats."

"We already have."

Barry went upstairs, grabbed some documents, locked himself in the toilet and started burning them. When he was done, he joined his family at the top of the stairs. Debbie picked up their daughter, hugged her and turned around. Barry watched the removal men clean out the house.

In *Doublecrossed*, the next visitor to arrive at the empty house was DEA agent Jacobsen.

"Barry, I'm sorry about the hearing," Jacobsen said.

"Where were you, man?" Barry said, sitting on the stairs.

"I'm sorry. They told us it was gonna be routine. Nothing could go wrong. They told us we couldn't come."

"They." Barry nodded. "They weren't ever on the street, were they, Jake?"

"Too dirty."

Barry started crying. "Why is this happening?"

"I don't know, Barry."

"What didn't I do for you?"

"You did it all."

"It's like open season on Barry Seal." Barry smiled sadly.

"I'm sorry. I can't help you."

"No. It don't matter."

"My hometown. They wanted to get me and they did."

"What about the Colombians?"

"I don't think the Colombians will try to kill me," Barry said. "It's just business."

CHAPTER 26

Assassination

Nobody expected Barry to last long at the Salvation Army halfway house. Most thought he'd cave in and seek sanctuary in the Witness Protection Program. But Barry confounded everybody with his resolve to stay put for the entire six months.

After the arrest of Max, the hit to kill Barry had been given to Cumbamba in May 1985. But Barry's entry into the Witness Protection Program had stalled things for the Colombians. On January 21, 1986, the shifting legal fortunes of Jorge Ochoa were such that he was under threat of extradition from Spain to Miami. On January 24, Barry started staying at the halfway house from 6 pm – which had been reported back to the Ochoas by the private investigator who'd attended Barry's sentencing hearing.

Fifteen days into his stay at the halfway house, a Colombian hit team flew to Mexico and illegally crossed the border into America. On February 16, Cumbamba arrived at the Kenner Airport Hilton. Using an alias, Miguel Velez, he rented room 312. The hit team arrived the next day. A 1982 grey Buick was bought for $6,500 in hundred dollar bills and registered to Mary Cook. Two Colombians checked in at the Jay Motel Lounge Restaurant, which cost $15.91 per night. From room 228, they could see the Salvation Army parking lot, a few hundred yards away.

On the morning of February 19, Barry called a friend who was a missionary pilot. "Joe, they're closing in."

"Barry, keep your eyes on Jesus."

On the same day, the Colombians received baseball caps and raincoats. Cumbamba drove Luis Carlos Quintero Cruz to the parking lot at the halfway house. Cumbamba reversed the Buick into a space on the lot three spaces over from three large white Salvation Army drop boxes for donations of clothes, located in the middle of the lot. Cumbamba and Quintero Cruz came out of the car to drop something in the donation boxes.

Back in the car, Cumbamba sat smoking, patiently awaiting Barry.

Barry's routine at the halfway house consisted of waking up early and leaving at 7 am. He returned at 6 pm, usually accompanied by a friend or with a friend following his car as an added precaution. He usually ate lunch at home with his family. The mail he read at home was full of bad news: his home was subject to a seizure warrant; now that he was a felon, the FAA was revoking his pilot's licence…

With the IRS having seized many of his assets, including a helicopter, two boats, three planes, his business office, his house furniture and a Mercedes from Lito's dealership, Barry was preoccupied with fixing his tax situation.

On February 19, 1985, Barry told a journalist, "This IRS thing has me very very time-limited. I've been with attorneys twenty-four hours a day. The whole time I'm over at the Salvation Army, I'm on the phone with them and it's gotten to be a very involved thing."

Returning to the Salvation Army on February 19, Barry used his car phone to call Bill Lambeth about buying a propeller for a plane. Sounding harried and troubled, Barry promised to call Bill back at 6:15 pm from the halfway house.

With so much weighing on his mind, Barry arrived at the halfway house. He went past the car with the Colombians and reversed the Cadillac into a space adjacent to the drop boxes. The Colombians were in a grey Buick on the other side of the drop boxes.

Just before 6 pm, Quintero Cruz had dropped a bundle into one of the drop boxes and hidden behind them, awaiting Barry. As Barry attempted to open his door, Quintero Cruz retrieved the bundle from the box. The outer layer was a raincoat, which he removed to access a MAC-10, which, because of its silencing, wouldn't make an explosive noise that would bounce off the buildings, just a cracking sound.

Quintero Cruz jumped towards Barry, until the MAC-10 was less than two feet from Barry's head. In two seconds, the gun sprayed twelve shots, making a sound like firecrackers. Three hit Barry in the left side of the head, two entering behind his ear lobe. More hit his body. He was left slumped and bleeding, with his hands over his ears.

A witness ran to Barry. Seeing a hole in Barry's head that appeared to have gone all the way through, he said, "Barry, can you hear me?"

No response.

While a Colombian certainly pulled the trigger, a hit man is only an instrument in the hands of the culprit. On the surface it seems that the hit man was working for the Medellín Cartel and Pablo Escobar. But Barry was operating in a world where appearances were often smoke screens. Before any conclusion can be drawn about the architect of the conspiracy, it's necessary to examine the lives of our two suspects – Pablo Escobar and George HW Bush – and finally, to consider information that has come to light from sources outside the US government and the mainstream media.

If you've read the first instalment of this War on Drugs trilogy, *Pablo Escobar: Beyond Narcos*, then you have the option of skipping the next section about Pablo and going directly to the section on George HW Bush unless you want to recap Pablo's story.

PART 2

THE MURDER SUSPECTS

MURDER SUSPECT 1
PABLO ESCOBAR

CHAPTER 27

Early Years

Pablo Escobar was born on a cattle ranch in 1949, the second year of The Violence, a civil war that saw millions of Colombians flee their homes and left hundreds of thousands dead. Slicing people up with machetes was popular and led to a new genre of slaughter methods with ornate names. The Flower Vase Cut began with the severing of the head, arms and legs. The liberated limbs were stuffed down the neck, turning the headless torso into a vase of body parts. A victim stabbed in the neck, who had his tongue pulled out through the gap and hung down his chest was wearing a Colombian Necktie. The turmoil affected nearly every family in Colombia. It accustomed Pablo's generation to extreme violence and the expectancy of a short and brutal life.

Pablo's parents were Abel de Jesús Dari Escobar, a hard-working peasant farmer who traded cows and horses, and Hermilda Gaviria, an elementary-school teacher. As her husband was mostly absent due to work, Hermilda cooked, cleaned and took care of her family. Pablo was the third of seven children.

One day, tiny Pablo wandered away from home. Hermilda found him under a tree, with a stick, playing with a snake.

"See, I'm not hurting you," Pablo said to the snake.

Gazing affectionately, Hermilda knew that Pablo was a sweet boy who loved animals.

The nearest school was so far away that Pablo and his brother, Roberto, had to wake up early. With no means of transportation, it took them an hour to walk there in worn-out shoes.

Rather that wear shoes with holes in them, Pablo decided to

go to school barefooted. His teacher sent him home. Humiliated, Pablo told his mother that he needed new shoes to stay in school. As she had no money, she deliberated her options and shoplifted a pair of shoes. At home, she noticed that each shoe was a different size. Disheartened, she confessed to a priest, who advised her to return the shoes and get them on credit.

She bought the shoes and arrived home, exhausted and anxious. With such a large family to feed, she complained about their lack of money.

"Don't worry, mom," Pablo said. "Wait until I grow up. I'll give you everything."

As The Violence between the Conservative and Liberal parties escalated, the family was warned to leave or else risk having their body parts re-assembled into art. But having no safe place to go, and loving the animals, the beautiful countryside adorned with wildflowers, and air that carried a taste of pine and resin from the forest, they chose to stay.

Pablo was seven when the guerrillas entered his village near the town of Rionegro, the Black River. Trembling, he heard machetes hacking the front door and threats of murder. He clung to his mother, who was crying and praying. His father said they would be killed, but at least they could try to save the kids. They hid the kids under mattresses and blankets.

The front door was so strong that the guerrillas eventually gave up trying to break in. Instead, they set fire to it. Wincing and coughing in a house filling with smoke, Pablo's parents braced to die. But soldiers arrived and the guerrillas fled.

With a burning building illuminating the street, the town's survivors were escorted to a schoolhouse. Pablo would never forget the charred bodies and the corpses hanging from the lampposts. Internalized in the terrified child, the horrors of The Violence would re-emerge years later, when he kidnapped, murdered and bombed to maintain his empire.

Growing up with six siblings, Pablo bonded the most with Roberto, who was two years his senior. Roberto was intelligent and had a passion for mathematics, electronics and cycling. Pablo enjoyed watching Roberto construct things such as radios, but rather than join in, he sat around for most of the day as if lost in thought.

Pablo and Roberto were sent from the family's ranch to live with their grandmother in the safety of Medellín, known as the City of the Eternal Spring due to a steady climate averaging around 22.2°C or 72°F. Downtown was a cluster of glass and steel skyscrapers separated by roads lined with trees. The surrounding expanse of houses grew more dilapidated towards the shantytowns, slums and garbage dumps – places crammed with displaced people where gangs of street kids, thieves and pickpockets roamed. The tough residents of Medellín worked hard to get ahead.

Pablo's grandmother was an astute businesswoman who bottled sauces and spices and sold them to supermarkets. Under her loving but stern hand, Pablo and Roberto had to go to church and pray every morning.

Although they loved the weather and the mountainous landscape, the second largest city in Colombia with all of its fast cars and over a million people intimidated the brothers, who were accustomed to the tempo of ranch life. They were delighted when their parents joined them, but their father disliked living in the city, so he returned to the countryside to work on other people's farms. Eventually, the brothers fell in love with Medellín.

The atmosphere at home was heavily religious. They had a figurehead of Jesus with realistic blood. After his mother told him Christ's story, young Pablo was so sad that when lunch was served, he put a piece of meat in his corn cake and took it to the figurehead. "Poor man, who made you bleed? Do you want a little meat?" This act convinced his mother that he was kind and religious. For the rest of his life, Pablo would always try to sleep with an image of Jesus nearby.

Hermilda enchanted Pablo with stories about his grandfather, Roberto Gaviria, who had smuggled whiskey. With long-range planning and a creative imagination, Roberto the bootlegger had outsmarted everyone, including the authorities. Pablo wanted to emulate his grandfather's success.

Growing up in a suburb of Medellín called Envigado, the kids built carts from wood and raced down hills. They made soccer balls from old clothes wrapped inside plastic bags, erected makeshift goalposts and played with the other kids in the neighbourhood. It was Pablo's favourite sport. A popular prank was to stick chewing gum on a doorbell, so that it rang continuously.

On the streets of Medellín, some of Pablo's leadership and criminal traits started to emerge. Although the youngest in his group, he'd take the lead. When the police confiscated their soccer ball, he encouraged the group to throw rocks at the patrol car. The police rounded up several of the group and threatened to keep them in jail all day. Only Pablo spoke up to the commander. He told them they hadn't done anything bad. They were tired of the ball being taken and they'd pay to retrieve the ball. Some of the kids in the group ended up in business with Pablo later on.

In his early teens, Pablo was elected president of his school's Council for Student Wellness, which demanded transportation and food for indigent students. He learned about the US meddling in South America for its own advantage, which often increased the suffering of the most poverty-stricken people. He hated that the poor were the biggest victims of violence and injustice.

During this time, he absorbed anti-imperialist phrases which became mantras for the rest of his life. He heard rumours that the CIA had facilitated the assassination of Jorge Eliécer Gaitán, a leftist presidential candidate who had defended workers' rights and promised an equitable land reform. Gaitán's death had ignited The Violence that had threatened Pablo's family.

Pablo started to despise the way that society was structured: a tiny percent of the population owned the majority of the land and wealth, while more than half of Colombians lived in poverty. Determined to prevent that from happening to him, he claimed he would kill himself if he had not made a million pesos by the age of thirty.

According to his brother Roberto in his book, *Escobar*, Pablo developed an interest in history, world politics and poetry. At the public library, he read law books. He practised public speaking on student audiences at lunchtime or on the soccer field. Roberto remembers him speaking passionately about becoming the president of Colombia and taking ten percent of the earnings of the richest people to help the poor to build schools and roads. To create jobs, he wanted to encourage Asian manufacturers to build plants in Colombia.

In school, Pablo grew restless. Distrustful of authority figures, he felt more at ease with the street gangs. For money, he experimented with small scams. Believing that school was a waste of time, he dropped out for two years. On the dangerous streets, he refined his techniques and learned to avoid the pitfalls.

Hermilda convinced him to resume his education, so he could get the three grades necessary to graduate. As he adored his mother, he went back to school. But he ended up in constant arguments with his teachers whom he viewed as absurd and foolish. Eventually, he was expelled.

After his mother scolded him, he responded, "Mother, I keep on telling you: I want to be big and I will be. I'm poor, but I'll never die poor. I promise."

By sixteen, Pablo was displaying an extraordinary amount of confidence on the streets. With a comb in his pocket, he often gazed at windows to inspect his reflection. In later years, he imitated the mannerisms of Al Capone and *The Godfather* played by Marlon Brando. His deep thinking was intensified by smoking marijuana. He grew quieter. When asked a question, he generally paused silently before replying. Some wondered whether he was imitating *The Godfather*, but it was a natural trait exacerbated when he was stoned.

Rationalising his banditry as a form of resistance to an oppressive society, he channelled his energy into criminal activity, which ranged from selling fake lottery tickets to assaulting people. With a rifle, he walked into banks and calmly told the staff to empty their safes. With a smile, he chatted to the tellers while awaiting the cash. Unable to perceive that Pablo had shed his sense of fear, some mistakenly ascribed his bravado to drugs. The results he achieved from his cleverness and farsightedness – including eluding the police – boosted his faith in himself.

A formidable combination of intelligence and street smarts enabled him to rise above his contemporaries, some of whom sought his advice and joined his gang. Those who were nervous or frustrated felt safe in his company. He earned their respect by remaining calm and cheerful in dangerous situations.

One said, "He was like a God, a man with a very powerful aura. When I met him for the first time, it was the most important day of my life."

In *Killing Pablo*, author Mark Bowden described Pablo as an accomplished car thief by age twenty. Drivers were forced out of their cars by his gang and the cars dismantled at chop shops. He dictated orders from home, managing the logistics and collecting the cash.

His gang started stealing new cars, which were impossible to resell if they had been reported as stolen. To get around this, he offered the police bribes. After a year, his relationship with them was so strong that the police chiefs followed his orders. Complaints about him reselling stolen cars were ignored.

Money from selling car parts was used to bribe officials to issue car certificates, so that the stolen cars could be resold without having to be chopped. The officials receiving the complaints about what he was doing were the same ones issuing him the titles for the new cars.

He started a protection racket whereby people paid him to prevent their cars from being stolen.

Always generous with his friends, he gave them stolen cars with clean papers. Those receiving new cars were told to pick them up from the factory. If the factory workers detected the forged paperwork, Pablo's friends told them, "These titles were made by Pablo," which prompted the workers to hand over the keys.

Pablo and his cousin, Gustavo, built race cars from stolen parts and entered rallies. Suspected of stealing a red Renault, Pablo was arrested in 1974, but he bribed his way out of a conviction.

Pablo ordered the murders of people who tried to prevent his accumulation of power, including those who denounced him, refused to abide by his rule or declined his bribes. He discovered that murder provided cheap and effective PR. Focusing people on their mortality or that of their families brought their behaviour into line. He killed without remorse, just to increase his reputation and earnings.

Some of the people who owed Pablo money were kidnapped. If the debt wasn't paid by family members or friends, the victim was killed. This enhanced his reputation and helped his business grow in a world of opportunists and cutthroats. He also kidnapped people and held them for ransom.

Diego Echavarría Misas was a powerful industrialist who lived in a remake of a medieval castle. Widely respected in the higher social circles, he yearned to be revered as a philanthropist. But no matter how many schools and hospitals he opened, the poor were not fooled by his attempts to mask his malevolence.

The workers in his textile mills toiled endlessly in cruel conditions for a pittance. He fired hundreds of them in an abusive manner and without a severance pay. Like many wealthy landowners, he expanded his territory by forcefully evicting peasant communities. Attempting to defend their homes, some peasants were imprisoned or murdered. The rest were forced to settle in the slums.

Pablo had heard enough about Echavarría. One day, his kidnapping became news. His family rapidly paid the ransom, but his fate remained a mystery. After six weeks, his body was found in a hole near Pablo's birthplace. He had been tortured, beaten and strangled. The poor celebrated his death.

Although many people believed that Pablo had brought them justice, with no evidence linking him to the crime, he was not charged. On the streets, people stopped to shake his hand or bowed to him in reverence. They began calling him "Doctor Escobar" and "The Doctor."

Roberto has claimed that the early stories of his brother's brutality are untrue accusations made by Pablo's enemies.

Pablo started to apply his organisational skills to contraband, a thriving business in Colombia, a country steeped in corruption. Medellín was known as a hub for smugglers. Those who got caught typically bribed their way free. If they were unable to pay a bribe, the police would usually confiscate their contraband rather than incarcerate them. It was the cost of doing business and customary throughout Colombia.

With numerous police on the payroll of crime bosses, it was hard to differentiate between the police and the criminals. The police not only gave their criminal associates freedom from jail, but they also committed crimes for the gangs, including kidnappings and contract killings. Shootouts sometimes occurred between different police on the payrolls of rival gangs.

The court system was the same. Judges who earned $200 a month could charge up to $30,000 to dismiss a case. Judges who refused were threatened or beaten. Court staff could be bribed to lose files, which was cheaper than paying a judge. If that didn't work, the judge was killed. The court system was considered the softest target in law enforcement, and Pablo would master the art of manipulating it.

Pablo was the underling of a powerful contraband kingpin who specialised in transporting cigarettes, electronics, jewellery and clothing in shipping containers from America, England and Japan. The goods were shipped to Colombia via Panama.

Having met Pablo at a soccer match, the kingpin asked him to be a bodyguard, in the hope of reducing worker theft. He told Pablo that the way to make money was to protect the merchandise for the guy with the money, and that was him.

Pablo bought the poorly-paid workers seafood and wine. He offered them half of his salary forever to work with him. If they stopped stealing, he'd come back and take care of them in two weeks. The workers agreed and returned the stolen goods they still had.

Specialising in cigarettes, Pablo drove across Colombia in a jeep ahead of half a dozen trucks transporting contraband. Along the way, he paid the necessary bribes to the police. Delighted with Pablo's performance, the kingpin offered him ten percent of the business. Pablo demanded fifty. The kingpin called Pablo crazy. Pablo said it was fair because the kingpin had sometimes lost more than half of the goods. Even after Pablo's fifty percent, the kingpin would still make more money because there would be no theft. The kingpin agreed to forty percent.

Through the contraband business, Pablo became adept at smuggling goods across the country, without paying government taxes and fees. Supervising two convoys a month earned him up to $200,000. He stashed his profits in hiding places in the walls of his home. He installed special electronic doors that only he could open. He recruited Roberto as an accountant, in charge of handling the payroll, making investments and depositing money into bank accounts with fake names. Over the years, money was invested in real estate, construction businesses and farms. As his brother was handling so much money, Pablo gave him a gun.

Giving half of his salary to the workers earned their respect and the name El Patrón or the Boss. He bought his mother a house, a taxicab for Gustavo and an Italian bicycle for his brother. He donated truckloads of food to the scavengers at the garbage dumps. He took about twenty members of his family to Disney World in Florida, where he went on all of the rides with his son.

When a policeman on Pablo's payroll was moved to another district, he snitched out the operation. The police waited to ambush a convoy of trucks. They would all get rich confiscating so many goods. Pablo had stopped for lunch and told the convoy to continue without him. Thirty-seven trucks were seized. A driver called Pablo who said to tell the other drivers not to speak to the police. With the police after him, he took a bus back to Medellín.

Lawyers got the drivers released but were unable to retrieve the merchandise.

Even though his contraband partnership with the kingpin was over, Pablo soon found a more lucrative business opportunity.

CHAPTER 28

Cocaine

In Peru, the Cockroach introduced Pablo and Gustavo to suppliers of cocaine paste who were offering it for $60 a kilo at a time when a kilo of cocaine was selling for up to $60,000 in America.

In Renault 4s, Pablo smuggled the paste from the Andean mountains, across three countries: Peru, Ecuador and Colombia. He had a separate Renault 4 for each country, with the relevant country's licence plate. Sometimes, he raced his cousin, Gustavo – who had penetrating dark eyes, a square face and a tidy moustache similar to Pablo's – to see who could get back to Medellín first. The winner kept all of the proceeds. The paste was hidden in a compartment installed above the passenger's-side wheel, which the checkpoint police never searched.

In a residential neighbourhood, the paste ended up in a house with covered windows, where it was transformed into cocaine. The cooks lived on the second floor. Most of the first floor had been converted into a kitchen. The cocaine was cooked in old refrigerators that Pablo had converted into ovens. Hoping for feedback on his first batch, he gave ten samples away. The majority said they preferred it to weed and requested more. Some said it gave them energy. Others said it calmed them down. Pablo didn't like it. He preferred smoking pot.

With the coca plant growing widely in the jungles and mountains of Peru, cheap paste was readily available. Due to drug laws, the price of cocaine in America was sky high. The US authorities were focused on marijuana and heroin coming in from Mexico, not cocaine. Pablo calculated that he could make more from a single load of cocaine sold in America than he could from a convoy of trucks smuggling normal contraband.

Testing the export business, Pablo discovered that he'd underestimated the demand for cocaine. He could sell any amount to any country, especially to America, the largest consumer of cocaine in the world.

Pablo's smugglers took drugs on flights and returned with large amounts of cash. Trucks replaced the Renault 4s. More workers were hired.

Vulture was one of Pablo's drivers. As he racked up profits from his trips, Vulture started showing off by buying an expensive car, a motorbike and clothes. This did not go unnoticed by one of his relatives in the DAS, the Colombian equivalent to the FBI. Vulture told his relative that he was transporting potatoes.

The DAS stopped one of Pablo's trucks and demanded the driver call his boss to pay a bribe. After Pablo and Gustavo showed up, they were arrested. The next day, Pablo's mugshot was on the front page of the newspaper. His mother sobbed for hours.

After spending eight days in jail, Pablo paid to be transferred to a facility with outdoor recreation, including soccer. He bribed the judge but after two months, it was decided that he would be tried in a military court which was more difficult to corrupt. His lawyer warned that he could get a long sentence. One night, Pablo told a guard that he needed to stretch his legs to reduce his stress. After being allowed onto the soccer field, he escaped.

The prison director called Pablo's mother, begging her to get her son to return, otherwise he'd end up in jail. When Pablo called her, she insisted that he return. Pablo and his mother showed up at the prison, with some x-rays of a sick person. Claiming he'd been ill, Pablo showed them to his military escorts, who were satisfied about his absence. In the end, Pablo bribed the judge. Pablo and Gustavo walked free. Sentenced to five years, the driver ended up in a prison with good facilities. Pablo gave the driver's family a house, a car and money.

Upon his release, Pablo resumed his cocaine enterprise, but now the police knew about it. He and Gustavo were pulled over by the two DAS agents who'd previously arrested them. They took him and his cousin to a remote area by a garbage dump, tied their hands together and forced them onto their knees. After roughing them up, the agents demanded a million pesos in exchange for their lives. While Gustavo went to get the money, Pablo offered more cash for the name of the person who'd arranged for them to kidnap him. He was surprised to learn it had been the Cockroach.

Once freed, Pablo plotted revenge that he would carry out himself. Being forced onto his knees at gunpoint was unforgivable. Emboldened by their success, the two DAS agents were about to kidnap one of Pablo's workers. They considered Pablo just another easy drug-trafficker target. Pablo's men kidnapped the agents and took them to a house. Pablo made them get onto their knees. As they begged for their lives, Pablo put a gun to their heads and shot them multiple times. The news reported the discovery of their bodies.

In 1974, Pablo fell in love with Maria Victoria Henao Vellejo, a local beauty. Because of her age, fourteen, and Pablo being twenty-five, Maria's mother was unenthused. He persisted, including showing up outside her home one night accompanied by a guitar player and serenading her. By 1976, she was pregnant, so they married. Three months after the marriage, Juan Pablo was born. It took two years for Maria's mother to warm to Pablo, but she did, accepting that he loved her daughter.

Pablo built his own gang, Los Pablos, with a fearsome reputation on the streets of Medellín. His organisation absorbed people who'd previously been rivals. When a war broke out between two cocaine traffickers in Medellín, resulting in workers and their family members getting killed, Pablo brokered a deal whereby they entered a partnership under him.

Initially, shipping cocaine to America was easy for Pablo and far more profitable than smuggling bulky marijuana. Up to forty kilos could be packed into used airplane tyres, which pilots would discard at Miami. They were taken to a dump, followed by one of Pablo's workers who would retrieve them. The cocaine was distributed through a network of Latinos in Miami.

Pablo no longer smuggled drugs himself. He paid others to do it. On the phone, he used code words such as emeralds and diamonds to frustrate the efforts of drug agencies and to avoid providing any verbal evidence that could be used against him.

To stay ahead of the DEA, he continuously changed his smuggling methods. He stopped using airplane tyres and had Colombian and US citizens board planes with cocaine in their suitcases or in specially made clothes. Holding up to five kilos, the suitcases had double walls. They were paid $1,000 and their flight tickets. Some wore shoes with hollowed-out bottoms. The shoes had been manufactured with the cocaine sewn inside. As well as passengers, Pablo recruited crew members, including stewardesses, pilots and co-pilots, who breezed through airports without getting searched. People in wheelchairs could smuggle up to $1 million worth of cocaine in the frames. Some smugglers dressed as nuns. Others posed as blind people with canes packed with cocaine. Some swallowed cocaine in condoms. If the condom opened, they died. Newspapers reported such tragedies.

With the authorities obsessed with eradicating the drug that had been demonised for decades in America – marijuana – cocaine slipped into the US unnoticed. The federal government had classified marijuana as a Schedule 1 substance, more harmful than cocaine, and equally as harmful as heroin, where it remains to this day.

Over time, instead of sending people with suitcases, Pablo just sent the suitcases. They were checked onto a flight and picked up at the other end. Airport officials were bribed with hundreds of thousands of dollars to look the other way. An official on a meagre salary ended up getting arrested with $27 million in his bank accounts.

To keep expanding, Pablo paid bigger bribes. To enable the police on his payroll to get promotions and pay increases, Pablo allowed them to confiscate massive amounts of cocaine. The media recorded the busts and reported them on the news. The government was delighted as such seizures enabled them to get more money from America to fight the War on Drugs. The confiscated cocaine was reported as destroyed, returned to Pablo and exported to the US. Corrupt governments all over the world still run this scam on US taxpayers.

Due to the smells released from making cocaine, Pablo moved his kitchens from residential areas to the jungle.

He moved into El Poblado, one of Medellín's wealthiest neighbourhoods with lots of white stucco houses, heavy on marble, glass and armed guards. The locals ate at fancy restaurants with views of the city lights and shopped at expensive boutiques. His brother urged him to stop and focus on real-estate investments, but Pablo was addicted to the power, money and lifestyle.

By offering high rates of return, Pablo attracted investors. An investment of $50,000 would be repaid with $75,000 in two weeks. If the drugs were busted, investors received half of their money back. To obtain investment capital, people sold their cars and houses or cashed in their savings.

Pablo set up a form of insurance whereby businessmen could invest a few thousand dollars for a share in a shipment of cocaine. After it was sold in America, the profits would be distributed. Pablo guaranteed their original investment even if the shipment was seized. For providing this insurance premium, he took ten percent of the American value of the cocaine. He even offered businessmen loans to invest.

Pablo was making millions, but things were still relatively small.

CHAPTER 29

Death to Kidnappers

The most powerful traffickers operating at the same time as Pablo included the Ochoa brothers – Jorge, Juan David and Fabio – who were alleged at the time to have played a larger role in the conspiracy to kill Barry than Pablo. This was reflected in the movie *Doublecrossed*, in which Pablo appeared as a sidekick to the Ochoas, and most of Barry's orders came from Jorge Ochoa, the leader of the family's cocaine business. In 1985, Barry testified that he worked for "the Jorge Ochoa cocaine cartel." The Ochoas began trafficking independently in the mid-1970s.

Jorge was quiet, strong on family values and didn't participate in drugs other than the occasional glass of wine. He collected vintage Harley Davidsons and attended horse shows. He had a knack of avoiding the law that served him well. The Ochoas lived at La Loma, a hilltop property south of Medellín, where friendly pet ponies ate out of visitors' hands, and also at Hacienda Veracruz, where they bred horses and had their own zoo.

Between 1981 and 1982, an alliance between the Ochoa family, Pablo Escobar and two other traffickers strengthened into what the US authorities eventually classified as the Medellín Cartel. The incident that cemented their relationship was the kidnapping of the Ochoa brothers' youngest sister, Martha Ochoa, by a guerrilla group called the M-19.

On November 12, 1981, the M-19 snatched Martha Ochoa from the campus of the University of Antioquia in Medellín, and demanded millions of dollars from the Ochoas. In response, Jorge Ochoa – seconded by Pablo – hosted a meeting, where he proposed the formation of an army, Muerta a Secuestradores, MAS, translated as Death to Kidnappers.

Also present were another two co-founders of the Medellín Cartel, Rodríguez Gacha and Carlos Lehder. Short stubby Gacha rose up in the emerald business, which had an even more violent reputation than cocaine. Killing anyone who got in his way, Gacha pioneered trafficking routes through Mexico and into the US. Of German-Colombian descent, Lehder was the man on the white Arabian stallion who'd forced Barry at gunpoint to fly a plane overloaded with cocaine.

Two hundred and twenty-three businessmen based all over Colombia attended the meeting and approved Death to Kidnappers. They included traffickers, smugglers and pilots. Each donated two million pesos and ten hit men. After the MAS meeting and the drafting of a communiqué, the participants attended a picnic at a ranch outside of Medellín, where they discovered that they had lots in common. Never before had they gathered like this to form public policy.

Copies of the MAS communiqué were loaded onto a plane, which flew towards a Cali soccer stadium on a Sunday afternoon, just prior to a match between Medellín and Cali. After the referee blew the starting whistle, leaflets descended from the sky onto the pitch. They described a general assembly, whose members would no longer tolerate kidnappings by guerrillas seeking to finance revolutions "through the sacrifices of people, who, like ourselves, have brought progress and employment to the country… The basic objective will be the public and immediate execution of all those involved in kidnappings, beginning from the date of this communiqué."

It offered twenty million pesos for information leading to the capture of a kidnapper and guaranteed immediate retribution. The guilty parties "will be hung from the trees in public parks or shot and marked with the sign of our group – MAS." Kidnappers in jail would be murdered. If that was impossible then "our retribution will fall on their comrades in jail and on their closest family members."

Pablo told a journalist, "If there was not an immediate and

strong response, the M-19 were going to continue screwing our own families... We paid law enforcement eighty million pesos for the information they had at that moment and the next day, they began to fall. My soldiers took them to our secret houses, our secret ranches, and people from law enforcement went there and hung them up and began to bust them up."

With hit men roaming the countryside, many of the M-19 and anyone suspected of being involved in the kidnapping of Martha were murdered in the tradition of The Violence in which Pablo had grown up, including the Colombian Necktie and the Flower Vase Cut. Within six weeks, over one hundred of the M-19 had been dealt with, putting the Colombian army to shame as they hadn't apprehended that many since the M-19 had started in 1974.

On December 30, 1981, a terrified woman was discovered chained to a steel gate, with a sign around her neck declaring that she was the wife of the M-19 boss who'd kidnapped Martha Ochoa. Her kidnapped daughter had been returned to relatives because the MAS Constitution prohibited harming innocent children.

On February 6, 1982, the MAS issued a statement about their patience wearing thin. On February 17, Martha Ochoa was released unharmed.

The MAS treated informants the same as kidnappers. According to Brian Freemantle in *The Fix*, the informant who told the DEA about the first MAS meeting didn't fare well. His hands were tied behind his back with barbed wire, and his tongue cut out before they killed him.

The success against the M-19 demonstrated what unity could achieve. The different groups started to see the benefits of not competing against each other. If they pooled their resources to ship cocaine to America, they'd all make more money. Independent operators put aside their differences and started cooperating in the manufacturing, distribution and marketing of cocaine, while continuing to run their own enterprises.

In future meetings, trafficking methods were streamlined. They offered government officials "plata o plomo" – silver or lead – meaning they could either accept a generous bribe or be killed. Their network had access to anyone in Colombia, so officials knew they couldn't avoid the death penalty. With the M-19 under control and the relevant officials accepting bribes, the cocaine business flourished out of Medellín. If the cartel leaders called a meeting, traffickers from across Colombia showed up. The American market was divided up between the Medellín and Cali Cartels. Cali had New York. Medellín had Miami. Los Angeles was split between the two.

With business forever expanding, new methods of outsmarting the authorities were required. Massive cocaine labs were built in the most inaccessible parts of the jungle. They grew into towns with their own housing, schools, dining facilities and satellite TV. Houses on wheels were used to disguise jungle runways. Cocaine was shipped in refrigerators and TVs with hollow insides. Electrical industrial transformers weighing more than 8,000 pounds were gutted and filled with up to 4,000 kilos. A 23,000 kilo shipment was mixed with dried fish. European and American chemists blended cocaine into items made out of plastic, metals or liquid, and other chemists separated the cocaine out at the destination. Cocaine was mixed with fruit pulp, flowers, cocoa and wine. Liquid cocaine ended up in all kinds of drinks. It was soaked into lumber and clothes such as jeans. Cocaine was turned black and mixed into black paint. It was chemically blended into PVC, religious statues and the fibreglass shells of boats. All of these methods were tested by drug-sniffing dogs.

Pablo bought planes to transport cocaine and cash, including DC-3s – fixed-wing propeller-driven airliners. He decided to invest in submarines. As buying a sub would have attracted attention, he commissioned his brother to build two, with the help of Russian and English engineers. The manufacturing was done in a quiet shipyard. The subs carried around 1,000 kilos. Unable to come close to the shore, they were met by divers who loaded the cocaine onto boats.

By 1982, Pablo was making $500,000 a day, rising to $1 million a day by the mid-80s. Millions were buried underground, but each year ten percent was lost due to rats eating it and water damage. He paid people to live in houses and apartments with up to $5 million stored in the walls, protected by Styrofoam. Using wooden cases wrapped in Styrofoam, millions were stashed below swimming pools in storage chests. Accountants in ten separate offices kept track of the money, some of which was invested in property worldwide, famous paintings and antique cars. Never forgetting the poor, he continued to build houses, schools, hospitals and to give away truckloads of food. He paid for college tuition and built soccer fields.

Refrigerators containing $7 million intended for Colombia were accidentally shipped to Panama. The money disappeared. Pablo calmly responded that sometimes he won, sometimes he lost. A plane with $15 million crashed in the jungle and exploded, turning the money into a bonfire. Workers who lost drugs or cash were given more drugs to make up for the loss. If they messed up again, they were killed.

In Medellín, plenty of killers were available to Pablo, whose reputation for extreme violence enabled his business to grow. According to Gustavo de Grieff, a former Colombian Attorney General, Pablo had sanctioned the use of a hot spoon to remove victims' eyeballs while they were still alive. Another approved method was to drive a heated spike or nail into a victim's skull, which was fatal when it reached the brain. One victim was tied to a tree with barbed wire, given a phone to explain his situation to his family, and tortured to death while they listened.

CHAPTER 30

Lara Bonilla

Hoping to achieve his childhood dream of becoming the president, Pablo ran for political office. While vowing to help the poor, he aimed to gain exemption from laws that would have allowed him to be extradited to America.

With so many of them on his payroll, Pablo was no stranger to politicians. Cartel members competed to own the most powerful ones, just like they outdid each other with luxury cars, homes and zoos. Politicians were approached by cartel lawyers with brown envelopes full of cash. If they declined the bribe, they'd receive a call asking if they'd prefer to be killed. With so many of their colleagues taking money, and the cocaine business bringing so much prosperity to Colombia, it was easy to say yes. Many of them felt that cocaine was America's problem because that was where it was mostly consumed. If they didn't want it, Colombia wouldn't produce it. Due to America's history in Central and South America – supporting right-wing death squads, assassinating democratically elected left-wing leaders, a blood-lust for foreign resources – the US was viewed dimly by many Colombians. Some saw cocaine as the lesser-developed world's atomic bomb against the US, and believed that imperialism would be destroyed from within by its own excesses.

Having created a power base for himself in the barrios of Medellín, Pablo was elected as an alternate to Congress in March 1982, which rendered him immune from prosecution under Colombian law.

Giving speeches as a politician, Pablo wore chino trousers, polo shirts and a gold Rolex. He spoke politely and softly at the openings of soccer pitches, roller-skating rinks, hospitals and schools he had invested in. He started a radio show, *Civics on the March*, and a program called *Medellín Without Slums*. One project, Barrio Pablo Escobar, consisted of five hundred two-bedroomed houses built over a garbage dump, complete with truckloads of free food. It was in north Medellín, a tough area where Pablo was extremely popular – a recruiting ground for young hit men and enforcers. While Pablo did the rounds, he was accompanied by two Catholic priests who were board members of *Medellín Without Slums*. The priests introduced him at public events, accompanied him in the slums and blessed a charity art auction he hosted at the Intercontinental Hotel, which was called Paintbrush of Stars.

Pablo hired publicists and journalists to boost his man-of-the-poor image. A column in his own newspaper, *Medellín Cívico*, lavished him with praise: "Yes, I remember him… his hands, almost priest-like, growing parabolas of friendship and generosity in the air. Yes, I know him, his eyes weeping because there is not enough bread for all of the nation's dinner tables. I have watched his tortured feelings when he sees street children – angels without toys, without a present, without a future."

In April 1983, a popular magazine, *Semana*, branded Pablo as "A Paisa Robin Hood." Pablo told *Semana*, "When I was sixteen, I owned a bicycle-rental business… then I started buying and selling automobiles, and finally I got involved in real estate… I didn't have any money, but as a community action member in my barrio, I promoted the construction of a school and the creation of a fund for indigent students."

The same month that Pablo was elected, March 1982, a new president came to power. His main goals included making peace with the guerrillas and improving housing and education. Drugs seemed to be off his agenda. With the majority of politicians taking donations from the traffickers, why ruffle any feathers? Besides, many previous presidents had taken drug money. Those who hadn't didn't stay in office for long. When the president announced that he was philosophically opposed to the extradition of Colombian nationals, the traffickers were delighted as they all dreaded the prospect of serving life sentences in America.

But the Reagan-Bush administration had other ideas. In 1982, Reagan announced, "My very reason for being here this afternoon is not to announce another short-term government offensive, but to call instead for a national crusade against drugs, a sustained relentless effort to rid America of this scourge by mobilizing every segment of our society against drug abuse."

Ramping up the War on Drugs, the Reagan-Bush administration tried to link the FARC guerrillas with marijuana trafficking, hoping to stir up war by labelling the 5,000-strong pro-Communist army as narco-guerrillas. The Colombians saw through the propaganda. The new Colombian president was upset because the outside interference had disturbed the peace negotiations with the guerrillas. The Americans changed their strategy. The Reagan-Bush administration had their emissaries search for a Colombian politician amenable to their goals. They settled on Rodrigo Lara Bonilla.

After studying law at the Externado University of Colombia, Lara was elected as the mayor of his hometown at age twenty-three. In August 1983, Lara – a member of the New Liberalism Party that he'd helped to create – became the minister of justice. His campaign against corruption upset his bribe-dependent contemporaries and attracted the interest of the DEA in Colombia, who egged him on to go after the traffickers by offering help and support.

On August 16, 1983, Pablo and his bodyguards arrived for the first time at Congress, which was packed with spectators, reporters and photographers. Even the hallways were crowded with people abuzz about a confrontation brewing between Lara and the traffickers. Dressed in a cream suit, Pablo was stopped at the door for not wearing a tie. Someone handed him one with a floral design, and he was allowed inside. People watched closely as he sat near the back. The house president requested the removal of his bodyguards. Pablo gave a nod and they left.

Pablo's ally, Jairo Ortega, started to address allegations of taking hot money from the traffickers. He asked Lara if he knew Evaristo Porras Ardila.

"No," Lara said, shaking his head.

Ortega said that Evaristo Porras – a resident of the Amazon border town of Leticia – had been incarcerated in Peru for trafficking drugs. In April, Porras had written a cheque for one million pesos to Lara as a campaign contribution. Holding up the cheque, he showed it to the ministers present for the debate. Copies of the cheque had been circulated. He added that Lara had thanked Porras for the cheque in a phone call. Ortega produced a tape recorder and played an unintelligible conversation.

"Let the Congress analyse the minister's conduct with this person who offered him a million pesos. Mr Porras is a recognised international drug trafficker, according to Peruvian police. But far be it from me to try to detain the minister of justice's brilliant political career. I only want him to tell us what kind of morality he is going to require of the rest of us. Relax, Minister. Just let the country know that your morality can't be any different from that of Jairo Ortega and the rest of us."

Cheering erupted in the gallery from Carlos Lehder, which others tried to hush. Sitting quietly in a swivel leather chair, Pablo watched, while occasionally picking his teeth or forcing an uncomfortable smile.

Thirty-five-year-old Lara stood to respond in a business suit and tie, his thick dark hair swept aside, his charming face clean shaved. Not in the habit of scrutinising the origin of incoming donations, he'd never heard of Mr Porras, nor could he recall any such telephone conversation.

"My life is an open book." Lara said that he was and always had been blameless, rendering him impervious to his enemies' claims. He would resign any moment that suspicion fell upon him "knowing that I will not be followed by complacent ministers affected by the blackmail and the extortion being perpetrated against Colombia's political class." He damned the act of casting suspicion on the alleged recipients of the money as opposed to the senders of it, including "those, who, yes, have to explain here or anywhere else in this country where their fortunes have come from… Morality is one thing, but there are levels: one thing is the cheques… that they use to throw mud at politicians. But it's another thing when somebody runs a campaign exclusively with these funds." Lara pointed an accusatory finger.

"[We have] a congressman [Pablo] who was born in a very poor area, himself very, very poor, and afterwards, through astute business deals in bicycles and other things, appears with a gigantic fortune, with nine planes, three hangars at the Medellín airport, and creates the movement Death to Kidnappers, while on the other hand, he creates charitable organisations with which he tries to bribe a needy and unprotected people. And there are investigations going on in the US, of which I cannot inform you here tonight in the House, on the criminal conduct of Mr Ortega's alternate."

Some of the respondents defended Pablo. They said that all of them were guilty of receiving tainted contributions. Pablo had been attacked, so that Lara might gain political capital.

"It was only when Representative Escobar joined our movement that all kinds of suspicion were thrown on the sources of his wealth," a congressman said. "I, as a politician, lack the ability to investigate the origin of any assets… Representative Escobar has no need to rely on others to defend his personal conduct, which, on the other hand, and as far as I know, has not been subjected to any action by the law or the government."

Simmering with anger, Pablo didn't respond. Re-joining his bodyguards, he left the chamber and walked into a swarm of reporters, whom he tried to dodge.

The next day, Lara received notification that he had a day to back up his claims with evidence, or else be sued. While Lara set about gathering evidence, he issued statements criticising drug-trafficking, which necessitated "a frontal fight, clear, open, without fear or retreat, running all the necessary risks." He classified the allegations of the cheque he'd received from Porras as a smokescreen. "My accusers could not forgive the clarity of my denunciation of Pablo Escobar, who through clever business deals has manufactured an enormous fortune... This is an economic power concentrated in a few hands and in criminal minds. What they cannot obtain by blackmail, they get by murder."

The media contacted Porras, who acknowledged donating a million pesos to Lara and admitted that he had been indicted by the Peruvian police for trafficking, which he put down to a youthful indiscretion. Working in the coca-leaf business for Pablo, Porras claimed that his wealth had originated from winning the lottery three times. Faced with Porras' testimony, Lara admitted receiving the cheque, which he said had been for a family debt. At Pablo's behest, a judge initiated an investigation into the cheque, which went nowhere.

Lara received help from a newspaper, *El Espectador*, which ran a story about Pablo's arrest for cocaine in 1976, including mugshots of Pablo and Gustavo. Pablo ordered his men to buy every copy of the newspaper, which only increased sales and encouraged the newspaper to publish daily stories about him. It described how he'd played the system by having his case transferred to various courts and judges, and how all of his criminal records had disappeared. The exposure led to an investigation into the murders of the policemen who'd arrested him. A new arrest warrant was issued for Pablo, but the judge who'd granted it was murdered in his car.

Lara obtained a recording of a DEA-assisted ABC News documentary about Colombia's biggest traffickers, including Pablo – who they claimed was worth $2 billion – and played it in Congress. While casting Lara a death stare, Pablo demanded proof of the allegations.

Rebutting Lara's accusations in an interview, Pablo said his money came from construction. While denying that he was a trafficker, he extolled the benefits that trafficking had brought Colombia such as creating jobs and providing capital for numerous projects that had contributed to economic growth. Insisting that the allegations of trafficking were untrue, Pablo showed a visa he'd recently obtained from the US embassy. Within days, the embassy cancelled the visa. Pablo lambasted Lara for becoming an instrument of US foreign policy.

Lara held his ground. He exposed how the traffickers had financed Colombia's main soccer teams. He tried to cancel the licences for 300 small planes they owned. He attempted to confiscate Pablo's zoo animals and named thirty politicians he believed had taken drug money.

On September 2, 1983, an arrest warrant for Carlos Lehder was issued after the Supreme Court ruled in favour of America. Having already disappeared, Lehder claimed he'd seen it coming, "because my friends in the Ministry of Justice alerted me regarding Lara Bonilla's intentions." He told reporters that the only way he would be extradited was over his dead body.

On September 10, Pablo was asked by a senator to quit politics, give up his parliamentary immunity and answer the charges against him. On September 11, Pablo refused, stating that he'd entered politics because, "only inside the government could a man best serve the community."

Within two weeks, a judge issued an arrest warrant for Pablo for conspiracy to murder the DAS agents who'd arrested him in 1976. Two had been executed in 1977. In 1981, hit men on motorbikes had assassinated the officer in charge.

In October, the Supreme Court ruled in favour of the extradition of two marijuana traffickers. Lara signed off on it, but the president refused to do so. He referred it to the Colombian courts. Lehder's extradition order remained unsigned.

Lara demanded that Congress remove Pablo's immunity from extradition. The newspapers reported Pablo's 1974 car-theft indictment, while championing Lara. The biggest newspaper asked, "How is democracy going to continue in Colombia if it is managed and manipulated by these criminals?"

On November 17, 1983, Pablo was fined 450,000 pesos for

the illegal importation of eighty-five animals, including camels, elephants, elk and a large Amazonian rodent called a capybara.

The evidence against Pablo was so overwhelming that there was nothing he could do to salvage his political career. He was forced out of the Colombian Liberal Party. He quit Congress in January 1984 and issued a statement: "The attitude of politicians is very far from the people's opinions and aspirations."

His presidential plan had backfired so badly that the media was exposing his cocaine business and the police were trying to muscle in on it. Fighting back in the courts, he managed to get his extradition warrant withdrawn on February 13, 1984.

After a politician pushing for Pablo's extradition was murdered, Lara made an announcement that upset the traffickers: "The more I learn, the more I know of the damage that the *narcos* are causing this country. I will never again refuse the extradition of one of these dogs. So long as Colombian judges fear drug traffickers, the *narcos* will only fear judges in the US."

Lara suspected that Pablo's guys were shadowing him. When he answered his phone, his own conversations were played back. He rebuffed offers of large sums of money. Death threats against him increased.

He hit back by busting cocaine labs across the country. With the help of the DEA, the Colombian authorities located a giant jungle lab called the Land of Tranquillity, which was mostly owned by the cartel leader Gacha. Over two years, it had produced cocaine worth $12 billion. Almost 200 people lived there. The authorities knew about it, but had been reluctant or unable to find it as it lay some 250 miles from the nearest road.

Supposedly, the raid had caused the cartel to urgently require the services of Barry. To get in the good graces of the Reagan-Bush administration, Barry had told the DEA that Jorge Ochoa was setting up facilities in Nicaragua because of the devastating effects of the raid, yet in *Cocaine: An Unauthorised Biography*, author Dominic Streatfeild quotes Jorge Ochoa as stating that they knew the raid was coming in advance, they'd removed all of the valuable stuff and the authorities had made up that they'd seized tons of cocaine as only chemicals were seized. Jorge denied ever moving cocaine through Nicaragua. Having seen Barry's photographs, he acknowledged that Pablo might have had something going on in Nicaragua.

In *Escobar*, Roberto states that Pablo had made a deal with the Nicaraguan government to build a lab on an island off the coast, but the lab was never built. The island was used for the refuelling of planes. If this is true, then it seems that Barry had been lying to the DEA and George HW Bush.

Pablo issued a statement to the US ambassador denying any role in the Land of Tranquillity: "I can only characterise your statements as tendentious, irresponsible and malintentioned without any basis in reality; they denigrate the good faith of public opinion. My conscience is clear." He accused Lara of being "the representative of your government in the Colombian cabinet."

After the raid on the Land of Tranquillity, the Medellín Cartel decided that it was time for Lara to go. The $500,000 contract went to Los Quesitos, a gang controlled by Pablo. Three of the gang's field commanders took a green Renault, loaded with guns, grenades and bullet-proof vests from Medellín to Bogotá. After settling into a four-star hotel, they discussed the hit over food in the company of the Snore, a Medellín hitman with lots of kills under his belt who was ready to serve as backup if the others failed. The hit would be performed on a motorbike, with Iván, a thirty-one-year-old drifter, as the shooter. Iván had a history of murder, robbery and assault. The driver would be a teenager called Byron, who was looking to earn a reputation among the big boys. Teenagers like these – poor and with nothing to lose – were easily recruited to perform hits. Unemployed or working jobs that paid $1 a week, they could earn thousands for each murder. For several days, the team waited, made calls back to Medellín and dined out.

The US emissaries encouraging Lara to extradite Pablo showed up with a bullet-proof vest. "You should be more concerned. You should take more precautions." Lara declined the vest, but they left it with him.

Aware of the threat, not just to him but to his wife and three little children, Lara beefed up security. "I am a dangerous minister for those who act outside the law," Lara said. "I only hope that they don't take me by surprise." Despite the tough talk, Lara called the US embassy and excitedly revealed that he was getting transferred out of the country to work as the ambassador to Czechoslovakia.

"You'll be safe there," the US Ambassador said. "All the terrorists are in the government."

As the transfer would take thirty days, Lara said he needed a place for him and his family to hide at because he felt that the Colombian government couldn't protect him anymore. The US embassy offered to put him in a Texas safe house owned by a rich businessman for as long as he needed it.

On April 30, 1984, Lara thanked a journalist friend for publishing an article about his work. "I am going to be killed today, but that article can be my will for the Justice Department." After playing his friend some samples of the fifty death threats that he'd received that morning, Lara said, "If I don't answer this phone, it will be because I am dead."

In the afternoon, Iván and Byron visited the shrine of Santa María Auxiliadora, near Medellín, to say a prayer. For good luck, Byron put a picture of the Virgin Mary into his underwear. At 7 pm, they got on a Yamaha motorbike and headed to Bogotá, armed with grenades and a MAC-10.

Sitting on a back seat, Lara was stuck in traffic with his bullet-proof vest next to him.

Iván and Byron stopped at an address they'd been given earlier that day. They were told people were talking about them in Medellín, which was code for "Find Lara and kill him." On the hunt for a white Mercedes-Benz limo, they found the roads still jammed. It was around dusk when they spotted Lara. Weaving around cars, they homed in from the rear and slowed down.

After extracting the MAC-10 from his jacket, Iván took aim at the figure in the back of the limo. Within seconds, the MAC-10 emptied its magazine, shattering the rear window, hitting Lara fatally seven times in the head, chest, arm and neck. Lara's escort limo pursued the assailants. A bullet hit the Yamaha's gas tank, setting it on fire. The motorbike crashed into a curb. Machine-gun fire exploded Iván's head. Next to the Yamaha, he dropped dead. Hit in the arm, Byron was arrested.

The president and his cabinet stayed up until 3 am, discussing what to do. No cabinet minister had ever been assassinated in Colombia. Perhaps cocaine wasn't just an American problem after all. Trafficking was ruining Colombia's reputation in the eyes of the world. With the justice minister gone, it would appear that the president had lost control of the country. Lara's death swung them in favour of extradition. In an emergency radio broadcast, the president declared war on the traffickers and said that drugs were "the most serious problem that Colombia has had in its history."

In the Rotunda of the Capitol Building, thousands visited Lara's closed coffin, which military guards took to the National Cathedral. Outside, mourners from all sections of society were crying and chanting that they loved Lara. In the cathedral, emotions ran high. Amid the top brass from the military and the government, the president appeared tense.

A plane transported Lara to his home city, where he was buried. At the funeral, the president said, "We have reached a point where we must reflect on what is our nation. What does the word citizen mean? Stop! Enemies of humanity! Colombia will hand over criminals wanted in other countries, so that they may be punished as an example." His eulogy received a standing ovation.

On May 8, 1984, the president signed an extradition order for Carlos Lehder. Traffickers would be tried in military courts and denied access to bail. Prison sentences would be increased, with limited possibility of parole. Suspected traffickers would have their gun permits cancelled.

Immediately, hundreds were arrested and jailed, including the Ochoa brothers' father, Fabio Sr. Property was seized. Helicopters landed at Hacienda Nápoles. With rifles and search dogs, troops in green battle fatigues stormed inside, provoking raucous cawing from Pablo's exotic birds. Seizing weapons and evidence, the troops trashed the property and handcuffed low-level workers, whom they lined up by a swimming pool. After the raid, they left the zoo animals to starve. Upon receiving complaints about the animals, the government reopened the zoo.

In response, the traffickers declared war on Colombia. All-out mayhem ensued: bombings, kidnappings, mass murders and death squads. The judge investigating Lara's death was killed.

US weapons manufacturers profited from the chaos by selling arms to every side. Through the CIA, they were accepting drug money as one of the biggest forms of payment. In public, George HW Bush was raising Pablo up the charts of enemy status in the War on Drugs, while in secret, the CIA was facilitating cocaine smuggling to finance a war in Nicaragua, cocaine that was flooding America. Such covert activity needed constant smokescreens, and a mass murderer such as Pablo was ideal. In the US media, his crimes allowed him to become the personification of the cocaine scourge, but journalists rarely mentioned that his empire existed because of a black market in cocaine worth billions that had been created by US drug laws; or that his weapons came from America. It was a no-lose situation for George HW Bush. Even though he knew from America's earlier experiences with the prohibition of alcohol that taking down Pablo wouldn't alter the flow of drugs, fighting traffickers not only justified military expenditure, but it enabled the US to extend its influence into Colombia, a country whose oil and other resources US corporations and bankers, perched like vultures, were eager to plunder.

CHAPTER 31

Panama

For a while, Pablo hid out in the jungle, until the Ochoa brothers, Lehder and Gacha fled to Panama to live in a large house by a golf club under the protection of Manuel Noriega, a military dictator and CIA informant whose hospitality had cost them millions. With a down payment of $2 million, Pablo had authorised the deal a few months before Noriega had come to power.

Known as Pineapple Face due to his pockmarks, Noriega had ended up ruling Panama by having a bomb – provided by the CIA – planted in the plane of his predecessor, whose leftist stance – he had believed in democracy and the rights of poor people – whiffed of Communism. A master of playing every side, Noriega had profitable relationships with the CIA and the Colombian traffickers, who were working together in the fight against Communism by supporting the Nicaraguan rebels. In an expectation of CIA protection, the cartel had contributed to the Nicaraguan cause. For America, Noriega provided security for the Panama Canal, with its American bases housing over 10,000 military personnel. His contributions to America's anti-Communism crusade included money laundering and hosting guns-for-drugs flights for the Nicaraguan rebels.

In 1982, Pablo had set up a deal with Noriega, whereby Panama was used as a trans-shipment point for cocaine heading to America, with Noriega collecting six-figure fees per load. Noriega also collected fees on the billions that the drug cartels – and intelligence agencies such as the CIA – laundered through Panama. It is alleged that Jeb Bush tapped into some of this hot money by establishing banking relationships between the CIA and the Medellín and Cali Cartels. Working in Venezuela for his CIA director father, Jeb supposedly disguised the drug money as oil industry revenues from front companies such as Texas Commerce Bank, a cartel favourite.

Protected by bodyguards assigned by Noriega, the cartel leaders entertained themselves by playing soccer on the golf course, working out at the gym and swimming. Eventually, they rented their own homes. It was around this time in Panama that Pablo and Jorge Ochoa had discussions with Barry.

Pablo had wanted to make Panama a temporary hub, but Noriega hadn't embraced the idea. The agreement had been to make Panama a transportation point, not an operations centre. Pablo got word from a Panamanian Colonel that Noriega was making overtures to the DEA. For the benefit of the cartel, Noriega had authorised the construction of a cocaine lab in Panama, but his military seized 16,000 barrels of ether destined for the new lab and arrested twenty-three Colombian workers. The angry cartel leaders demanded an explanation, but were told that Noriega was in Europe.

Through President Fidel Castro, a meeting was arranged for the Colombians and Noriega in Cuba. Before Noriega arrived, the cartel attended a preliminary conference with the Panamanian government. After the meeting, Noriega released the Colombian prisoners and returned $3 million in cash and lab equipment to the cartel.

Growing homesick and distrustful of Noriega, the cartel tried to reach an agreement with the Colombian government, whom they asked to consider the possibility of their re-incorporation into Colombian society in the near future. Their memorandum offered a history of drug trafficking in Colombia and asserted that their organisations "today control between 70 and 80 percent of Colombia's drug traffic," which equated to "an annual income of around $2 billion." Pablo offered to move billions from overseas accounts into the Colombian banking system and to dismantle the cocaine empire, but the deal was refused.

On June 15, 1984, the cartel lost 1.2 metric tons of cocaine packed in freezers and perfume cartons to US Customs agents in Miami. A Panamanian charter company owned the cargo jet transporting the cocaine. The next week, Panamanian authorities confiscated 6,159 drums of ether.

Pablo advised his fellow Colombians to leave Panama. Private planes and helicopters arrived. The Colombians dispersed to Medellín, Brazil and Spain. According to Roberto, Pablo and his brother went to Nicaragua. Pablo took 1,100 kilos of cocaine with him, aiming to convert it into cash.

Even though extraditions to America had begun, things had settled down a bit in Colombia since the aftermath of Lara's death. The majority of those who'd been arrested in the raids following Lara's death had been released due to a lack of evidence and the usual corruption.

Giving an interview from abroad, Pablo said, "People who know me understand very well that I am involved in industry, construction and ranching... the fact that I attack extradition does not make me extraditable."

The pressure on the authorities from the traffickers had never relented. They had obtained the president's private telephone number – which had spooked the president – and were issuing threats.

Outside a courthouse, a man approached the judge who'd indicted the cartel for Lara's murder and requested a temporary dismissal. "Ask for whatever you want, and they'll put it wherever you want it, in Colombia or outside the country... Then you can relax. Neither your life, nor the lives of your family members will be in danger." The judge refused. Climbing into a taxi, he was shot dead by five men in a Mazda.

Armoured vehicles transported US embassy staff. Their children went to school on a bus protected by army jeeps with machine guns. On the roads, the staff kept their eyes peeled for motorbike assassins. Some kept their windows down, so they could listen for the distinct sound of a motorbike approaching. In their guarded living quarters they heard guns fired every night. An empty car aimed at the embassy rolled down a hill, hit a curb and exploded, sending flames three hundred feet into the air. Embassy staff was reduced to a bare minimum.

Any locals working with the Americans were killed in grotesque ways. One had pins inserted under his fingernails, before being shot in the head and left on the street with a sign around his neck: "Killed for Being a DEA Informant." After the DEA got word that a guerrilla hit team had been contracted by Pablo to kidnap key members, they closed their Medellín location.

In the latter half of 1984, Pablo thought it was safe to return home. He convened a meeting of seventy important people, ranging from traffickers to priests, who arrived with 200 bodyguards. Extradition was discussed. Pablo proposed that Medellín should have a united group of bodyguards divided into zones. Among the big four founders of the Medellín Cartel, Gacha's power was rising, while Lehder's was falling. Lehder was assigned to oversee jungle operations and to maintain relations with the guerrillas guarding the labs.

A little after midnight on the night of the meeting, a Mercedes arrived at the farmhouse. A well-dressed woman emerged. She knocked on the door and claimed to have flowers for Dr Hernandez. Roberto told her that she was at the wrong address. He warned his brother that he'd never seen anyone in the flower-delivery business arrive in a Mercedes-Benz. Pablo dismissed it as nothing. Roberto instructed the bodyguards to start shooting in the air if any strangers showed up.

Around 2 am, shots were fired. Pablo and his brother ran out of the back of the farmhouse. A shot grazed Roberto's leg and pieces of brick hit him in the face, causing lots of bleeding. They came across one of their bodyguards returning in a car. They escaped in it along with Gustavo.

A trafficker from the city of Cali, which had a history of rivalry with Medellín, had attended the meeting at the farmhouse and subsequently snitched Pablo out, hoping for a government guarantee against extradition.

The colonel in charge of the raid had been paid $50,000 a month by Pablo. Pablo sent him a message, "Now you are against me and you know what I think about that."

Jorge Ochoa got into trouble in Spain, where he'd emigrated with the boss of the Cali Cartel and settled in an 8,000-square-foot mansion, complete with a swimming pool, tennis courts, a disco and four Mercedes-Benz. An informant told Spain's Special Prosecutor for the Prevention and Repression of Drug Trafficking that Ochoa was in Madrid under a fake name: Moisés Moreno Miranda. On November 15, 1984, the two Colombian bosses and their wives were arrested. Attempting to capitalise on the windfall, the Americans made overtures to the Spanish in the hope of getting the Colombians extradited. The stage was set for a lengthy legal battle.

In volatile Colombia, even forming an army called Death to Kidnappers didn't always serve as a deterrent. In 1985, Pablo's father was kidnapped by policemen. On his way to visit one of Pablo's farms, he was pulled over by six men in a jeep. After tying up the workers accompanying him, they drove him away. They wanted $50 million.

After she found out, Pablo's mother spent hours yelling and crying and praying. Pablo put out the word that if his father ended up with a single bruise the ransom money they got wouldn't be enough to pay for their own burials.

Remaining composed, Pablo formed a plan to capture the kidnappers. His father needed medicine for open-heart surgery. Many of the two-hundred drugstores in Medellín had security cameras. He installed cameras in those that didn't. He offered a reward for photos of anyone buying the heart medicine his father needed. Two kidnappers were identified. As the kidnappers used payphones, Pablo gave hundreds of radio transmitters to people with instructions to listen to a certain radio station. Whenever the kidnappers called Pablo's mother, the station announced a song dedicated to Luz Marina. After hearing this, the people with the transmitters rushed out to the nearest payphones.

Over eighteen days, Pablo's brother negotiated the ransom down to $1 million. The money was delivered in duffel bags with electronic tracking devices, which the kidnappers took to a farm. The house was surrounded and assaulted from every direction. Three of the kidnappers were captured and sentenced to death by Pablo. His father was released unharmed.

Perhaps things weren't as safe in Colombia as Pablo thought. He went everywhere with bodyguards, moved around a lot and took extra precautions.

CHAPTER 32

The Extraditables

After the MAS had started to annihilate the guerrillas responsible for kidnapping Martha Ochoa, Pablo had met their leader, Ivan Marino Ospina. Not only did each side agree not to attack the other, but, as a show of good faith, Ospina gave Pablo the famous sword of the liberator Simón Bolívar, a Venezuelan military leader who'd helped Colombia gain independence from Spain in 1810. The founder of the M-19, Jaime Bateman, had stolen the sword – a symbol of unfulfilled liberation – from a museum in 1974 and announced that it would not be returned until the government agreed to peace with the M-19. Initially, Pablo hung it on a wall. Eventually, he gave it to a nephew to hide.

Relations between the guerrilla groups and the cartel were generally in a state of flux; however, since the handing over of the sword, the friendship between Pablo and the M-19 leader, Ivan, had lasted. With the M-19 known for committing spectacular attacks against the government, they came to mind when Pablo thought of targeting the government's files on extradition, which were housed in the Palace of Justice in Bogotá. If Pablo could destroy or intimidate the Colombian judiciary system in a sensational way, then maybe he could take over the entire country. He would do the unthinkable: go after the Supreme Court.

By September 1985, six Colombians out of 105 on the US list had been extradited, and nine were in jail. Pablo formed a group called the Extraditables with the motto: "Better a grave in Colombia than a jail cell in the US." The cartel leaders made a blood pact that they would commit suicide rather than rot away in an American prison. Their preferred method was to shoot themselves behind the ear, which allowed a bullet easy access to the brain by circumventing the skull.

Since his early arrests, Pablo had refined his intimidation tactics against judges. A judge assigned to a narcotics case would be visited by a bright young well-dressed lawyer, carrying a briefcase. On the judge's desk, he'd put a brown envelope.

The lawyer would say something like, "You have a choice. You can have lead, bullet in your head, or silver, some money as a payoff. It's your call." If the judge prevaricated, the lawyer would reach inside his briefcase and take out a photo album containing pictures of the closest family members and friends of the judge: their children leaving home in the morning, going to school, playing in the playground, talking to friends… The threat of their entire family being wiped out persuaded most judges.

Pablo was about to refine his tactics again. The Extraditables sent letters to the Supreme Court justices, demanding that they declare the extradition treaty illegal. The letters were designed not to give any evidence to the police. Block letters were used. They were signed by the Extraditables or a first name such as Manuel. When Pablo wasn't writing on behalf of the Extraditables and he wanted people to know that he'd authored a letter, he wrote in his own handwriting, signed his name and added his thumbprint. Some people wondered whether Pablo was the Extraditables, whereas others thought that he was a front for them.

The Extraditables obtained the justices' private phone numbers and threatened them. With a ruling due on extradition, the justices were afraid. More letters came for the justices stating that the Extraditables knew everything going on in their lives.

"We declare war against you. We declare war against the members of your family. As you may suppose, we know exactly where they are – we will do away with your entire family. We have no compassion whatsoever – we are capable of anything, absolutely anything."

In the Palace of Justice on November 6, 1985, pomp and circumstance was in full swing in the Protocol Salon of the National

Palace. National anthems were being played. Armed grenadiers were marching in the courtyard. At first, the gunfire was difficult to hear over the noise, but the sound of marching boots made people question what was going on.

At 11:40 am, dozens of guerrillas with rifles, machine guns and grenades jumped from a truck and stormed the Palace. They blasted at security guards and joined their comrades who'd entered the night before in civilian clothes. In no time, they had almost 300 hostages, including most of the justices. Other hostages included lawyers, secretaries, shopkeepers and shoeshine people. The guerrillas blocked stairwells with furniture and mounted machine guns on top. They issued a demand for the highest court in the nation to put the president on trial for failing to keep his promise to establish peace.

The police on the scene rescued some hostages, but were repelled with gunfire. The army showed up with tanks, grenade launchers, helicopters and hundreds of troops with hard helmets and rifles, who positioned themselves in rows against various walls for cover. They blasted rockets at the massive building with its masonry façade, making holes in the walls. Debris littered the sidewalk. Tank fire and rockets pounded the entrance door. Helicopters landed on the roof, and troops alighted to sniper fire coming through the skylights. Troops who managed to get inside couldn't get past the blocked stairwells and received machine-gun fire. A day went by with the guerrillas in control of the building.

The next day around 7 pm, smoke started filtering through the building. Burning files ignited a fire, which spread to the wooden building dividers. Gagging and coughing, some of the people hiding on the top floor went downstairs, where the guerrillas captured them. They were thrown on top of sixty hostages compressed into a bathroom, who were traumatised by the likelihood of imminent death. Some were bleeding. Others had stopped breathing. The room stank of sweat and bodily fluids.

The next afternoon, troops braced to go inside. Instead of complying with the guerrillas' demand for negotiations, the president had authorised a military assault. After a tank rammed the front door, troops charged in. The guerrillas sifted through the corpses to find the living, whom they ordered to get up. Hostages shoved out of the door were annihilated by the army. Grenades toppled some of them, leaving them injured and bleeding or dead. Guerrillas threw corpses down the stairwell, including one of the justices who looked dead but was still alive, his artificial leg shattered by a bullet. After the guerrillas left that area, the injured justice crawled to the cellar and up a flight of stairs. Mustering energy, he raised himself and his arms. "Don't shoot!"

Approximately one hundred died in the bloodbath, including eleven justices: half of the Supreme Court. All of the guerrillas died, as well as eleven police and soldiers. Some of the survivors disappeared immediately afterwards, with the government suspected of killing them.

At first, the cartel's role wasn't obvious. Roberto Escobar stated that the Extraditables had financed the operation for the destruction of the records – not mass murder – and the traffickers had offered to double the fee to the guerrillas if the government negotiations had worked out.

Survivors, including the justice who'd been thrown down the stairs with the corpses, criticised the government for not negotiating. When the president eulogised in a church for the dead justices, the survivors didn't attend.

Afterwards, some people quit working for Pablo, others for the government, including many judges.

The violence increased into 1986, with journalists, prosecutors and judges getting killed by hit men on motorbikes.

CHAPTER 33

War

Sensing weakness in its rival, the Cali Cartel started to move against the Medellín Cartel in the late 1980s. Both had different organisational structures. The Medellín was an alliance between independent operators, whereas Cali was run by a four-man executive board. Below the board were accountants, engineers and lawyers, and then the workforce. The executives, some of whom had law degrees, considered themselves sophisticated. They were known as the gentlemen of trafficking, whereas Medellín members were called thugs. The head of the New York DEA told journalists, "Cali gangs will kill you if they have to, but they prefer to use a lawyer."

In 1988, the Cali Cartel rebuffed Pablo, who wanted both cartels to join forces against the government. Instead, the Cali Cartel cut a deal with the authorities whereby its business operations would be left alone in exchange for providing information about the Medellín Cartel. The Cali Cartel told the enemies of the Medellín Cartel the whereabouts of Pablo's safe houses and hiding places. These enemies included special units of the Colombian police assigned to find Pablo and Colombian paramilitaries. These authorities were supposedly after Pablo to stamp out his illegal cocaine business, yet were working with the Cali Cartel, who were in the same business as Pablo, and were expanding thanks to the authorities they were helping.

After eating dinner one night, Pablo left his family in Monaco, a building made from reinforced steel. He hid out at a farm ten miles away. At 5:30 am, a bomb went off at Monaco that woke people up two miles away. The building was destroyed. By the time Roberto showed up, Pablo said he already knew who was responsible. Half an hour after the explosion, he'd received a call from the Cali Cartel's Gilberto Rodriguez Orejuela, who said he'd heard about the bomb and wanted to know if he and his family were OK. Rumours were circulating that the bomb had been planted by DAS agents, but Pablo suspected Gilberto.

Pablo knew that Gilberto had spent time in prison in Spain with a bomb-maker for the Basque guerrillas. Pablo tracked the bomb-maker down, asked him to train some of his workers and promised him excellent prices on cocaine to sell in Spain. After the bomb-maker agreed, Pablo asked him if he'd ever had any experience working in Colombia. The man replied that he'd met someone in jail who'd brought him to Colombia to train some guys to make a bomb to be used against the government. Surrounded by armed bodyguards, Pablo said that the bomb has been used against him. The bomb-maker's face turned white. Pablo told him not to worry, and urged him to start to train Pablo's workers in bomb manufacture.

When the Cali Cartel found out that Pablo knew, Gilberto called Pablo, protesting that he hadn't done anything. Pablo told him to stop lying and to get ready to be hit.

At 4 am, a car bomb exploded by Pablo's mother's house. Cut by glass, she was hospitalised. His six-months-pregnant sister had also been asleep on the fourth floor. In hospital, she gave birth to a baby that had to live in an incubator for several weeks. Another sister on the fifth floor was treated for shrapnel wounds.

The Cali Cartel offered a band of killers from Medellín $5 million to kill Pablo, who managed to hire the killers himself by exposing Cali for being tight with money. Pablo ordered the fire-bombing of the drugstores Cali laundered their money through.

By 1989, bombs were exploding almost daily, and international mercenaries, including ex-SAS members, had joined the hunt for Pablo.

CHAPTER 34

The Cathedral

Pablo adopted a strategy of kidnapping elite hostages and negotiating with the government. He wanted to surrender to a prison he had built for himself, called La Catedral del Valle, stationed on a mountainous slope over the Honey Valley, 7,000 feet above sea level, which would give the guards and the occupants a bird's-eye view of any threats. The area was foggy in the evening and at dawn, which made a surprise raid from the air more difficult and provided a means for the occupants to slip away unnoticed if they needed to flee. They could easily lose their pursuers in the surrounding forest, which was teeming with wildlife such as armadillos, sloths and huge iridescent butterflies.

The building and 30,000 square metres of land had been registered in the name of one of Pablo's friends, a trusted old ironmonger. Pablo wanted only local guards and for the police and army to have nothing to do with it. The mayor of Envigado approved the transfer of the building into a prison called the Cathedral.

The building had cement floors, tile roofs and green metal doors. Formerly a farmhouse, the administration section included three little rooms: a kitchen, a courtyard and a punishment cell. It had a big dormitory, library, study and six cells with their own bathrooms. The large dayroom included four showers, a dressing room and six toilets. Seventy men had been working around the clock, remodelling it. Due to its inaccessibility, furnishings had arrived on mules: water heaters, military cots, tubular yellow armchairs, potted plants…

Despite its secure location, Pablo wanted a standing army of bodyguards inside the prison, just in case anything unexpected happened. "I won't surrender alone." He stated that he wouldn't abandon his associates to be slaughtered by the Elite Corps, while omitting to say that by keeping his network close he could continue to run his operation. As added insurance, Pablo and Roberto buried weapons near their designated cells. "One day we'll need them," he told Roberto.

Pablo arrived in a helicopter. When he got out, fifty men in blue guard uniforms aimed their guns at him.

He responded like thunder: "Lower your weapons, damn it!"

The guns were lowered before their commander issued the same order.

They walked to a house containing the official delegation, more of Pablo's men who'd surrendered and his wife and mother.

The prison director shook Pablo's hand. "Señor Escobar. I'm Lewis Jorge Pataquiva."

Pablo pulled up a trouser leg, revealing a Sig Sauer 9 mm pistol with a gold monogram inlaid on a mother of pearl handle. The spellbound crowd watched him remove each bullet and throw it on the ground. The gesture was designed to show confidence in the warden whose appointment had worried Pablo. On a portable phone, Pablo told his brother that he'd surrendered. Addressing the journalists present, he said his surrender was an act of peace. "I decided to give myself up the moment I saw the National Constitutional Assembly working for the strengthening of human rights and Colombian democracy."

By spending some of the millions he'd smuggled into the prison, it wasn't long before Pablo started to modify his surroundings to suit a man of his stature. He kept his cash in milk cans inside containers of salt, sugar, rice, beans and fresh fish, which were permitted inside because they were classified as food rations. Excess money was buried near the soccer field and in underground tunnels accessible by trapdoors in the cells. When his employees needed paying, helicopters transported cash out of the Cathedral.

He added a bar, lounge and disco, where he hosted parties and weddings. Famous people, models, politicians and soccer players danced and cavorted in the Cathedral. He installed a sauna in the gym, and Jacuzzis and hot tubs in the bathrooms. In his bedroom, he had a circular rotating bed and two other beds for his family. One of the biggest benefits to Pablo of no longer being on the run was the time he could spend with his family. Above his bed was a gold-framed portrait of the Virgin Mary.

Large items such as computers and big-screen TVs were smuggled in by Roberto's son, who drove a truck laden with crates of soda disguising the contraband. The truck brought women in, too. Despite rules restricting visits to official days, people were always sneaking in. Vans with fake walls held up to twenty people. This method of entry was ideal for people who wanted to keep their visits a secret, such as criminals and politicians.

Pablo's extensive record collection was there, including albums signed by Frank Sinatra from when Pablo had visited him in Las Vegas, and Elvis records purchased during a Graceland trip. His books ranged from Bibles to Nobel Prize winners. He had novels by Gabriel García Márquez and Stefan Zweig, a prominent Austrian writer from the 1920s. His movies on videotape included *The Godfather* trilogy and films starring Chuck Norris. Most of the prisoners had posters on their walls, whereas Pablo hung valuable paintings on his. His closet was full of neatly pressed jeans, shirts and Nike sneakers, some with spikes on in case he had to flee. Pablo never tied the laces of his sneakers – it was said that if he did, then something life-threatening was imminent. In case of danger from above the prison, a remote control allowed Pablo to turn off all of the internal lights.

Further up the slope, cabins were built for privacy with female visitors and as hideouts in case the prison was attacked. They were painted brightly and had sound systems and fancy lamps. Paths were made into the forest to allow a quick getaway and to enable the prisoners to walk where the air was freshest.

As the location included a direct sightline to his family's home, he mounted a telescope so he could see his wife and children while talking to them on the phone. A playhouse was constructed for his daughter and filled with toys.

The soccer field was renovated, night lights installed and wires positioned above it to sabotage helicopter landings. Despite having a bad knee, Pablo played centre forward; his associates made tactful allowances for this such as passing him the ball to score winning goals. The professional teams who came to play against Pablo and his men were careful never to win. Pablo had a replacement on standby in case he grew tired. When he regained his energy after resting, he'd join back in. The guards served the players refreshments. Sometimes his lawyers had to wait hours to see him if he was playing soccer.

The introduction of two chefs known as the Stomach Brothers addressed Pablo's concerns about getting poisoned. He enjoyed beans, pork, eggs and rice. He'd installed exercise equipment such as weights and bikes for the prisoners to get in shape, but as they were no longer on the run and had access to endless food and alcohol, they started to gain weight.

The Cathedral became known as "Club Medellín" or "Hotel Escobar." *Hustler* magazine published an illustration of Pablo and his associates partying in prison, throwing darts at a picture of President George HW Bush. Pablo obtained the illustration and hung it on his wall.

Communications were a priority. Pablo had cell phones, radio transmitters, a fax machine and beepers. Roberto has denied allegations by other authors that Pablo used carrier pigeons.

With the government protecting him instead of hunting him down, Pablo's cocaine business thrived.

A DAS agent working as prison security discovered that the Cali Cartel had bought four bombs from El Salvador, and was attempting to buy a plane to drop them on the Cathedral. From then on, the guards fired at any planes flying too close to the prison.

To address legal problems, Pablo had thirty lawyers working

for him almost full-time. He was facing an indictment for being the intellectual author of the murder of the presidential candidate, Galán. One of Pablo's men was arrested in New York for traveling with a fake passport, and was accused of being a player in the bombing of Avianca Flight 203. During a raid of one of Pablo's properties, the authorities found paperwork linking Pablo to the assassination of the journalist, Guillermo Cano.

When he wasn't meeting his lawyers, Pablo was usually on the telephone or reading. He tried to learn Mandarin. At nights, he sat in a rocking chair and watched the lights come on in Envigado, while thinking about his family.

He received endless letters from people asking for help, business advice and money. If their stories checked out, Pablo often sent them cash. A teenager sent a photo of herself in a wedding dress and a letter offering her virginity in exchange for Pablo paying her college fees, so she could become a lawyer. After her story was confirmed, he paid the fees, without taking her offer up. People also gathered at the prison gate with notes for Pablo, seeking his assistance.

On December 1, 1991, Pablo celebrated his forty-second birthday with a party in the Cathedral, where his guests ate caviar and pink salmon while listening to live music. His gifts included a Russian fur hat from his mother. Photographed wearing it, he declared it would be his trademark.

Pablo took trips to watch soccer games at the stadium he'd built in Medellín. The police diverted traffic to allow his vehicles access. He went Christmas shopping at a mall. He spent the one-year anniversary of his surrender at a nightclub with family and friends.

When the government attempted to build a maximum-security prison based on the American model to transfer Pablo to, no construction company would accept the job. One said, "We're not going to build a cage with the lion already inside." Finally, a company owned by an Israeli security expert attempted to build it, with supposedly incorruptible workers from afar. Watching the work crew, Pablo's men started writing down their licence-plate numbers, and eventually attacked them, causing many to quit. The project was abandoned.

In early 1992, the attorney general's office published photos taken at Hotel Escobar, including waterbeds, Jacuzzis, big-screen TVs... The embarrassed president commissioned an investigation, but the justice minister found that the furnishings were legal because each prisoner was allowed a bed and a bathtub, and TVs were permitted for good behaviour.

"I want all of these things taken out immediately!" the president said. "Tell the army to go in there and take everything. Escobar has to know we're not kidding."

No government department wanted the job. "No way," the minister of defence said. "I cannot do it because I don't have the people." When it was pointed out that he had 120,000 troops, he still refused the assignment.

Due to the deal struck with Pablo, the police couldn't do it. The DAS said that they couldn't act because they were only allowed inside the prison in the event of a riot.

In the end, a lawyer was told to take a truck and some workers, and to go to the prison and get the goods. "What have I ever done to you?" the lawyer responded. "Why'd you give me this assignment?"

Banking on the truck not being allowed to enter the prison, so he could turn around and go home, the lawyer set off. When he arrived, the prison gate opened and Pablo waved them in.

Upon being told why they were there, Pablo said, "Certainly, Doctor. I didn't know these things bothered you. Please, take everything out." Pablo and his men helped them carry the goods until everything was gone.

The lawyer rushed to his boss with photos of the bare prison. While the president was examining the photos, all of the goods were heading back to the Cathedral.

Pablo claimed that his imprisonment was a personal sacrifice for the good of all of the traffickers – for whom he'd single-handedly got rid of extradition. Due to the benefits they were receiving, they were expected to compensate him by paying a tax. In prison, Pablo was tuned into everything going on outside thanks to his extensive communications network. Those who tried to cheat him out of the tax or were perceived to have swindled him in any way were dealt with harshly.

Pablo's friends, Fernando Galeano and Kiko Moncada, ran two of the biggest trafficking groups that Pablo taxed. They were smuggling cocaine into America via a route that Pablo had established through Mexico. Word trickled back to the Cathedral that they'd been short-changing Pablo, who viewed their deceit as a prelude to a takeover of his organisation. Pablo learned where they stashed their money. His men confiscated $20 million. After denying Pablo's allegations, Galeano and Moncada asked for it back. He told them that he wanted to discuss it in person at the prison.

Pablo gave Galeano and Moncada a lecture about everything that he'd done for them. According to Roberto, they were killed after they'd left the Cathedral: Popeye killed Moncada and Otto shot Galeano. Within days, their brothers were also killed. Their distraught families begged for their corpses to give them proper burials, so Pablo told them where to find them.

Pablo wanted all of the property belonging to their organisations. Their employees were told that they worked for Pablo. Their key people were smuggled into the Cathedral through a secret tunnel to attend a meeting, many of them thinking they would die.

"I'm declaring an emergency," Pablo said. "Your bosses are already dead. Now you'll turn over all their resources to me. If you lie, you'll die very painfully." He reminded them that he was the boss. He said that they'd all be safe provided they paid him the tax.

The DEA recorded a version of events based on an informant's statement:

Escobar argued that while he and his close associates were in jail and needed money for their expensive war with the Cali Cartel, Galeano and Moncada preferred to store money until it became moldy rather than use it to help their friends… Escobar convinced cartel members who genuinely liked Moncada and Galeano that if the two men were not killed, the Medellín Cartel would be in a war with itself, and they would all perish.

Word got out about the murders of Galeano and Moncada, which made the president appear weak for not taking any action. Two of Pablo's biggest enemies – George HW Bush and the Cali Cartel – were putting relentless pressure on the government to eliminate Pablo once and for all by moving him to another prison, where he could be assassinated, or by extraditing him to the US, where he would never get out of prison.

Roberto told Pablo that he felt something bad was imminent. He asked Pablo to look into it. Government and army people on Pablo's payroll confirmed that he needed to abandon the Cathedral. He was told that George HW Bush was threatening to invade Colombia on the grounds that the government was incapable of extraditing Pablo.

Military trucks were spotted heading for the Cathedral. Pablo received a message that officials were coming to speak to him.

The weapons buried by Roberto and Pablo – prior to their arrival at the Cathedral – were unearthed. In addition to the pistol in his pants, Pablo slung an Uzi over his shoulder. Approaching the perimeter, they relied on the fog for cover. With soldiers nearby, Roberto used wire cutters on the electrified fence, making a gap big enough for a person to slip through.

While preparing to escape, Pablo kept trying to contact the president.

"Either we flee or we all die," Pablo told his men. He and Roberto entered a hidden room and grabbed lots of cash. To thwart the spy planes, Roberto used his emergency remote control to plunge the prison into darkness, which terrified everybody inside including the hostages.

Pablo listened to radio stations report different stories. One claimed he'd been captured and was on a plane to America. Another said the military had taken over the Cathedral and lives had been lost.

Concerned about his family hearing these reports, he called them. "Don't worry. Don't listen to the news. The situation is being resolved directly with the president." After hanging up, he called and reassured his mother. Pablo crouched down, grabbed his shoelaces and finally tied them. "Roberto, let's put our radios on the same frequency."

With darkness, fog and rain providing cover, Pablo told his men to simply walk out through the hole that Roberto had cut in the fence, one after the other, five minutes apart. Hoping to blend in with the military units surrounding the prison, most of the men had put on army fatigues. Pablo went first. He positioned himself to watch the others emerging and everything going on around them.

Due to the poor visibility, Roberto got lost. After wandering around afraid, he found the hole in the fence at around 2 am.

The group set off down a wet slippery surface that presented a risk of injury or death. Confronted by a rock face, the brawniest went first and allowed the others to stand on their shoulders. While thorny vegetation prickled them, they held hands going down another slope. After two hours, visibility improved as the fog thinned. Realising they'd gone in a circle and hadn't achieved much distance from the prison, they traded expressions of shock and frustration. They needed to keep moving because they could easily be shot. Pablo estimated that they had two hours left to evacuate the area.

The sun was up when they reached a neighbourhood called El Salado. People were going to work and children to school. In filthy ripped clothes, Pablo and his men emerged like vagrants. They headed for a farm belonging to Memo, a trusted friend.

They knocked on the door. The groundskeeper answered, but didn't recognise them. Once it dawned, he let them in. They stripped off the soaked clothes compressed to their weary bodies. While their clothes were washed, they finally rested.

Almost an hour later, there was frantic banging at the door. Bracing for a gunfight, they grabbed their weapons and took aim. The door opened. In came the neighbours with a hot breakfast for the visitors. Other neighbours patrolled the streets to watch out for the army. Pablo and his men cleaned themselves, shaved and put on fresh clothes.

The raid netted five of Pablo's men. Twenty-seven guards were charged with suspicion of cooperating with Pablo.

Drinking coffee at Memo's house, Pablo listened to the radio reports, while helicopters buzzed overhead. Roberto's son called a radio station and stated that they were hiding in a tunnel under the prison with weapons and food. He told a reporter that Pablo would surrender and return to the Cathedral if the original terms were reinstated.

Hoping to unearth the tunnel, the government sent construction equipment to the prison, so that the troops could start digging. Explosives were detonated in the fields.

Pablo gazed at the activity through a window. "The only thing they'll find is the money in the barrels," he said, referring to $10 million that had been buried.

The radio reported that Pablo had ordered the assassination of all of the top government officials. Hoax bomb threats and evacuation drills at schools were widespread.

On TV in the evening, the president called for calm and promised to protect the escapees' lives if they surrendered, but he never mentioned reinstating Pablo's original deal.

Some US news outlets reported that Pablo and his men had stormed out of the prison in a hail of gunfire with their weapons blazing. These stories increased support for George HW Bush to send soldiers to Colombia to apprehend Pablo and to incarcerate him in America.

When darkness came, the men left Memo's and trekked through the woods. At the Cathedral, explosions were still going off as the troops searched for the tunnel. At another farm, Pablo called his family and urged them to ignore the news. They ate and set off again.

Outside a farm, five German Shepherds launched at them. They couldn't shoot the dogs because the noise would have alerted the authorities. One bit El Mugre on the leg, drawing blood. Pablo threw some snacks at the dogs, which distracted them. He stayed with the dogs while the others moved on and then followed everyone.

At 3:30 am, they arrived at a friendly farm. A driver took Roberto to see his mother, so that he could explain the situation. He didn't want to stay long, but she insisted on making some food for him and Pablo. Unable to say no, Roberto positioned himself at a window and watched out for the police.

When Roberto returned to the farm, some of the group had moved on because Pablo felt they'd be harder to find if they split up. More soldiers were constantly arriving in the area around the Cathedral, hoping to flush them out. For two days, they stayed at the farm, watching TV reports and listening to the radio.

On July 24, 1992, Pablo recorded a statement, offering to surrender if he could go back to the Cathedral. He said the arrival of the troops had taken them by surprise. "As for the aggression carried out against us, we won't take violent actions of any nature yet and we are willing to continue with the peace process and our surrender to justice if we can be guaranteed to stay at the Envigado jail [the Cathedral], as well as handing control of the prison to special forces of the United Nations."

At the end, he said he was in the jungles of Colombia, which prompted the government to send soldiers and helicopters there.

They had been at the farm for twenty days when 5,000 soldiers were dispatched to the area. With helicopters arriving, they ran into the forest and escaped into the jungle. Unable to ascertain their location, the army kept dropping bombs but missing them. For twelve days, they slept on hammocks, occasionally awakened by the explosions going on around them.

CHAPTER 35

Los Pepes

Pablo's escape was an opportunity for George HW Bush to distract the public from domestic issues and to boost his popularity. Catching the person he'd labelled the biggest cocaine trafficker in the world would surely increase his chances of re-election. The DEA in Bogotá sent a cable to Washington:

The BCO [the local US embassy] feels that Escobar may finally have overstepped his self-perceived illegitimate boundaries and has placed himself in a very precarious position. Escobar's gall and bravado may lead to his ultimate downfall. But then again, the GOC [government of Colombia] has always bowed to Escobar's demands in the past. This current situation again provides the GOC with an opportunity to demonstrate its dedication to bring all narco-traffickers to justice, including the most notorious and dangerous cocaine trafficker in history, Pablo Escobar.

Amid hyped-up threats that Pablo might assassinate him and set bombs off in America, George HW Bush dispatched Delta Force, Centra Spike, the DEA, the FBI, the ATF, the CIA, the Bureau of Alcohol, Tobacco and Firearms, the army, navy and the air force after Pablo. Out of all of the agencies, Centra Spike quickly obtained results by flying planes over Medellín with technology that picked up Pablo's calls.

Pablo responded to America's involvement with a fax:

We, the Extraditables declare: that if anything happens to Mr Pablo Escobar, we will hold President Gaviria responsible and will again mount attacks on the entire country. We will target the United States Embassy in the country, where we will plant the largest quantity of dynamite ever. We hereby declare: the blame for this whole mess lies with President Gaviria. If Pablo Escobar or any of the others turn up dead, we will immediately mount attacks throughout the entire country. Thank you very much.

George HW Bush approved a $2 million reward for information leading to Pablo. The US Embassy in Colombia offered $200,000 and relocation to America for any useful information. Advertised on TV, the reward program included pictures of Pablo and his henchmen.

The Centra Spike eavesdropping enabled the authorities to determine that Pablo was using at least eight cell-phones. He viewed himself as a victim of a violation of his agreement with the government and wanted to return to the Cathedral. Pablo's freedom enabled the Americans to retarget him for assassination. Delta Force came and trained the Colombians. Centra Spike got back on the case. His enemies multiplied.

The CIA worked with a death squad called Los Pepes (People Persecuted by Pablo Escobar), which included former members of the Medellín Cartel and policemen frustrated by the limits of the law that prevented them from responding to Pablo with the same level of deadly force that Pablo had been using upon them. Los Pepes' mission statement was to retaliate against Pablo, his family and his associates for each and every time he'd committed a terrorist act, which injured innocent people. The Cali Cartel provided intelligence to and financed Los Pepes.

Possessing inside knowledge about Pablo's organisation, Los Pepes kidnapped, tortured and murdered anyone associated with Pablo whom they could get their hands on, including family members, his workforce and even lawyers and accountants. Many of his workers defected to the Cali Cartel, which continued to flourish. The Americans claimed to be in Colombia to suppress the cocaine supply, yet they were passing intelligence over to

Los Pepes and the Cali Cartel, who were increasing the cocaine supply to America.

Using terror and torture methods taught to the Search Bloc by Delta Force, members of Los Pepes, including policemen, went on the rampage murdering and bombing. One of Pablo's mother's properties was burned down and several of Pablo's properties were torched. Bombs exploded outside the apartments where Pablo's family was staying. A bomb at a ranch house injured his mother and aunt.

In a note, Pablo blamed Colonel Martinez, the new head of the Search Bloc:

Personnel under your supervision set car bombs at buildings in El Poblado, where some of my relatives live. I want to tell you that your terrorist actions will not stop my struggle under any circumstances. Your threats and your car bombs against my family have been added to the hundreds of young people that you have murdered in the city of Medellín in your headquarters of torture in the school Carlos Holguin. I hope that the Antioquian community becomes aware of what you do with the dynamite you seize, and of the criminal actions undertaken by men who cover their faces with ski masks. Knowing that you are part of the government, I wish to warn you that if another incident of this nature occurs, I will retaliate against relatives of government officials who tolerate and do not punish your crimes. Don't forget that you, too, have a family.

The warning from Pablo didn't deter Los Pepes, who were just getting started on annihilating the personnel of the Medellín Cartel. Having been provided Medellín Cartel organisational charts by the CIA and Centra Spike, Los Pepes knew exactly whom to target to maximise damage. They even made public announcements of what they were going to do to Pablo's associates, and offered rewards for information.

In February 1993, a manager low down in the cartel hierarchy was found dead with a sign attached to his neck: "For working for the narco-terrorist and baby-killer Pablo Escobar. For Colombia. Los Pepes." They started to kill up to six of Pablo's employees and associates a day, including a director of the National Police of Colombia, who was on Pablo's payroll. They shot the man in charge of financing operations multiple times in the head. Pablo's warehouse stocked with antique cars worth $4 million was torched. On February 28, 1993, the Search Bloc killed a brother-in-law of Pablo.

Rattled by Los Pepes, Pablo desperately wanted to get his family out of the country. Knowing that his family was his weakness, the US authorities intervened to prevent them from leaving.

Los Pepes killed the brother of a man who dealt in real estate for Pablo and bombed properties belonging to Pablo's bankers and lawyers. On March 4, 1993, the corpse of a lawyer was discovered with a note from Los Pepes threatening the rest of Pablo's legal team, two of whom were swiftly killed, including Roberto Escobar's lawyer, whom they got after he'd exited a prison he'd been visiting. They tortured and killed one of Pablo's top lawyers and his eighteen-year-old son. Kidnapped by fifteen men with machine guns, the father and son were found in the trunk of a car, shot in the head, their hands taped together, with a note from Los Pepes: "Through their profession, they initiated abductions for Pablo Escobar. What do you think of the exchange for the bombs in Bogotá, Pablo?"

Pablo's top lawyers resigned. But one thought he could outsmart Los Pepes by continuing to work undercover. In Medellín, he was walking with his brother when Los Pepes shot him twenty-five times. One lawyer fled the country. Pablo responded with periodic bombs, but he was losing his ability to fight back as the violence spiralled out of his control. No one dared stand up to Los Pepes, including the authorities who made up plenty of their membership.

On April 29, 1993, Pablo wrote a letter to the attorney general:

Los Pepes have their headquarters and their torture chambers in Fidel Castaño's house, located on El Poblado Avenue near the country club... There they torture trade unionists and lawyers. No one has searched the house or confiscated their assets... The government offers rewards for the leaders of the Medellín cartel and for the leaders of the guerrillas, but doesn't offer rewards for the leaders of the paramilitary, nor for those of the Calí cartel, authors of various car bombs in the city of Medellín.

In the note, Pablo complained that the murders and kidnappings by Los Pepes were not investigated by the government nor had any arrests been made. He offered to turn himself in if the government agreed to certain guarantees.

The Colombian government threatened to clamp down on Los Pepes. In response, Los Pepes announced that they had disbanded, but the killing didn't stop. On July 14, 1993, Los Pepes castrated Roberto Escobar's prize stallion worth millions, and executed its rider and trainer.

CHAPTER 36

Demise

Aware that the end was near, Pablo left a recording for his daughter telling her to be a good girl and that he would protect her from heaven. The authorities were relying on Pablo calling his family, so that they could trace the calls back to his location. Concerned about Los Pepes, Pablo made numerous calls to his son. Centra Spike and the Search Bloc traced the calls to Los Olivos, a neighbourhood in Medellín near the football stadium, consisting mostly of two-storey homes. The Search Bloc set up surveillance in Los Olivos.

Pablo spent his forty-fourth birthday, December 1, 1993 at building number 45D-94 on Street 79A, a two-storey house that he owned. He had one bodyguard, Limón. His cousin, Luzmila, was his cook. When Pablo wanted to make phone calls, Limón drove him around in a yellow taxi, which had given Pablo a false sense of security. Birthday congratulations kept Pablo on the phone longer than usual with his family. He celebrated with restaurant food and champagne.

To throw his pursuers off his trail, Pablo had decided to hide in the jungle. He wanted to say goodbye to his mother first, so he risked going to her apartment in the early morning. He told her that it was the last time he would see her in Medellín. His plan now was to form a new group, establish an independent country and be its president. Without crying, his mother said goodbye.

On December 2, 1993, Pablo woke up around noon and ate spaghetti. He sent his cousin to buy supplies he would need in the jungle: stationery and toiletries. In a taxi, he made phone calls. On the phone, he got out of the taxi and returned to the apartment, making the mistake of speaking for longer than five minutes.

At 1 pm, pretending to be a radio journalist, Pablo called his family. His wife, Maria Victoria, was crying. Numerous of their family members and associates had been killed by Los Pepes. The family was distraught.

"So, what are you going to do?" Pablo said.

"I don't know," she said, still crying.

"What does your mother say?"

"It was as if my mother fainted," she said, referring to a few days ago at the airport when the family had unsuccessfully tried to flee to Germany. "I did not call her. She told me bye, and then–"

"And you haven't spoken to her?"

"No. My mother is so nervous..." Maria Victoria said the murders committed by Los Pepes had traumatised her mother.

"What are you going to do?" Pablo said softly.

"I don't know. I mean, wait and see where we are going to go and I believe that will be the end of us."

"No!"

"So?"

"Don't you give me this coldness! Holy Mary!" Pablo said.

"And you?"

"Ahhh."

"And you?"

"What about me?" Pablo said.

"What are you going to do?"

"Nothing... What do you need?"

"Nothing," Maria Victoria said.

"What do you want?"

"What would I want?"

"If you need something, call me, OK?"

"OK."

"You call me now, quickly," Pablo said. "There is nothing more I can tell you. What else can I say? I have remained right on track, right?"

"But how are you? Oh my God, I don't know!"

"We must go on. Think about it. Now that I am so close, right?" Pablo said, referring to his proposal to surrender to the government.

"Yes," Maria Victoria said. "Think about your boy, too, and everything else, and don't make any decisions too quickly. OK?"

"Yes."

"Call your mother again and ask her if she wants you to go there or what..." she said. "Ciao."

"So long."

At 3 pm, Pablo called his son, who said that a journalist wanted to know what conditions Pablo would be satisfied with in order to turn himself in. Members of the Search Bloc started to go street to street, hoping to detect Pablo's location.

"Tell him, 'My father cannot turn himself in unless he has guarantees for his security...'"

The call lasted for so long that the Search Bloc was on Pablo's street, driving up and down. They noticed a bearded man behind a second-story window, phone in hand, watching the traffic. After a few seconds, the man disappeared into the house.

"This is the house!"

They radioed to Colonel Martinez who yelled, "Stay exactly where you are! Station yourself in front and back of the house. Don't let him come out!"

All units of the Search Bloc sped to the house.

There have been many accounts of what happened next.

A sledgehammer knocked down the front door. Six Search Bloc members stormed inside, shooting at a garage space empty other than a taxi. Charging up the stairs, one member of the team fell as if shot, startling the rest, but he had only slipped.

The authorities reported that Limón had escaped through a window onto an orange-tile roof. As he fled, Search Bloc members behind the house sprayed gunfire. Shot multiple times, he careened off the roof onto the grass.

Pablo tossed his sandals and leapt down to the roof. Not wanting to end up like Limón, he stayed against a wall, which blocked clear shots at him even though marksmen were all over the place. Aiming to escape down a back street, Pablo hastened along the wall.

Shots erupted. The gunfire was so intense from all sides of the house that it tore up the bricks and the roof and some members of the Search Bloc thought they were under attack by Pablo's bodyguards and radioed for help.

Pablo fell.

The shooting stopped.

"It's Pablo! It's Pablo!"

Troops approached the blood-soaked corpse and flipped it over.

"Viva Colombia! We've just killed Pablo Escobar!"

"We won! We won!"

In the book *Escobar*, Roberto described the police barging in downstairs and Pablo sending Limón to investigate. Shot multiple times, Limón died while Pablo made it to the roof, looked around and saw he was surrounded. Having pledged to never be captured or killed, he shot himself in the head to deprive the government of being able to claim that they had killed him.

Pablo was shot three times: in his back, leg and above his right ear. Roberto believes the wound above the ear was the suicide shot.

Troops shaved a Hitler moustache onto Pablo's face and posed for pictures with him.

While the upper classes celebrated, the news devastated the poor. At the funeral, over 5,000 rushed to touch the coffin. Pablo's wife had to be evacuated. Along the streets, ten thousand joined the procession. For the first year, his grave had an armed guard.

Pablo's death had no impact on the cocaine flowing into America.

Pablo wouldn't have thought twice about ordering the assassination of Barry Seal. He ordained the death penalty for informants, some of whom were tortured in the most brutal ways such as having their tongues yanked out through their necks. Some had their eyeballs removed with hot spoons. Others had their skulls penetrated with sharp instruments. Pablo had the motive and the means to kill Barry, but his hit men had repeatedly failed. In the end, they succeeded because of outside help from co-conspirators in the US government. To ascertain the identities of the architects of Barry's death, it's necessary to examine the life of a suspect responsible for murder on a far grander scale than Pablo: George HW Bush.

MURDER SUSPECT 2

GEORGE HW BUSH

CHAPTER 37

War Hero

On September 2, 1944, anti-aircraft fire was strafing a blue sky with a few puffy clouds above Chichi Jima, one of the Bonin Islands in the Pacific. Chunky grey US bombers were dodging flak, dropping their loads, some hitting the island causing explosions; others splashing into the dark-blue sea, causing water to spurt into the air. With a target map strapped to his knee, George HW Bush was at the controls of an Avenger torpedo bomber with a canopy over its top that provided a view of a green island dense with vegetation and the aquamarine water of the bay. Aiming to drop a bomb on a Japanese radio tower, Bush felt a jolt, as if a giant fist had punched the underbelly of the plane. Bailing out of the plane, abandoning his crew of two, Bush gashed his forehead as it struck the tail assembly.

In another bomber, approximately a hundred feet in front of Bush's, a rear turret gunner, Chester Mierzejewski, had a pristine view of Bush's plane getting hit by anti-aircraft fire. Chester was so close that he could see Bush's face in the cockpit. A puff of smoke quickly dissipated and Bush parachuted out.

Chester claimed that the bomber was never on fire and "no smoke came out of his cockpit when he opened his canopy to bail out… I was hoping I would see some other parachutes. I never did. I saw the plane go down. I knew the guys were still in it. It was a helpless feeling… I think Bush could have saved those lives, if they were alive. I don't know that they were, but at least they had a chance if he had attempted a water landing." When there is no fire, it's standard procedure to attempt a water landing. Afterwards, Chester was debriefed by an intelligence officer, but his statement never made it into the official record. "I told him what I saw. I don't understand why it's not in the report."

Another witness in the same bomber as Chester, gunner Lawrence Mueller, stated that no one in the debriefing room had said anything about a fire. "I would have put it in my logbook if I had heard it."

The bomber story became raw material for the Bush propaganda machine, which churned out several variations:

In 1987, the incident was described in Bush's campaign autobiography. With flames rippling towards the fuel tanks, Bush risked his life unloading four bombs on targets and flying out to sea. There was no mention of his crew until he parachuted onto the South Pacific, inflated his raft and began searching for them. Only after being rescued by a submarine had he learned that neither had survived. One had gone down in the plane. The other had jumped, but his parachute had failed to open.

In a 1980 authorised biography, Nicholas King claimed that Bush's parachute had failed to open properly and had become momentarily fouled on the tail of the plane after Bush had hit the water. There was no mention of his forehead injury.

In *George Bush: The Life of a Lone Star Yankee* (1997), the award-winning historian Herbert S Palmer wrote an account based on interviews with Bush and from reading Bush's personal papers and diaries: Bush had jumped prematurely and pulled the ripcord. His head struck the horizontal stabiliser at the plane's rear and his parachute ripped as it became snagged on the tail.

In another account, Bush claimed that he'd seen his rear gunner machine-gunned to death, while the plane was on fire. In a taped interview, Bush stated that one of the crew had jumped and his parachute had streamed. The other man had been killed in the plane and was slumped over.

In a book commissioned by Bush to extol his wartime glory, *Flight of the Avenger* (1991), Joe Hyams described Bush jumping from a burning plane at approximately 3,000 feet, his parachute opening successfully and him landing on the water. This account was a damage-control response to a 1988 interview with Chester Mierzejewski published in the *New York Post*.

Upset by Bush's false claims of war heroics made during the 1988 presidential campaign, sixty-eight-year-old Chester sent a letter, informing the vice president that his recollections differed from Bush's official story. After not receiving a response, Chester broke his forty-four year silence in the *New York Post*, "That guy is not telling the truth."

When the paper double-checked Chester's account with former Lieutenant Legare Hole, the executive officer of Bush's squadron, they were told, "The turret gunner in Melvin's plane [Chester] would have had a good view. If the plane was on fire, there is a very good chance he would be able to see that. The pilot can't see everything that the gunner can and he'd miss an awful lot."

Regardless of the facts, Bush was awarded the Distinguished Flying Cross and his bravery was parlayed into political capital. A grainy film showing submarines rescuing him was aired numerous times during his 1964 Senate campaign in Texas. During the Gulf War of 1990-91, Bush achieved record heights of worship for his military prowess. As his business associates cashed in on bombing Iraq, Bush compared Saddam Hussein – whom the CIA had installed as the leader of Iraq in the 1960s – to Adolf Hitler.

CHAPTER 38

War Profiteering and Eugenics

For almost a century, the Bush family has engaged in profiting from war with as much zeal as Barry Seal possessed for flying. To understand why Barry would end up transporting arms shipments covertly for the interests represented by George HW Bush – and become a liability to Bush for knowing too much – it's necessary to examine the history of the Bush family's war profiteering.

America entered World War I in 1917. In 1918, Samuel Bush – Bush's grandfather – became the chief of the Ordinance Small Arms and Ammunition Section of the War Industries Board. His duties included providing government assistance to weapons companies. Later that year, he became the director of the board's Facilities Division. The War Industries Board funnelled taxpayers' money to weapons manufacturers and holders of raw materials and patents. As thirty eight million people died in the war, the recipients of the taxpayers' money made billions.

In *War is a Racket* (1935), Major General Smedley Butler detailed the abnormal profits generated during World War I. "Only a small 'inside' group knows what it [the war racket] is about. It is conducted for the benefit of the very few, at the expense of the very many. Out of war a few people make huge fortunes." He added that World War I created 21,000 new millionaires and billionaires and that the most profitable operators were the bankers. He cited the du Pont family who manufactured gun powder. Their average earnings for 1910 to 1914 were $6 million a year, whereas their average profit during the war years, 1914 to 1918, was $58 million a year, an increase of more than 950 per cent. Du Pont's revenues from the sale of powder and explosives soared from $25 million in 1914 to $319 million by 1918, totalling $1.245 billion over five years. The same leap in profits happened for the producers of ships, planes, engines, steel, copper, nickel, leather, sugar, coal, mosquito nets, undershirts and hobnailed service shoes.

The weapons manufacturers didn't just arm their own countries in a patriotic quest to defend their homelands. They armed every side in the war. Before the war had even started, their salespeople were manipulating world leaders into fighting each other, so they could maximise their sales. Hearings in 1934 exposed culprits such as Remington Arms and the British Vickers company, who were attacked for being "Merchants of Death."

In 1916, eight years before the birth of his son, George HW Bush, Prescott Bush was invited to join Skull and Bones, a Yale senior-year secret society with bizarre death-worshipping rituals, founded by children of the Wall Street elite. Several Bonesmen who graduated in 1917, including Prescott, were hand-picked to join Brown Brothers Harriman, the largest private investment bank in the world, which cashed in on World War I. Instrumental in the selection of Prescott was Percy Rockefeller, a co-owner of Remington Arms. Prescott was groomed by master warmongers and profiteers. World War I was kind to Prescott's associates, but Prescott's ability to profit from slave labour and the slaughter of millions would really shine during World War II.

With the Skull and Bones order originating at the University of Berlin, many of its US members supported financing and arming Hitler. Just like the Nazis, they believed in eugenics: the interbreeding of elites to improve the genetic quality of the human population, and the sterilisation or extermination of people with inferior genes such as the mentally ill, alcoholics, gypsies, Jews and people of colour. If the horses they interbred could display superior characteristics, then surely the same applied to humans – or so they thought. Prescott supported and helped to finance the American Eugenics Movement, which lobbied for the successful passage in many states of sterilisation laws for anyone judged unfit.

Inspired by the American Eugenics Movement, Hitler wrote, "There is today, one state in which at least weak beginnings toward a better conception of immigration are noticeable. Of course, it is not our model German Republic, but the United States… I have studied with great interest the laws of several American states concerning prevention of reproduction by people whose progeny would, in all probability, be of no value or be injurious to the racial stock."

By the time the US had entered the war, Prescott was the managing partner of Brown Brothers Harriman, which had helped finance Hitler's rise and was still laundering Nazi money.

In *George Bush: The Unauthorized Biography*, Webster G. Tarpley and Anton Cheitkin revealed the extent of Prescott's Nazi collaboration. In 1922, USA railway magnate W Averell Harriman met the Thyssen family in Berlin with a view to founding a German-USA bank. The Thyssens owned banks that allowed them to transfer their money from Germany to the USA via the Netherlands. Fritz Thyssen was fascinated by Hitler's public-speaking skills. He donated $25,000 to the German National Socialist Workers' Party, giving Hitler an early boost. In 1931, Thyssen joined the Nazi Party. His steel company was at the heart of the Nazi war machine.

In 1926, Harriman and the Thyssens set up the Union Banking Corporation (UBC) with Prescott at the helm. That same year, Prescott was promoted to vice president and partner at Brown Brothers Harriman. Both firms allowed the Thyssens to send money to the US from Germany via the Netherlands. UBC ended up securing Nazi money. When the Nazis needed to retrieve it, Brown Brothers Harriman sent it directly to Germany. As the executive of both companies, Prescott was a primary banker for the Nazis.

After Hitler invaded Poland, Prescott ended up with a controlling interest in the Consolidated Silesian Steel Corporation – later changed to Silesian American Corporation – which used the slave labour of Auschwitz. While mostly Jewish prisoners

– starved and skeletal – were worked to death and finally exterminated, Silesian coal enabled the Nazis to rampage across Europe. According to Dutch intelligence, Prescott managed some of the Auschwitz labour to maximise his profits. At least 1.1 million people died at Auschwitz. Instructed to take showers, they were shaved and herded naked into chambers, sometimes to music being played by a live band. After getting sealed in, they were gassed with the pesticide Zyklon B. The proceeds from the sale of their jewellery, belongings and the gold extracted from their teeth helped to finance the Nazis.

On June 14, 1940, Auschwitz was opened, thanks in part to the joint enterprise of the German company IG Farben and the Standard Oil Company of New Jersey (later renamed Exxon). The initial purpose of Auschwitz was the production of artificial rubber and gasoline from coal. The principal manager of the IG Farben-Standard Oil cartel was William Stamps Farish, the grandfather of the man who would later become George HW Bush's money manager. In 1942, William Farish pleaded no contest to charges of criminal conspiracy with the Nazis, and was fined $5,000, which was nothing compared to the millions he'd made from Hitler. Standard Oil was also fined $5,000, and several of its subsidiaries. Patents Farish had provided the Nazis had been illegally withheld from the US military. With US soldiers dying, Farish was summoned to the Senate committee investigating the national defence program.

Before he testified, the chairman, Senator Harry Truman, told reporters, "I think this approaches treason."

Farish protested that he had not been disloyal, but after the hearings, it emerged that Farish had prevented the US Navy from acquiring patents he'd given to the Nazis, and also that he'd supplied gasoline and tetraethyl lead to Germany's air force and submarines. Communications showed he'd intentionally deceived the US government. While Prescott's Nazi banking facility was quietly seized and shut down, the attention on Farish intensified. A heart attack saw him off on November 29, 1942. After Farish was lambasted for fuelling Nazi aircraft, his son, a lieutenant in the US Air Force, was humiliated. Training in Texas, he died in an accident six months later. The family fortune earned from the Nazis went to the grandson Will Farish, who used some of it to help launch George HW Bush's political career.

In October 1942, the US authorities confiscated Nazi bank funds from the New York UBC, whose president, Prescott Bush, was charged with running Nazi front groups in the US. Two of the remaining five directors of UBC were Skull and Bonesmen; the other three were Nazis. UBC was essential for the financial operation of the German Steel Trust, which had produced huge amounts of war material for the Nazis, including more than a third of their explosives. The firm was condemned as a financial and commercial collaborator with the enemy and its assets were seized. This is documented in The National Archives and Library of Congress. As investigators followed the paper trail, more companies were seized, including Silesian American Corporation.

It became apparent that the Nazi invasion of Poland in 1939 had in part been made possible by war material produced by the business interests of Prescott and his associates. During war, profits are maximised by investing in opposing sides, and true to the pattern established in World War I, Prescott and his associates had provided the technology for oil to be pumped from wells in Baku, which had enabled the Soviets to attack Poland from the East.

Yet again, it emerged that Remington Arms had been providing guns to both sides. Mr Pryor, the executive committee chairman of Remington Arms, was also a founding director of UBC, working in tandem with Prescott's Nazi banking facility. Remington was probed by US Senate arms-traffic investigators, who stated that, "German political associations, like the Nazi and others, are nearly all armed with American... guns... Arms of all kinds coming from America are transhipped in the Sheldt to river barges before the vessels arrive in Antwerp. They then can be carried through Holland without police inspection or interference.

The Hitlerists and Communists are presumed to get arms in this manner. The principal arms coming from America are Thompson submachine guns and revolvers. The number is great."

Thyssen – whose bullets had been used to kill Allied soldiers and whose factories had employed slave labour – was arrested and interrogated. The chief interrogator was a plant, who banked with the Thyssens. Thyssen's war profits were preserved and parlayed into a multi-billion-dollar empire. The Thyssens are one of the wealthiest families in the world.

In 1947, the manager of a Thyssen-owned Rotterdam bank threatened to blow the whistle on the UBC money-laundering scheme when he discovered that he was sitting on a pile of hidden Nazi assets. After being fired by the Thyssens, he fled to New York City where he naïvely intended to talk to Prescott Bush. Two weeks later, his body was found in New York.

In 1996, a Dutch journalist, Eddy Roever, went to London to interview a baron involved in the money-laundering scheme. The baron was a neighbour of Margaret Thatcher. Two days later, Roever's body was found. Retired US intelligence agent William Gowen commented on the deaths of the Rotterdam bank manager and Roever: it was only a coincidence that both healthy men had died of heart attacks immediately after trying to uncover the truth about the Thyssens.

If Barry Seal had been born a few decades earlier, his covert operations would have included transporting American arms to the Nazi private armies that overthrew the German Republic, all with the blessing of Prescott Bush. By the time George HW Bush obtained the presidency such activity was performed by the CIA.

By banking for Hitler, Prescott multiplied the wealth of the Bush dynasty. Despite violating laws that banned US companies from trading with enemies, he never suffered any punishment. He even managed to claw back $1.5 million of the seized money. He was the perfect role model for his son, George HW Bush, who felt destined to continue the family tradition.

CHAPTER 39

Early Bio

Fifteen years older than Barry Seal, George HW Bush was born on June 12, 1924 in Milton, Massachusetts. Although the stock-market crash of 1929 had depleted the fortune built by Prescott Bush on the back of World War I, the family, including five children, lived luxuriously in an eight-bedroom Victorian home with four servants, a chauffeur and a view of two acres of lawn. His mother, Dorothy, raised her children to win at all costs. Prescott was a binge drinker who beat his boys with a belt, a razor strap and a squash racket.

At Phillips Academy in Andover, a boys' prep school used as a stepping stone to Yale University, Bush excelled at sports, but was mediocre in the classroom. Prior to his graduation, the US entered World War II. Despite his parents' concerns, Bush insisted on joining the Navy's air program. The prerequisite of having completed two years of college for entry was no obstacle as Prescott had established the career of the Navy Secretary for Air. In an accomplishment that would have impressed Barry Seal, Bush became the Navy's youngest pilot.

In June 1944, flying a Grumman TBF Avenger he'd nicknamed Barbara on a combat mission against the Japanese, his plane lost oil pressure. He made an emergency landing on the sea, where he was rescued after floating for a few hours. That year, he flew fourteen missions near Guam. He nicknamed his next plane Barbara II – the one that was hit by flak which he parachuted from, abandoning his colleagues.

On January 6, 1945, Bush still had a battle scar on his forehead when he married Barbara Pierce at the first Presbyterian Church in Rye, New York. She wore her mother-in-law's long-sleeved white-satin dress and veil. Bush had donned his Navy midshipman's dress blues. After honeymooning on Sea Island, Georgia, Bush returned for special combat training in anticipation of the final Allied assault on Japan. Barbara prayed for the war to end and rejoiced when it did while her husband was still training. After celebrating in the streets, they thanked God at a nearby church.

After Yale and Skull and Bones, Bush tried to get a job with Procter & Gamble, but failed the interview. Utilising the Skull and Bones network, Prescott got his son a job at Dresser Industries, a large oil-equipment manufacturer and a subsidiary of Brown Brothers Harriman, where Prescott had served as a director for twenty-two years.

In January 1949, Bush flew to Texas, where he started work as an equipment clerk at a Dresser subsidiary, International Derrick and Equipment Company. While working for Dresser, he lived in various places in Texas and California with his family, which had expanded with the births of George W and Robin, the latter named after Barbara's mother, who had recently died in a car crash.

Bush co-started the Bush-Overbey Oil Development Company Inc in 1951, which specialised in swindling farmers out of their land for a pittance and reselling it to big buyers such as oil companies at inflated prices. Bush and Overbey chose land based on leaked geological information or after observing major oil companies drilling there.

In 1953, he co-founded the Zapata Petroleum Corporation, which drilled in the Permian Basin in Texas. Zapata struck so much oil that its shares rose from seven cents to $23 dollars, delighting its investors.

By now, there were three children thanks to the addition of Jeb, but one morning, Robin woke up pale and said, "I may go out and sit in the grass and watch the cars go by or maybe I'll just lie in bed." The doctor diagnosed her with leukaemia. Her white blood cell count was the highest the doctor had ever seen. "You should take her home, make life as easy as possible for her, and in three weeks' time, she'll be gone."

The next morning, the Bushes flew Robin to New York to see Bush's uncle, Dr John Walker, a former cancer specialist who was the president of Sloan-Kettering Memorial Hospital. He recommended treatment to extend her life in case a medical advancement occurred in the field of childhood leukaemia. Brave Robin lasted for seven months of painful bone-marrow transplants and blood transfusions. She died with her parents present. Her body was donated for research. The shock turned twenty-eight-year-old Barbara's hair grey. In the following years, Barbara gave birth to three more children.

In 1954, Bush was named president of the Zapata Offshore Company, a subsidiary that specialised in offshore drilling. Big oil companies hired its services. The CIA used it as a front for some of its activity and money laundering. This fledgling relationship with the CIA would lead to Bush getting to know and employing the services of Barry Seal.

CHAPTER 40

JFK Assassination

High-profile people in power require others to do their dirty work. George HW Bush had at his disposal a stable of CIA good ol' boys, including Barry Seal. Bush was working for the CIA at least as early as 1961, but many researchers believe that he was recruited in his Yale days when he was in Skull and Bones.

The Bush family's relationship with the CIA goes back to its first director, Allen Dulles, a lawyer who helped facilitate the laundering of Nazi money with Prescott Bush. Allen Dulles was the CIA director fired by JFK, whom LBJ put in charge of the Warren Commission investigating JFK's assassination. Allen's brother, John Foster Dulles, was Prescott Bush's lawyer during the Nazi days.

Throughout the Eisenhower presidency, 1953-61, Prescott was a confidential ally of the Dulles Brothers. They concocted schemes to overthrow foreign governments by any means possible in order to further their business interests, which included the United Fruit Company.

In 1954, they toppled the democratically elected president of Guatemala, who'd come to power by offering land reform – detailed in Chapter 3. Under the guise of fighting Communism, the CIA removed the president and installed a ruthless dictator.

The CIA tried to oust the leader of Cuba, Fidel Castro, in numerous ways – detailed in Chapter 3 – including using George HW Bush's company, Zapata, whose Scorpion platform fifty miles away from Cuba provided an ideal training post for anti-Castro Cubans. According to the book *Prelude to Terror* by Joseph Trento, Bush was given a list of names of Cuban oil workers that the CIA wanted placed in jobs. CIA money and payments were filtered through Zapata, according to John Sherwood, ex-chief of CIA anti-Castro operations. "We had to pay off politicians in Mexico, Guatemala, Costa Rica and elsewhere… Bush's company was used as a conduit for these funds under the guise of oil-business contracts."

Bush was a major organiser and recruiter for the Bay of Pigs invasion, codenamed Operation ZAPATA. Colonel Fletcher Prouty – a former Pentagon high ranking official who was the basis for the Colonel X character in Oliver Stone's *JFK* – obtained two Navy ships for the operation that were repainted to non-Navy colours and renamed HOUSTON and BARBARA. Zapata's worldwide oil rigs enabled Bush to vanish for weeks at a time on CIA business.

Anyone getting in the way of the Bush clique tended to end up dead. Prime targets were foreign leaders and even domestic ones such as JFK.

A few hours after JFK's assassination, George HW Bush called the Houston FBI field office, identified himself and claimed that his location was Tyler, Texas. He reported that James Milton Parrot, a young Republican, had talked about killing JFK. An FBI memo declassified in 1993 stated:

Mr George H W Bush, President of Zapata Offshore Drilling Company, Houston, Texas, residence 5525 Briar, Houston, telephonically furnished the following information to writer by long-distance telephone call from Tyler, Texas. Bush stated that he wanted to be kept confidential but wanted to furnish hearsay that he recalled hearing in recent weeks, the day and source unknown. He stated that one James Parrott has been talking of killing the president when he comes to Houston. Bush stated that Parrot is possibly a student at University of Houston and is active in political matters in this area. He stated that he felt Mrs Fawley, telephone number SU2-5239, or Arline Smith, telephone number JA9-9194 of the Harris County Republican Party Headquarters would be able to furnish additional information regarding the identity of Parrott. Bush stated that he was proceeding to Dallas, Texas, would remain in the Sheraton-Dallas-Hotel and returned his residence on 11-23-63. His office telephone number is CA2-0395.

Following up on the lead, FBI agents went to the house of Parrott, an unemployed twenty-four-year-old Air Force veteran who'd been honourably discharged. His mother said he wasn't home and provided an alibi. "She advised that James Parrott had been home all day helping her care for her son Gary Wayne Parrott whom they brought home from the hospital yesterday... Mrs Parrott advised that shortly after 1 pm a Mr Reynolds came by their home to advise them of the death of President Kennedy, and talked to her son James Parrott about painting some signs at Republican Headquarters on Waugh Drive."

Upon further questioning, both Reynolds and Parrott claimed that Reynolds had visited between 1:30 and 1:45 pm. But decades later in 2007, Reynolds told an interviewer that he had not gone to Parrott's house that day. He said he'd been asked to accompany Parrott to the local Secret Service office. The encounter was documented as follows:

There was a young man who came around headquarters... and somebody said that he had made a threat against Kennedy and this was, I believe, this came up after the assassination... The end result was, it was suggested I contact the Secret Service, the local Secret Service, and I accompanied this young man... And we went down, and this was kind of a strange kid, mild-mannered, quiet kind of, seemed to be living in another world, and I took him down one day, escorted him down there.

When the FBI showed up to question him, Parrott was painting "Bush for Senate?" signs. Parrott admitted picketing members of

JFK's administration. He denied threatening the president. As a member of the right-wing John Birch Society, he'd opposed Bush during Bush's campaign for GOP chairman of Harris County. The FBI decided that Parrott hadn't been involved in a conspiracy to kill JFK. So why had Bush sent them on a wild-goose chase?

Bush's call to the FBI had placed him in Tyler, Texas, approximately 100 miles away from the JFK assassination crime scene in Dallas. One theory is that Bush had dropped Parrott's name to the FBI as payback. Another theory is that Bush was joining in the hunt for the killer to camouflage his own role in the conspiracy. To camouflage their activity, killers sometimes join in the search party for their own victims or other false suspects. Bush may have been attempting a more sophisticated form of that strategy.

Two decades later, during Bush's 1988 presidential campaign, Parrott emerged as a volunteer for Bush, lending weight to the theory that Parrott was acting as a fall guy, enabling Bush to establish his Tyler, Texas location.

So what were Bush's actual movements around the time of JFK's assassination? Bush had booked two nights at the Dallas Sheraton: November 21 and 22. He and his wife spent November 21 in Dallas and took a private plane to Tyler, where Bush was scheduled to speak at a Kiwanis Club luncheon.

Aubrey Irby, the vice president of the Kiwanis Club (and later president of Kiwanis International during Bush's vice presidency) told author Kitty Kelley her version of the events on November 22. In *The Family: The Real Story of the Bush Dynasty*, Kitty Kelley wrote that Bush had started to deliver a speech to a hundred men gathered at Tyler's Blackstone Hotel. The head bellhop tapped Aubrey on the shoulder and said that JFK had been shot. Aubrey told the club president, who leaned over and told Bush.

After halting his speech, Bush said, "In view of the President's death, I consider it inappropriate to continue with a political speech at this time. Thank you very much for your attention." Bush sat down. Aubrey considered Bush's behaviour magnanimous. Recounting the tale in 2007, Aubrey described Bush as having been matter-of-fact and supremely well composed.

In her 1994 memoir, Barbara Bush published a letter that she had purportedly written on the day of JFK's assassination:

Dearest Family, Wednesday I took Doris Ulmer out for lunch. They [Al and Doris Ulmer] were here from England and they had been so nice to George in Greece. That night we went to ...

I am writing this at the Beauty Parlor, and the radio says that the President has been shot. Oh Texas – my Texas – my God – let's hope it's not true. I am sick at heart as we all are. Yes, the story is true and the Governor also. How hateful some people are.

Since the Beauty Parlor the President has died. We are once again on a plane. This time a commercial plane. Poppy [Bush] picked me up at the beauty parlor – we went right to the airport, flew to Ft. Worth and dropped Mr. Zeppo off (we were on his plane) and flew back to Dallas. We had to circle the field while the second presidential plane took off. Immediately Pop got tickets back to Houston and here we are flying home. We are sick at heart. The tales the radio reporters tell of Jackie Kennedy are the bravest I've ever heard. The rumors are flying about that horrid assassin. We are hoping that it is not some far right nut, but a "commie" nut. You understand that we know they are both nuts, but just hope that it is not a Texan and not an American at all.

I am amazed at the rapid-fire thinking and planning that has already been done. LBJ has been the president for some time now – two hours at least and it is only 4:30.

My dearest love to you all,

Bar

According to Russ Baker, who wrote *Family of Secrets: The Bush Dynasty, America's Invisible Government and the Hidden History of the Last Fifty Years*, the first and only Bush family acknowledgment of where Bush was on that day came in a classic form: from the wife in the most innocuous swathing. That it didn't surface until 1994 is also peculiar. To whom the letter was mailed is unknown or whether an original exists or how it was unearthed thirty years after JFK's assassination. She wrote "Dear family," but all of her children were ten years old or younger, and why would she mail them a letter if she were flying home and probably would have been home before the letter arrived? Was she sending it to her parents? Unlikely, because her mother was dead. Her father had remarried, but Barbara Bush wasn't known to be particular close to them. She hadn't attended her mother's funeral. Although the letter has details, it didn't document Bush's call to the FBI about the potential assassin James Parrott. The letter did achieve one thing: it recorded that they were in Tyler, Texas during the assassination.

According to Roger Stone in *Jeb! and the Bush Crime Family*, Bush was in Dallas on the evening of November 21, attending an oil contractors' association meeting.

In 1976, Bush, now the director of the CIA, received a letter asking for help, which casts even more suspicion on Bush and his knowledge of the JFK assassination:

Maybe you will be able to bring a solution into the hopeless situation I find myself in. My wife and I find ourselves surrounded by some vigilantes; our phone bugged; and we are being followed everywhere. Either FBI is involved in this or they do not want to accept my complaints. We are driven to insanity by this situation . . . tried to write, stupidly and unsuccessfully, about Lee H. Oswald and must have angered a lot of people . . . Could you do something to remove this net around us? This will be my last request for help and I will not annoy you anymore.

G. de Mohrenschildt.

The staff at the CIA asked Bush if he knew G. de Mohrenschildt. Bush responded in a memo to the staff:

I do know this man De Mohrenschildt. I first men [sic] him in the early 40'3 [sic]. He was an uncle to my Andover roommate.

Later he surfaced in Dallas (50's maybe) . . . Then he surfaced when Oswald shot to prominence. He knew Oswald before the assassination of Pres. Kennedy. I don't recall his role in all this.

By not recalling, Bush was downplaying the extent of his relationship with de Mohrenschildt, who came from Russian nobility. His family had made a fortune from oil. Working for the czar, his father had been the governor of Minsk. His uncle and father had run the Swedish Nobel Brothers Oil Company in Baku, Russian Azerbaijan on the southwestern coast of the Caspian Sea, where, during World War I, Prescott Bush and his associates had provided the technology for the oil that had enabled the Soviets to attack Poland from the East. Back then, Baku hosted half of the world's known oil reserves and major players such as the Rockefellers were trying to get in on the action.

Born in 1911, George de Mohrenschildt had moved to the US and worked for Humble Oil, a company co-founded by Prescott Bush. By 1952, he was living in Dallas and a member of the Dallas Petroleum Club. He regularly attended the Dallas Council on World Affairs, which Bush's friend Neil Mallon started in 1951. He helped expand American oil interests in Cuba and other locations of interest to the CIA. He had a knack of taking business trips to locations where a political event or upheaval significant to the CIA was imminent. In 1961, as exiled Cubans and their CIA support team prepared for the Bay of Pigs invasion in Guatemala, de Mohrenschildt and his wife passed through Guatemala City on a month-long walking tour of the Central American isthmus. Another time, they appeared in Mexico just as a Soviet leader arrived on oil business and they just happened to have a meeting. Another time, they were in Haiti shortly before an unsuccessful coup was launched against its president.

According to the author Edward Jay Epstein, in 1961, the Dallas CIA told de Mohrenschildt that Lee Harvey Oswald was living in Minsk, a Russian city. He was asked to get information about Oswald and in return the CIA would help him with an oil deal in Haiti. In the summer of 1962, when Oswald was back in Texas, de Mohrenschildt started to become close to Oswald and eventually became his mentor. He helped Oswald find jobs and apartments, took him to meetings and social gatherings, and assisted him and his Russian wife, Marina, and their baby in various other ways. He provided information to the CIA about Oswald and in March 1963, his Haitian oil deal went through.

In 1964, de Mohrenschildt and his wife testified to the Warren Commission, which spent more time with them than any other witness except for Oswald's widow. The Warren Commission helped portray de Mohrenschildt as an eccentric, while steering him away from naming his powerful friends and associates. One relationship he never disclosed to the Warren Commission was that with Bush. The Warren Commission concluded that de Mohrenschildt's relationships were all coincidences that had nothing to do with the assassination.

Bush replied to de Mohrenschildt:

Let me say first that I know it must have been difficult for you to seek my help in the situation outlined in your letter. I believe I can appreciate your state of mind in view of your daughter's tragic death a few years ago, and the current poor state of your wife's health. I was extremely sorry to hear of these circumstances. In your situation I can well imagine how the attentions you described in your letter affect both you and your wife. However, my staff has been unable to find any indication of interest in your activities on the part of Federal authorities in recent years. The flurry of interest that attended your testimony before the Warren Commission has long subsided. I can only speculate that you may have become "newsworthy" again in view of the renewed interest in the Kennedy assassination, and thus may be attracting the attention of people in the media. I hope this letter has been of some comfort to you, George, although I realize I am unable to answer your question completely.

On March 29, 1977 – months after Bush wrote his response – de Mohrenschildt visited his daughter at a family friend's house in

Manalapan, Florida, between West Palm Beach and Boca Raton. While in Manalapan, he was interviewed by Edward Jay Epstein for a feature story in *Reader's Digest.* The House Select Committee on Assassinations (HSCA) investigator, Gaeton Fonzi, showed up at Manalapan while George was out doing the interview. Fonzi was an investigative reporter from Philadelphia hired by the HSCA. He left his business card with de Mohrenschildt's daughter.

When de Mohrenschildt arrived home for lunch, his daughter told him in Spanish that Fonzi had visited and to not tell the maid and gardener. She gave him the card and went shopping. Later that afternoon, de Mohrenschildt's corpse was found in his upstairs bedroom with a self-inflicted gunshot wound. No one heard the gun go off. There was no suicide note. The next day, he was supposed to have testified before the House Select Committee on Assassinations. After his death was ruled a suicide, he was cremated within a week. Among his personal belongings, in an address book, was an old listing for George H W Bush at 1412 W. Ohio; also Zapata Petroleum Midland.

Just like Barry Seal, he died in possession of Bush's contact details.

Another JFK assassination connection is John Crichton, a former intelligence operative, and later, an oil-company investor, who became friends with Bush in 1964. According to Fabian Escalante, a former chief of Cuban counterintelligence turned author, Vice President Nixon had paired Bush and Crichton to raise funds for Operation Forty, a Bay of Pigs CIA assassination squad. Crichton rubbed shoulders with the elites of Texas and had worked during his military days with many of the Dallas police. His directorships included Dorchester Gas Producing Company, whose other director D H Byrd owned the Texas School Book Depository Building that Oswald had just coincidentally started to work at two weeks before JFK drove by.

Crichton was involved with JFK's Texas travel arrangements. The driver of the pilot car in Kennedy's motorcade was Deputy Police Chief George Lumpkin, who'd worked under Crichton in the Dallas Army Intelligence unit. Crichton provided the interpreter for Oswald's wife, Marina. According to author Russ Baker in *Family of Secrets*, Marina's words were mistranslated to implicate Oswald. The Warren Commission never asked Crichton to testify. In 2007, Crichton died. The George Bush presidential library holds his papers, which are all sealed.

Not only was he evasive when asked about his relationships with people such as de Mohrenschildt, but when Bush was president he claimed that he had never asked for any CIA files on the JFK assassination. Under the Freedom of Information Act, it was revealed he had submitted numerous requests for such files – when he was CIA director – as if trying to gather a range of information.

On September 9, 1976, he asked whether Lyndon Johnson had been told by a former CIA director that Cubans were involved in the assassination. On September 15, 1976, Bush asked his deputy director to look into reports that linked Jack Ruby with the Mafia boss Santos Trafficante Jr. Bush wrote, "A recent Jack Anderson story referred to a CIA cable, the subject matter of which had some UK journalist observing Jack Ruby visiting Trafficante in jail (in Cuba). Is there such a cable? If so, I would like to see it."

Bush was close to the former CIA head, Allen Dulles, who had a grudge against JFK, as well as being tight with the Texas elites heavily invested in oil and weapons manufacturing, with close ties to intelligence operations that had used assassination teams in attempts to overthrow foreign governments. Bush was in Dallas on November 21, and maybe even on the morning of November 22, yet since then, he has claimed that he can't remember where he was on those dates. He created a record of being in Tyler, Texas by sending the FBI on a wild goose chase after James Parrott, and through his wife's letter that materialised decades later. Lastly, JFK's attitude towards the war and the CIA stood in the way of the pattern of profiteering dating back to Prescott and the Nazis that multiplied the wealth of the Bush dynasty and from which they continue to profit to this day.

It seems that Bush at the very least had insider knowledge of the JFK assassination or at the most was a co-conspirator. Anyone who'd go so far as to conspire to kill a president would easily order the assassination of Barry Seal.

CHAPTER 41

CIA Director

After CIA Director William Colby spoke too honestly with congressional investigations, a decision was made to get rid of him. Colby made the mistake of putting the American Constitution before the CIA. He believed the CIA had a moral and legal obligation to cooperate with Congress. Colby's natural replacement was someone esteemed for subterfuge: George HW Bush.

Bush wanted to become the Vice President – a title he considered his birth-right – which a CIA directorship would have precluded. On December 18, 1975, President Ford told Bush that he'd been ruled out of the candidacy for Vice President, and that Ford had written a letter stating such to the committee chairman. Bush convinced Ford to alter the letter to make it appear as if Bush had withdrawn from the candidacy.

The amended letter stated, "He [Bush] and I have discussed this in detail. In fact, he urged that I make this decision. This says something about the man and about his desire to do this job [CIA director] for the nation…"

The next day, Bush was approved for the CIA directorship. He was sworn in on January 30, 1976.

Frank Church, whose committee was investigating CIA assassinations, commented on Bush's appointment, "There is no question in my mind but that concealment is the new order of the day."

Lucien Nedzi, a Democratic congressman in Michigan, wrote to President Ford, "The director of CIA must be unfettered by any doubts as to his politics. He must be free of the appearance, as well as the substance, that he is acting, or not acting, with partisan political considerations in mind... Accordingly, I respectfully urge that you reconsider your appointment of Mr Bush to this most sensitive of positions."

Richard Nixon wrote to Bush: "You will be tempted greatly to give away the store in assuring the members of the Senate Committee that everything the CIA does in the future will be an open book. I think you will be far better off to stand up and strongly defend the CIA and the need to maintain, particularly, its covert activities."

Bush replied: "I couldn't agree more. We must not see the Agency compromised further by reckless disclosures."

The Church Committee was investigating how the CIA had used the media to manipulate the public. Senators requested the names of journalists on the CIA payroll. On February 12, 1976, Bush stated that he would remove from the CIA payroll all "full-time or part-time news correspondents, accredited by any US News service, newspaper, periodicals, radio or TV network station."

In April, the Senate Select Committee on Intelligence Activities found there were at least twenty-five journalists and reporters still on the CIA payroll. When called to account over his earlier statement, Bush responded that he'd only referred to correspondents accredited by US News services. This excluded a large number of freelance reporters, editors, news executives and foreign news organisations still on the CIA payroll.

Two senators drove to the CIA headquarters in Virginia and demanded Bush release the names of the journalists still on the CIA payroll. Bush responded that the CIA was "not at liberty to reveal the names."

On February 18, 1976, the *New York Times* reported that, "Bush now had more power than any other director of Central Intelligence since its creation."

Bush approved Executive Order 11905, authorising the CIA to conduct foreign counterintelligence activities in the US. He obtained money from Saudi Arabia for covert operations that

Congress had refused to finance. He oversaw a CIA plot that cost $10 million to overthrow the government of Jamaica, which included illegal arms shipments, inciting violent demonstrations and three assassination attempts on Prime Minister Michael Manley. Even the reggae-singer Bob Marley got caught up in the violence on December 3, 1976, when three men entered his house and shot him.

With Bush at the helm, CIA-backed operations against Cuba included supporting a Cuban exile terrorist group called CORU, which blew up Cubana de Aviación Flight 455 on October 6, 1976. After taking off from Barbados, a bomb exploded, killing all seventy-three people on-board, including the Cuban Olympic fencing team. Not quite as many as the 110 deaths due to the bomb aboard Avianca Airlines Flight 203 credited to Pablo, but Bush would far outshine Pablo in other murder methods, especially war.

For years, the CIA planned terrorist attacks in order to blame them on Cuba by manufacturing evidence. A US army memorandum dated March 1962 called *Possible Actions to Provoke, Harass or Disrupt Cuba*, included "downing a US plane and blaming it on Mr Castro," or demonstrating "convincingly that a Cuban aircraft has shot down a chartered civilian airliner." Sinking a warship "could be blamed on Cuba." Cuban exile terrorists could be used by the CIA to fly by the island to "distract local pilots with radio conversations with the aim of causing the crash." Another plan was to "sink a boatload of Cubans en route for Florida."

General Noriega accused CIA director Bush of sanctioning a bomb in Panama that destroyed a car owned by William Drummond, a prominent US resident of the American occupied Canal Zone. Drummond had been criticising the negotiations between the US and Panama. The CIA allegedly arranged the blast to pressurise US residents to end their resistance to the treaty.

"The US embassy in Panama didn't known about Bush's scheme and got nervous," Noriega said, "so Bush had to calm the embassy down: he created a problem to solve a problem." Noriega described Bush as "a cold-blooded killer."

After Jimmy Carter was elected in 1976, Bush asked to stay on as CIA director, but Carter replaced him.

CHAPTER 42

Vice President

Aiming to become the president, George HW Bush further ingratiated himself with the most powerful and wealthy entities: the banks, oil companies, pharmaceutical companies, intelligence community… He announced his candidacy on May 1, 1979.

He didn't consider his almost seventy-year-old opponent, Ronald Reagan, much of a threat. The two contenders had roughly equal support until Bush revealed his true colours at a debate. Originally, the debate was only supposed to include Reagan and Bush. With Bush refusing to contribute, Reagan ended up paying the costs of the debate. Having spent $3,500, Reagan decided to open the debate up to four more candidates.

Disgruntled by Reagan's initiative, Bush sat at the edge of the stage, refusing to talk to the other candidates. Attempting to get Bush to talk, a senator said, "If you don't come now, you'll be doing a disservice to party unity."

Bush replied, "Don't tell me about unifying the Republican Party. I've done more for this party than you'll ever do." He continued to rebuff the other candidates.

The audience yelled for all of the candidates to get the debate started. On the microphone, Reagan urged the same.

"Turn Mr Reagan's microphone off," a newspaper editor yelled.

"I'm paying for that microphone, Mr Green," Reagan said.

The audience applauded wildly, while Bush, according to William Loeb, "looked like a small boy who had been delivered to the wrong birthday party." Confronted with Reagan's action, Bush appeared weak.

By May 1980, Reagan had twenty-nine states and Bush only

four, so he quit the race and handed his support to Reagan, convinced that Reagan would make him the vice president. Having being passed over for the vice presidency by Nixon once and twice by Ford, Bush figured that his birth-right was overdue. But instead, Reagan wanted Ford for vice president. Reagan and his wife, Nancy, disliked Bush.

"Why can't I pick someone I like?" Reagan told his aides. "I'm wary of a man who freezes under pressure. George froze that night. That haunts me."

After Ford declined the vice presidency, Reagan called Bush. "George, it seems to me that," Reagan said, grimacing, "the fellow who came the closest and got the most votes for president ought to be the logical choice for vice president. Will you take it?"

Reagan later wrote in his memoir, "He [Bush] didn't have a moment's hesitation."

When Reagan made the official announcement of Bush as vice president, everyone cheered, except for his wife, Nancy, who was standing next to him at the lectern.

After the media questioned Bush about his political differences with Reagan, he promptly changed his stance on abortion, the Equal Rights Amendment, school bussing and school prayer – as if to prove that he had a soul.

To help oust President Carter at the November election, the Reagan-Bush camp made a secret deal with Iran, whereby Iran agreed not to release fifty-two American hostages being held at the US embassy since November 4, 1979. In the media, Bush railed against the lingering hostage crisis. As Carter had been promising their release by the election, his credibility was damaged when the hostages weren't freed. FBI and CIA documents released under the Freedom of Information Act showed that Bush played a major role in an arms deal worth $150 million. In return for not releasing the hostages, weapons were shipped to Iran illegally via Israel.

Reagan won the election. In his first inaugural address on January 20, 1981, he addressed the recession: "In this present crisis, government is not the solution to our problems; government is the problem."

However well-intentioned, Reagan was showing signs of fatigue. He napped for several hours a day and left matters of policy and control to Bush, who had planted numerous loyalists in the administration, many from the CIA. His CIA associates believed that if Bush were the president things would run more smoothly for them, but they knew that Bush only had a slim chance of becoming the president from the position of vice president.

Bush schemed to put Reagan's power in his own hands. An order was presented to Reagan for signing, which granted Bush powers over crisis management. Many of Reagan's advisers were opposed to the order, including Secretary of State Alexander Haig. Nevertheless, on March 25, 1981, Bush was named the leader of the US crisis management staff as part of the National Security Council system. It didn't take long for a crisis to occur.

On March 30, 1981, Ronald Reagan exited the Hilton Hotel in Washington DC, surrounded by Secret Service agents in grey suits and an outer circle of police in dark uniforms. People on the pavement yelled greetings at the president, who smiled and waved. When he was almost at his limo, a noise erupted that Reagan thought was firecrackers. Two people fell wounded to the ground. Others instinctively crouched.

A Secret Serviceman grabbed Reagan by the waist and threw him headfirst into the limo. Reagan landed on the seat. The Serviceman dived on top of him. Police and Secret Servicemen piled onto John Hinckley Jr, a twenty-two-year-old holding a .22 revolver.

As his limo took off for the White House, Reagan felt a pain in his chest. He told the Secret Serviceman on top of him to get up as he suspected he'd broken a rib. When the Serviceman moved, Reagan coughed bright-red frothy blood onto his hand.

"I guess the broken rib has pierced the lung." Reagan coughed blood into a handkerchief. The limo headed for George

Washington Hospital. With his handkerchief soaked red, he used the Secret Serviceman's handkerchief, which quickly filled with blood.

At the hospital's emergency entrance, Reagan got out of the limo and walked in. "I'm having a little trouble breathing," he said to a nurse. His knees went out. He collapsed. They put him on a trolley and used scissors to cut his new suit off him.

Reagan prayed.

A bullet had entered Reagan's side, pierced his lung and was lodged near to his heart. He'd been hit while diving into the limo. The bullet had hit a rib, causing extreme pain. It had tumbled and stopped one inch away from his heart. He lost almost half of the blood in his body. The medical staff thought that he wasn't going to make it.

When informed about the shooter Hinckley, and Hinckley's mental condition, Reagan added Hinckley to his prayers.

As with the JFK assassination, all of the shots were immediately credited to a lone gunman, even though people reported shots coming from a position above and to the right of Hinckley. NBC correspondent Judy Woodruff said that at least one shot had been fired from an overhang above Reagan's limo. Most of the photos and footage of the shooting have disappeared, however one photo does show what appears to be a sniper on the balcony above and behind Reagan.

At the time of the assassination attempt, Bush had been at the Hyatt Regency in Fort Worth, delivering a plaque as part of the designation of a national historic site. After Secretary of State Alexander Haig informed the vice president about the assassination attempt, Bush flew to Washington to take control of the government.

In the Situation Room, Bush asked for a condition report on the president, any others wounded, the assailant and the international scene. The reports were handed over. Immediately, Bush announced that there had been no conspiracy. Just five hours after the attempt on Reagan, on the basis of fragmentary early reports, before the suspect had been properly questioned and before a full investigation had been carried out, Bush had declared that it was all the work of a lone gunman.

But the JFK-style assassination attempt failed by Reagan surviving.

Bush desperately didn't want anyone to know about his family's ten-year relationship with the Hinckley family.

On March 31 and April 1, 1981, newspapers started reporting that Bush's son, Neil Bush, had been scheduled to dine with Scott Hinckley, the brother of the lone gunman, at Neil's home on the day after the assassination attempt.

The *Houston Post* reported that Neil Bush "knew the Hinckley family because they had made large contributions to the Vice President's campaign." Neil said he "could not recall meeting John Hinckley Jr." Neil's wife Sharon said that the Hinckleys "are a nice family… and have given a lot of money to the Bush campaign."

The next day, Neil Bush hosted a press conference to correct inaccuracies reported in the *Houston Post* article. He claimed that the 1980 campaign records showed no contributions from the Hinckleys. The scheduled dinner with Scott Hinckley was downgraded to a dinner with a close female friend to whom Hinckley was only attending as a companion. Neil added that he'd only met Scott Hinckley once at a surprise party in 1981.

According to Charles Overbeck in his essay "Reagan, Hinckley, and the Bushy Knoll Conspiracy," the Hinckleys had been contributing to Bush as far back as 1970. John Hinckley Sr had raised money for Bush's campaign to get the presidential nomination from Reagan.

According to the author Barbara Honegger, the Secret Service had been warned about Hinckley's designs on Reagan two months before the shooting. In October 1980, Hinckley had flown to Nebraska to meet an American neo-Nazi and flown to Nashville to stalk President Carter, but was arrested at the airport with three handguns in his suitcase. He only spent five hours in custody. Mentally-unstable Hinckley had attempted to transport weapons over state lines and into a city visited by the president, yet had been released with a fine.

Just as LBJ stood to gain the most from the assassination of JFK, Bush stood to gain the most from the death of Ronald Reagan.

Following the shooting, Bush continued to expand his power. On May 14, 1982, a secret memorandum signed by Reagan formalised Bush as chief of all covert action and made him the de facto head of US intelligence. According to the memo, "National Security Decision Directive 3, Crisis Management, establishes the Special Situation Group (SSG), chaired by the Vice President. The SSG is charged… with formulating plans in anticipation of crises."

The memo also introduced the Standing Crisis Pre-Planning Group (CPPG), which funnelled intelligence to Bush and the SSG. Its members included representatives of Bush, the National Security Council (NSC), the CIA, the military and the State Department. It was to "meet periodically in the White House Situation Room." Its objective was to identify potential crises and present plans and policy options to resolve crises to the SSG under Chairman Bush. It was also to give Bush and his associates "recommended security, cover, and media plans that will enhance the likelihood of successful execution." CPPG members' names were to be provided to Oliver North, who operated as the middleman for Bush and Barry Seal.

In August 1982, Bush hired Donald Gregg and Felix Rodriguez from the CIA – both familiar faces to Barry Seal. When Bush had been the CIA director from 1976 onwards, Greg had worked under him. Another Bush loyalist, Rodriguez had been a CIA assassinations manager. Rodriguez operated out of the vice president's office.

The group Bush assembled included several of the co-conspirators in the death of Barry Seal.

CHAPTER 43

Gulf War

On the back of his campaign promise, "Read my lips. No new taxes," George HW Bush was elected president in November 1988. Within two years, he broke the promise. His popularity waned so much that at the mid-term elections the Republicans lost nine seats.

Prime Minister Margaret Thatcher reminded Bush that nothing works as well as war to boost ratings. According to Kitty Kelley, Thatcher told Bush that her popularity surged thanks to the invasion of the Falklands Islands in 1982. "I stayed in office for eight years after that,"Thatcher said.

War would enable Bush to achieve the two things dearest to him: increase his approval rating and the profits of the companies run by his family and their associates, especially in the military and oil sectors.

In mid-1990, Saddam Hussein – a CIA-installed leader and a US ally – was amassing troops on Iraq's border with Kuwait, waiting for the green light from Bush to launch an invasion. On July 24, 1990, the State Department emphasised that the US had no commitment to defend Kuwait. On July 25, 1990, Saddam Hussein was told by Ambassador April Glaspie, acting on behalf of Bush, "We have no opinion on the Arab-Arab conflict like your border disagreement with Kuwait... I have direct instructions from the president to seek better relations with Iraq."

By July, 1990, Iraq had 100,000 troops on Kuwait's border. On August 2, Iraq invaded Kuwait with Bush's tacit approval.

The invasion couldn't have come at a better time for Bush. He just needed to stir things up a little more before he could take any action. In August, Bush told the Saudi ambassador, Prince Bandar, that he had satellite photos provided by the Pentagon showing Iraqi troops gathering on the Saudi border. Deceived by the fake photos, the Saudis permitted US troops on their soil, which was viewed by many in the Islamic world as infidels defiling holy territory. The Saudis also poured billions into the war effort.

The CIA-controlled media followed suit, drumming up hysteria against Saddam Hussein. Televised speaking to Congress, an innocent-looking fifteen-year-old Kuwaiti sobbed as she described witnessing Saddam Hussein's soldiers snatching babies from their incubators in a hospital in Kuwait City and tossing them on the floor to die. She was known only by Nayirah as her full name had to be kept confidential to prevent reprisals against her family in occupied Kuwait. Her testimony was circulated in a media kit prepared by Citizens for a Free Kuwait. It made headlines worldwide. In November, Bush repeated the story to US troops to motivate them to slaughter Iraqis. The PR exercise was highly successful. The sobbing teenager hadn't even been in Kuwait at the time of the invasion. She was the daughter of the Kuwaiti ambassador in Washington. The firm Hill and Knowlton had coached her on what to say.

The University of Massachusetts conducted research useful to Bush. They surveyed public opinion and correlated it with the public's knowledge of the basic facts about US policy in the Middle East. They concluded that the more television people watched, the fewer facts they knew. The less people knew in terms of facts, the more likely they were to back the Bush administration. Dee Alsop of the Within Group bragged that his job was to "identify the messages that really resonate emotionally with the American people." Alsop found the biggest emotional reaction came from emphasising "the fact that Saddam Hussein was a madman who had committed atrocities even against his own people and had tremendous power to do further damage and he needed to be stopped." Alsop even used audience surveys to adapt the clothing and hairstyle of the Kuwait ambassador, so he'd be more likeable to TV viewers.

The Gulf War began with an extensive bombing campaign on 17 January, 1991. The Coalition flew over 100,000 sorties and dropped 88,500 tons of bombs, far exceeding Pablo's bombing capabilities. News stations such as CNN showed the precision bombing of military infrastructure, while dismissing civilian casualties as collateral damage. An investigation by Beth Osborne Daponte estimated total civilian fatalities at about 3,500 from bombing and 100,000 from the war's other effects.

The US claimed that only 148 troops were killed in action, but a multiple of that died slowly and agonisingly from a group of mysterious illnesses that has become known as Gulf War Syndrome. One of those affected was Joyce Riley – the spokesperson for the American Veterans Gulf War Association – who has campaigned tirelessly on the issue.

Joyce Riley came from a military family. Her father had been a belly gunner on a B-17. Every night before she went to bed, he played the US Air Force song:

Off we go into the wild blue yonder,
Climbing high into the sun
Here they come zooming to meet our thunder
At 'em boys, Give 'er the gun!
Down we dive, spouting our flame from under
Off with one helluva roar!
We live in fame or go down in flame. Hey!
Nothing can stop the US Air Force!

Wanting to improve the world by helping the sick, Joyce studied nursing at the University of Kansas and graduated with a Bachelor of Science. As a director of nursing in four institutions, she specialised in medical surgical nursing and organ transplantation. She assisted in heart, lung, liver and kidney transplants and helped cancer patients. She flew around the US transporting organs to operating rooms.

By 1990, the year of Bush's Gulf War, Joyce was in the military serving as a flight nurse, but she wasn't dispatched to the Middle East. In one day, she received ten injections and wrote in her journal, "I would have taken a hundred shots today just to save my country." She knew about people passing out receiving shots, but she didn't know what it meant.

Six months after the vaccinations, Joyce became so ill that she could barely walk or function. After the Gulf War ended in February 1991, Joyce was hospitalised in Houston and told that she had an illness like MS. As she hadn't been deployed to the Middle East and therefore hadn't been exposed to oil-well fires or chemical or biological weapons, she suspected that her illness might be related to the vaccines. She decided never to take a vaccine again as long as she lived or to give any vaccines.

Within six months of taking their vaccines, other nurses became sick. When Joyce told her superiors, she was told she had a mental problem. "There are so many of us who are sick here," Joyce said. "So many! What are we gonna do?"

"They're not sick," said Colonel Mountain, the commander of the unit. "You're not sick. Nobody's sick."

Joyce and the sick nurses went to the US Department of Veterans Affairs (VA). The VA told them that because they were in the reserves, they were ineligible for treatment. Joyce was shocked, not because of the lack of treatment, but because she wanted to find out why they were all sick.

Further research led her to discover that the Reagan-Bush administration had sold chemical and biological weapons worth billions to Iraq before the Gulf War. Aware that Saddam Hussein had repeatedly used chemical weapons on Iranian soldiers and Iraq's Kurdish minority, the Reagan-Bush administration helped Iraq develop its chemical, biological and nuclear weapons programs. Joyce even obtained the batch numbers and dates that the weapons were sold. With billions from oil revenues and loans from its Arab neighbors, Iraq became one of the biggest arms importers in the world. Countries competed to sell arms to

Saddam Hussain as he built a million-man army and spent over $50 billion on military hardware.

By attacking Iraq, a country that Bush had helped to arm – a manoeuvre that probably made Prescott Bush smirk in his grave – US weapons manufacturers reaped billions of dollars from US taxpayers and money staked by Saudi Arabia and Kuwait. Destabilising the Middle East made the price of a barrel of oil soar from $15 to $42, generating billions in revenue for the multinational oil companies controlling the oilfields in which the Bush family and their associates held investments.

Joyce also discovered that huge profits were being made from the Gulf War by pharmaceutical companies – another fertile area of Bush family investments and directorships. She found out about secret vaccine trials undertaken by the Tri-Service Vaccine Task Force, and that the Bush government was doing experiments with the same chemical and biological weapons they'd sold to Iraq in order to develop a vaccine that would be effective against what they knew the troops would be exposed to.

Joyce believes that anthrax, hepatitis B and experimental vaccines made numerous soldiers sick, a situation that was exacerbated in cases were the shots had been administered on the same day. The military introduced a new policy. You could get compensation for MS if you reported it within one year of leaving the military. MS is rarely seen in the male population from seventeen to twenty, but numerous Gulf War veterans in that age bracket started to have symptoms of a demyelinating disease – a disease in which the myelin sheath comes off the nerve ending and it misfires horribly. It's like having a seizure where you're awake and alert, but your body can't stop doing the things it's doing.

Joyce took all of the documents to her attorney and spread them out on a big table.

Examining the documents, he turned pale. "I'm no longer your attorney. I will not watch after you. I cannot do anything for you. I couldn't handle the tax audit that I'd get if I helped you." She never saw him again.

Joyce travelled across the country speaking at veterans' groups such as the American Legions and the Veterans of Foreign Wars. Her tour infuriated Bush's Department of Defense. The commander of the American Legion in Washington DC issued a memo banning Joyce from any American Legion venue on the grounds that she was falsely trying to make veterans think that they were sick. They ejected her from their facilities. Other organisations tried to destroy her credibility. She had a sign on her car: American Veterans Gulf War Association. She got stopped by the police so much that she had to remove the sign.

In one state, a highway-patrol pulled her over.

"What's wrong, officer?" she said.

"Ma'am, I could get fired for what I'm doing," the policeman said. "I'm not supposed to stop you. I don't have a reason to stop you."

"What's the matter?"

"Ma'am, I think I've heard you. Are you the nurse on Art Bell [a radio show]?"

"Yes."

"I just had a baby born that's deaf. I wanna know have you heard about any other babies that have been born deaf because their parents had served in the Gulf War?"

"Yes, I'm sorry to tell you."

The officer's eyes filled with shock and sadness. "Because I called the DOD and the VA, and they told me that no other babies had been born deaf."

"They're lying to you."

He began to cry.

She received a letter from a veteran, who'd been a highway patrolman for twenty-nine years. Never in his career had he felt the need to shoot anybody. After Desert Storm, he had an urge to kill himself or someone else. Thinking he was crazy, his wife left him after over twenty years of marriage. He felt his life was ruined and wanted to die. Joyce offered to contact his wife. She explained about the prevalence of Gulf War syndrome. It wasn't her husband's fault. He needed help. They reconciled and sent Joyce a thank-you letter with a picture of them.

In California, Joyce was speaking at a Veterans auditorium about the large amount of veterans coming home from the Gulf War with herpes, yet they hadn't been unfaithful. The audience was shocked. A couple on the third row began to cry and hold each other. Joyce stopped the meeting. "Can I help you? What's going on?"

"I'm a pastor of my local church here," the man said. "I was a chaplain in the Gulf War. I came home from the Gulf War with herpes and I was never unfaithful to my wife. My wife and I have gone through hell because she could never trust me. She never believed me."

"Now we have a marriage again," his wife said, in-between sobbing. "If only I would have known this."

In Indiana, Joyce was talking to a group about veterans' children who had been affected by Gulf War illness. Uniforms brought home from the Gulf War were contaminating kids. The uniforms contain depleted uranium and traces of chemical and biological weapons, none of which washed out.

"If anybody brought home uniforms," Joyce said, "be very careful of the equipment that you have and where you store it. The chemicals in the uniforms and equipment can affect your family members, and make them ill."

At the back of the room, a lady started crying. Joyce called a break and approached the lady. "What's going on?"

"When my husband came back from the war," she said, "shortly after that, my son started behaving really bizarre and started throwing up and being sick. They told me he was just imagining it and acting out. He was really sick and he's only four, but they put him in a psychiatric facility and started giving him all these drugs. He got worse and worse on the drugs and he's in that psych facility now. He's been there for two months and they're saying that it's just because he wants to be sick for whatever reason. Now I know why my son is really sick, but I can't get him out of there."

"Do you have any of your husband's equipment?" The woman began to get hysterical and couldn't talk. "What's the matter?"

"All of my husband's uniforms and all of his equipment are stored under my boy's bed."

"Oh dear God! You've got to get that out of there."

"I'm going to the hospital right now. I'm going to tell them what you just told me and I'm going to get my son out of the hospital." The mother was able to retrieve her son.

A US representative sent his team to see her talk. During the meeting, five team members furiously scribbled notes. At the half-time break, they called her over. "The representative has a message for you."

"Really," Joyce said.

"The representative wants you to know that he's not gonna support you."

"Well, nobody else has either... But why is he not gonna support this?"

"He says you know a lot about this, but you don't know it all. If you knew the rest of the story and the public knew, it would bring down this country as we know it. His message to you is, 'Keep doing what you're doing. Don't stop.'"

Joyce helped make a documentary, *Beyond Treason*, about Gulf War illness. It included testimony from Lieutenant Doug Rokke, a US Army Health Physicist Nuclear Medicine Sciences Officer with expertise in nuclear, biological and chemical warfare operations. He stated that exposure to depleted uranium was a major cause of his Gulf War illness. The US military granted him disabled status due to depleted uranium and other exposures. "All of the Iraqi equipment and a lot of the US equipment contained radiological components. When that equipment was blown up, the radiological materials were released into the environment, exposing and contaminating. And then to top it all off, we used uranium munitions known as depleted uranium. They've been used back in 1973 by the Israelis against the Egyptians, but during Gulf War One, Desert Shield and Desert Storm, we took it to a totally new level. The use of radioactive materials on the battlefield. Deliberately taking tons and tons, actually taking over 350 tons of solid radioactive materials and dispersed it across Kuwait, Saudi Arabia and Iraq. Taking our radioactive waste and throwing it in somebody else's backyard."

Depleted uranium has a half-life of 4.468 billion years. Iraq and all of the countries contaminated with it since the Gulf War will be toxic for a while – exacerbated by Bush's son who employed the same war strategies as his father. Dust storms recycle the DU onto civilian populations. DU is invisible and the particles are so small that they get through the protective masks and clothing issued by the military.

Birth defects and cancer rates, including leukaemia, have skyrocketed in Iraq. In 2004, Fallujah was bombarded, causing cancer and infant mortality rates to exceed those reported after atomic bombs were dropped on Hiroshima and Nagasaki. Babies have been born with organs outside their bodies, one eye on the forehead, known as Cyclops babies, limbs growing out of heads, multiple heads, spina bifida, brain dysfunction, spinal conditions, unformed limbs and cleft palate… The first question parents in Iraq have started asking isn't about the sex of their baby, but rather, whether it's normal. Many mothers have watched their babies die shortly after birth. Some women in Fallujah have avoided pregnancy.

Joyce got a call from a navy commander at the Pentagon about her documentary, *Gulf War Illness Fact or Fiction*. "I want you to know that you are not to give out that documentary to anyone in the military."

"Pardon," Joyce said. "What's inaccurate in it?"

"It's not that. It's that you are one of us. It's not allowed to be given out."

"No, sir. If you think I'm going to participate in the wholesale manslaughter of our military, you're wrong. Until you can show me what's inaccurate, I'm going to continue to give it out." Immediately, Joyce had a thousand extra DVDs made because she feared her home would be raided and her inventory seized.

Bush's Department of Defense tried to sabotage her talks. Joyce was asked to speak at a college in Michigan. The night before, Joyce received a call from the college: "Joyce, we've got a problem. The DOD has called here three times. They don't want you to speak and they told us not to allow you to speak."

"Really! What are you going to do?"

"We've decided that if they would call three times to tell us that we shouldn't hear it, we probably need to hear it."

"Great. I'll be there."

Joyce arrived at the college at 4 pm for dinner with the PR people and the alumni. The PR director was summoned to the phone. When he returned, he told Joyce, "We've got a problem. The DOD just landed at the airport in a DOD plane. They're coming to the meeting."

"Fantastic. That is the best thing that I could imagine."

Before the talk, he said, "Are you sure you want to do this? Three people from the DOD are here."

"Absolutely! Everything I have to say is true and accurate or I wouldn't be saying it."

Joyce entered a full auditorium. After introducing herself, she said, "How many of you are students?" Numerous hands shot up. "How many of you are professors?" They raised their hands. "How many of you all were paid to be here tonight?" Not one hand went up. "I understand there are three people from the DOD here, from the Secretary of Defense's Office and I'd like to have them recognised." No hands went up. "Since I'm only a captain and I understand that Lieutenant Colonel Thompson is here, I defer the rank. I'd like for you to be recognised, sir. I don't want to continue until you're recognised." For a few seconds, it remained quiet until suddenly, three people stood up on the back row. "I want to welcome you here tonight and I want you to know that I'm going to say some of the most damning evidence ever against the Department of Defense and I'm going to prove it with your own documents. But before I begin, I want you to agree that if there is anything that I say that's inaccurate here tonight, I want you to stop me or it will stand as accurate." Joyce began to speak and go through all of the documents. Not once did any of the men stand. At the end of the three hours, they scurried away.

Upset by Joyce, the DOD called a press conference. They invited media people who'd attended Joyce's talk. In a light blue uniform, Colonel Thompson did a PowerPoint on the magnificence of the military and how wrong Joyce Riley was.

After ten minutes, an investigative reporter stood up. "Colonel Thompson, I think I need to stop you and tell you that I don't think there's one person in this audience who believes a word that you're saying. Is it true, like Captain Riley said, that the US sold weapons to Iraq before the Gulf War. Is that accurate?"

"There's no way that we could possibly know that because that's all compartmentalised information. I'm sure Joyce doesn't have anything that could prove that."

"You saw her show the evidence of the sale of those biologicals to Iraq last night. There's not a person believing anything that you are saying here."

An aide emerged from the side of the curtain. "Colonel Thompson, you're needed in Washington immediately. Your plane is ready to leave."

The colonel abandoned the press conference.

As an increasing amount of troops got sick from Bush's Gulf War, Joyce refused to shut up. She started her own radio show, *The Power Hour*, talking about Gulf War illness. She received letters from thousands of ill people, who were being told there was nothing wrong with them. The government had lied to them so continuously that they didn't understand their situations. They'd served their country their whole lives. They were told to obey and take orders and if they got sick they'd be taken care of. After registering as sick, they were told they had mental problems and placed on psychotropic drugs manufactured by companies that had contributed to Bush's election campaign. This didn't make any sense to them. It made financial sense to the companies supplying vaccines and drugs. SSRI drugs were being used to keep veterans quiet and so their illnesses could be classified as mental. The abandonment by the military is one of the causes of so many veterans committing suicide.

"They're just writing me off," a veteran said on a call to Joyce. "I'm non-commissioned. I've been in the military for twenty-seven years and they won't take care of me. I'm going to be going over to the VA one last time because now I'm in a wheelchair. I cannot walk. So now they're gonna have to listen to me. My wife is gonna take me over there and our children are gonna go over there and we're gonna get an answer today regardless."

"Great. Call me after you go the meeting with them and let me know."

He went to the meeting. "I'm in a wheelchair. Now will you guys believe me that I am sick and I don't have a mental problem?"

The doctor went over to the veteran's wife. "Look, I hate to have to tell you this, but we gave your husband a psych evaluation and we think he's a latent homosexual and that's why he's doing this to himself."

Angry, the veteran's wife grabbed the physician's white jacket. "How dare you say that to my husband in front of his family! You know that is so far from being true!" The family was ejected from the VA hospital.

Joyce became familiar with the tricks of the medical staff who'd stop at nothing to convince veterans that their problems were psychological. The first thing they did was to give psych evaluations, so they could always find a fall-back reason for the illness. If that didn't work, they humiliated or embarrassed them.

While the Bush dynasty fortune increased from war profiteering, officials continued to tell veterans that the government had played no role in their Gulf War illness, even though the government knew it was a lie. In Senate Report 103-97 chaired by John D. Rockefeller IV in 1994, the government acknowledged that soldiers are routinely experimented on without prior knowledge or consent and lasting harm was caused to many veterans:

During the last 50 years, hundreds of thousands of military personnel have been involved in human experimentation and other intentional exposures conducted by the Department of Defense (DOD), often without a servicemember's knowledge or consent. In some cases, soldiers who consented to serve as human subjects found themselves participating in experiments quite different from those described at the time they volunteered. For example, thousands of World War II veterans who originally volunteered to "test summer clothing" in exchange for extra leave time, found themselves in gas chambers testing the effects of mustard gas and lewisite [an organoarsenic compound that causes blisters]. (Note 1) Additionally, soldiers were sometimes ordered by commanding officers to "volunteer" to participate in research or face dire consequences. For example, several Persian Gulf War veterans interviewed by Committee staff reported that they were ordered to take experimental vaccines during Operation Desert Shield or face prison. (Note 2)

The goals of many of the military experiments and exposures were very appropriate. For example, some experiments were intended to provide important information about how to protect US troops from nuclear, biological, and chemical weapons or other dangerous substances during wartime. In the Persian Gulf War, US troops were intentionally exposed to an investigational vaccine that was intended to protect them against biological warfare, and they were given pyridostigmine bromide pills in an experimental protocol intended to protect them against chemical warfare.

However, some of the studies that have been conducted had more questionable motives. For example, the Department of Defense (DOD) conducted numerous "man-break" tests, exposing soldiers to chemical weapons in order to determine the exposure level that would cause a casualty, i.e., "break a man." (Note 3) Similarly, hundreds of soldiers were subjected to hallucinogens in experimental programs conducted by the DOD in participation with, or sponsored by, the CIA. (Note 4),

(Note 5) These servicemembers often unwittingly participated as human subjects in tests for drugs intended for mind-control or behavior modification, often without their knowledge or consent. Although the ultimate goal of those experiments was to provide information that would help US military and intelligence efforts, most Americans would agree that the use of soldiers as unwitting guinea pigs in experiments that were designed to harm them, at least temporarily, is not ethical.

Whether the goals of these experiments and exposures were worthy or not, these experiences put hundreds of thousands of U.S. servicemembers at risk, and may have caused lasting harm to many individuals.

Despite the low battlefield casualty figures touted by the media during the Gulf War, Joyce calculated that hundreds of thousands of service-people became ill and six thousand have died so far as a result of Gulf War illness. She estimated that more than fifty percent of the military was experimented on. Joyce estimated civilian deaths to be 300,000 worldwide from millions infected.

These figures push the total deaths attributable to decisions made by Bush into the hundreds of thousands.

The deaths were kept off Bush's balance sheet by his administration paying millions to organisations such as the Rand Corporation to do research that concluded there is no evidence that Gulf War illness exists. When confronted with over 100,000 sick veterans, the government was able to say that they went to the Rand Corporation, an independent organisation, who found no link.

The Department of Defense became the biggest purchaser of SSRI drugs in the world. Medicated to the hilt, troops still died at record levels due to suicides and homicides. Presently, veterans from the recent wars in the Middle East are committing suicide at the rate of over twenty per day. The government continues to pretend that the causes are unknown.

After years of campaigning, on the day before Thanksgiving,

Joyce went into an emergency room. They did an MRI and CT scan. She was told, "You have spinal cancer, really, really badly." They began emergency radiation on Thanksgiving Day.

"This must be bad if you're doing it on Thanksgiving," she told the oncologist.

"If we didn't do it today, you probably wouldn't be here."

Even cancer didn't deter Joyce from exposing the crimes committed on the service-people during Bush's Gulf War.

The only country to indict Bush as an alleged war criminal was Japan in 1997, after sixteen Japanese citizens were barred from the US due to alleged war crimes during World War II. Due to his attacks on Iraq and Panama, Bush was at the top of the list of ten Americans – including Reagan and Oliver North – banned from Japan for "war crimes, crimes against humanity and violations of human rights."

The first Gulf War resulted in over 100,000 deaths, eclipsing Pablo's 4,000. In this context, the death of Barry Seal would have been insignificant to a master of wholesale slaughter such as Bush.

CHAPTER 44

Protecting Paedophiles

Waging war and dropping bombs can boost a leader's ratings – as Margaret Thatcher pointed out to Bush – but protecting paedophiles has never been popular with the public. It has been alleged that Bush did so during his presidency, putting more children at risk. One victim claimed that Bush engaged in paedophilia, and allegations have been made about some of his inner circle.

The brave and tireless campaigning of Noreen Gosch – whose son was snatched from a street – helped to expose the Franklin paedophile ring, but agencies under President Bush obstructed any form of justice for the victims.

In 1982, Noreen was living the normal life of housewife with three kids in West Des Moines, Iowa. She enjoyed baking cookies and going to ball games.

On September 5, her twelve-year-old, Johnny, left the house at about 5:45 am to deliver Sunday newspapers. He headed down the street, pulling a little wagon with his dog riding along with him. When he got to the street corner, a man in a car stopped him and asked for directions. Having been instructed not to talk to strangers, Johnny didn't engage with the man. Other kids on the corner saw Johnny walk away from the stranger.

The stranger did a U-turn, sped back up the street and stopped where the boys were gathering their papers. The stranger turned off his engine, opened the passenger door, put his feet on the curb and chatted in slurred speech to the boys.

Johnny turned towards sixteen-year-old Mike. "This man is nuts. There's something wrong with him. I'm scared and I'm leaving." Johnny threw his papers into the wagon and took off down the street.

The other boys left. A forty-four-year-old lawyer had parked his car to get his son's papers. He saw the stranger and the licence plate. Unaware of what was going on, he departed.

Mike heard Johnny's dog growl. The stranger got back in his car, slammed the door, started the engine, raised his hand and clicked the dome light three times. Mike saw Johnny walking along, and another stranger, about 6-foot-3, emerge from in-between two houses. The second stranger started following Johnny, who went around the corner, out of Mike's sight. A few seconds later, a car door slammed, tyres screeched, and the original stranger's car ran a stop sign, turned left and headed out of town.

During the twelve minutes that Johnny was absent from his home, Noreen and her husband, John, had been sleeping. For thirteen months, Johnny had always woken his dad up before going on his newspaper round, but that day he hadn't. It was the only day that he'd gone out alone.

The phone started to ring because neighbours hadn't got their papers.

Assuming Johnny was running late, John told Noreen that he'd go out and help him. John left, only to screech back onto the drive a few minutes later. "Call the police immediately! Johnny's gone! Somebody took him! His wagon is up on the street corner full of papers! Not even the bundle ties have been cut!"

Noreen called the police to report a missing child. Awaiting the police, Noreen called her other two children and asked them to come home. One was working at Pancake House; the other was at a college in a nearby town. She asked her friends to help her search for her son. She called the *Des Moines Register* district manager of her area, Johnny's boss at the newspaper, who brought a register of the names of all of the boys who had been delivering newspapers that morning. Noreen called them all.

The police arrived forty-five minutes after she had called them. By then, she had a description of the stranger and his car, a partial licence plate number and every detail that every witness could remember. She filled out and signed a missing person's report.

"Did your son ever run away before?" a policeman asked.

"He's never run away, period. Why would you say such a thing? Didn't you just listen to me? What I told you! What the witnesses had said."

The policeman recoiled as if to say, *How dare you talk to me like that!* "I have to go back to the station." He left at about 8:30 am.

Noreen organised search parties and contacted the media. Thousands of people searched for Johnny in the state parks, cornfields and anywhere a body could have been dumped.

Twenty of the searchers showed up at Noreen's house, furious. "I thought you wanted help," one said.

"I do want help," Joyce said, confused. "What's wrong?"

"The police chief just showed up at one of the state parks, drunk, and got on top of a picnic table and shouted through a bullhorn, 'Everyone go home! Johnny Gosch is nothing but a damn runaway!'" Much later, that police chief was shamed and lost his job. Eventually, he was arrested for shoplifting.

Realising that the police weren't going to help her, Noreen called the FBI. Two agents arrived at her home. Sitting at a table, they explained, in-between slurping coffee, that they couldn't investigate the case because there was no crime.

"I have no son," Noreen said. "What are you going to do about it?"

"The police chief told us that this case does not require the FBI, so we will not be in the case."

For the next few days, Noreen suffered from confusion and turmoil. Every fifteen minutes, her phone rang, day and night. Local TV stations began to show Johnny's picture. The news spread throughout Iowa and other states that a young boy had been snatched off the street.

The local police did nothing. Noreen walked into the police station and demanded to speak to the chief. "If there had been a bank robbery, would you have called it runaway money for the first seventy-two hours or would you have begun to work on it?" she said. The chief told her to leave the station.

At least now she knew she was on her own. Within a week, she was interviewing private investigators. The investigator she chose set up surveillance at the location of the kidnapping, and began to monitor cars at the same early time at which Johnny had been taken. Two squad cars showed up and arrested the investigator for vagrancy.

Noreen returned to the police chief. "If you aren't going to work on my son's case that's your choice, but step aside 'cause I am. I don't want to see or hear again that my private investigators have been disturbed or arrested. They're licensed in Iowa to operate, so you need to back off if you're not going to do your job."

The investigators gathered information. One did house-to-house interviews, during which a neighbour described seeing a van parked in the wrong direction on the street with its motor running. Its loud engine had drawn his attention, so he'd watched it through his window. He saw a car pull up next to the van, and two men load something long wrapped in a blanket from the car to the van. Then they all left. Unaware a kidnapping had occurred, he just thought it odd at the time. Noreen decided not to share the information with law enforcement because she believed that somebody would come forward with that piece of information. If it hadn't been broadcast by the media, she'd know that the person was authentic.

Six months after Johnny's disappearance, another boy was kidnapped. The parents received a call on their son's cell phone demanding a ransom. The FBI sent numerous agents to Des Moines. They found the child within thirty-six hours.

The next day, a special agent led his FBI team into Noreen's home. "We really had to work on that case because there was a human life at stake," he said.

Noreen was shocked. "Well, what do you think my son is? Don't you think his life matters?"

"Mrs Gosch, there's something you don't understand. The other family are very wealthy. They're very prominent in Des Moines. We had to search for their son because they are more prominent people than you are."

Noreen picked up a cup of hot coffee and threw it across the room. It just missed the agent's face.

"I can see that you're distraught. Is there anything I can do for you?"

"Yes. You can get the hell out of my house! Don't ever come back! If you're not going to investigate my son's case, then step aside because I'm coming through. I'll find out what happened to my son, regardless of whether you accept the information or whether you don't. I will at least know before I die."

Reflecting on what he'd said, Noreen realised he'd done her a favour. He'd told her the bottom line.

Over the years, Noreen received leads that raised her hopes, but went nowhere.

Nine long years later, Paul came forward. He'd been tortured and sexually abused as part of a pornography and prostitution ring. In jail, accused of perjury and sex crimes, he had told his lawyer that he'd participated in Johnny's kidnapping.

The lawyer tried to call Noreen, but Johnny's dad, John, answered because Noreen wasn't home. John didn't tell Noreen. She only found out about Paul two years later.

Noreen met Paul and read his diaries, including the entry about Johnny's kidnapping. Paul said they had a van parked a couple of blocks from the kidnapping site. Johnny had been loaded from a car into the van, which had transported Johnny to a location in Iowa. As the information matched what Noreen's witness had seen, she knew Paul was authentic.

Noreen took Paul's information to the police and the FBI, who refused to act because Paul was "a nut" with no credibility. They said he had multiple personalities due to the abuse and programming he'd suffered, and not one word of his statement could be taken as fact.

Noreen noticed that Paul had never wavered from his story under questioning over the years. After eleven years, what Paul had said about Johnny remained the same, verbatim. When asked about something he had no knowledge of, Paul had always said,

"I'm sorry. I don't know about that." He never made up stories or changed any words, which impressed. Noreen.

From Paul's statement, Noreen concluded Johnny's kidnapping was highly organised. Two weeks before the kidnapping, a neighbour had seen Johnny being photographed on his way home from school. The car had out-of-state plates. The photographer had leaned out of the window and used a camera with a long telephoto lens. The neighbour had reported it to the police, who said it wasn't a crime to take photos.

The morning of the kidnapping, the kidnappers had those photos. About four years older than Johnny, Paul had been in the back seat. They'd used a child to lure a child. Johnny had come close enough to the car for them to pull him in.

Paul revealed that the two vehicles involved in Johnny's kidnapping had rendezvoused at a farmhouse outside of Sioux City, Iowa. For two weeks, Johnny was kept in the basement of the old farmhouse. On film and at gunpoint, Paul and another young man sexually abused Johnny. After two weeks, a man called the Colonel arrived and paid a lot of cash to the kidnappers. Paul was under the impression that the Colonel was taking Johnny back to Colorado and the West Coast.

Paul didn't see Johnny again until 1986, during an orgy at a ranch belonging to the Colonel. It was in a remote area in the mountains. Adults were having sex with kids. Johnny's hair had been dyed black. They'd switched his name to Mark. Paul said kids were flown all over the country to wealthy paedophiles, who requested kids by description. The kids were constantly moved around.

Noreen complained bitterly to her state senators that the FBI had continued to refuse to investigate the case. Her senators got in touch with the FBI office in Washington. The FBI was forced to do a house-to-house search. A neighbour reported that the FBI agents were disgruntled and mouthing off about Mrs Gosch for having forced the search upon them. They hadn't intended to search at all.

Why, Noreen wondered, *would a police chief not investigate and try to find Johnny, and why would the FBI refuse to investigate a bona fide kidnapping case with multiple eyewitnesses? Why do they keep saying we have no crimes?* Noreen was sick of hearing that phrase. *Are they stupid? Do they not know how to investigate a case like this? Are they naïve? Are they compliant in protecting a bigwig that is a paedophile? Or are they involved in it themselves?*

Noreen recalled that shortly after Johnny had been kidnapped, there'd been an article in the *Des Moines Register* about the kidnapping of two girls, thirteen and fourteen, who'd been taken to Omaha and put into a pornography ring. They were returned and the kidnappers were arrested. Noreen took the clipping to the police chief and asked him to investigate the lead.

"I don't have a feel for that, so I'm not going to do anything," he said.

"Can you call the police chief of Omaha just to ask about it? Omaha is only two hours away. If they came here for the girls, they could have come here for my son, too." The police chief and the FBI refused her request.

Noreen hosted a press conference. She read the clipping from the paper and recited the reaction from the police chief and the FBI. Four days later, she received the first of many death threats. "If you don't stop rocking the boat and making waves, you're going to die."

What boat did I rock? Noreen thought. *What wave did I make?* She realised the wave was asking about Omaha. She was knocking on the back door of the Franklin Credit Union scandal, years before the story erupted. The authorities in Des Moines were not going to let the story break by solving Johnny's case.

Noreen found out that the police chief she'd been dealing with was good friends with the police chief in Omaha, Nebraska. They both had allegedly attended orgies in Omaha together, where they used young boys and girls. The police chief of Omaha had been accused of impregnating an underage girl at a party. It finally made sense to Noreen why the police chief had told everybody searching for Johnny to go home and why he wouldn't investigate the Omaha connection. Noreen felt sick, but also thankful that she finally knew what she was dealing with and what the obstacles were.

She pledged to keep Johnny's story alive and let as many people as possible know that children were being abducted from the streets for sex rings. She started the Johnny Gosch Foundation to help raise money for private investigators to keep searching for Johnny. She developed a program: In Defense of Children. She gave up her life to go on the road, speaking in schools, churches, civic organisations and network TV shows. In five years, she did 700 speeches.

She wrote legislation for the State of Iowa. The Johnny Gosch Bill provided for any family with a missing child to have an immediate investigation started. No more waiting seventy-two hours. The FBI would be called in to start work immediately. Her second bill provided for victims of sexual abuse to testify via video camera, rather than having to recount everything in open court in front of their assailant. She introduced a children's Bill of Rights to help protect sexually-abused children. Her laws were passed in other states bordering Iowa, codifying procedures for missing and abused children.

Around this time in Washington DC, the National Center For Missing Children was being formed. Parents of missing children, including Noreen, were flown to Texas to testify before the Justice Department on video, explaining what went wrong in their cases, who was responsible and why they hadn't done their jobs. Noreen related the mistakes on Johnny's case. She ended her speech with, "If the FBI was not going to investigate missing children's cases, then the Justice Department should cut their funding. They should take that amount of money and give it to an organisation to start a missing children's centre, so that those of us who have missing children will have some government agency to turn to for assistance."

The room fell silent. John Walsh, the grieving parent who

hosted *America's Most Wanted*, rushed over to Noreen. "I can't believe you said that. I can't believe you said to cut their funding."

"John, I meant it. If they're not going to do their job, cut their funding and give it to someone who will. I'm very serious about it. Why does everybody think the FBI is a sacred cow that you can't challenge? They didn't do their job for my son. They didn't follow their own code of ethics for the criteria of a kidnapping case. Perhaps if they would have moved a little swifter, Johnny would be with me today."

She wanted Johnny's kidnapping to stand for something and progress to be made in the system, so other parents wouldn't have to suffer. Every time she did a TV show or a speech, leads and information trickled in. With the help of her investigators, she slowly assembled the jigsaw. She discovered what had happened to Johnny, why, who was responsible and how they profited from children.

"Kiddie porn is a multi-billion dollar business in this country," Noreen said. "The only reason it is is because of supply and demand… Somebody has to supply the children to the paedophiles who have this thing for young children and the money to pay for it. My son just happened to be one of them." Noreen concluded that the police didn't investigate Johnny's kidnapping because of their involvement in the paedophile ring.

In December 1996, Noreen was invited to a talk show in LA with other mothers who'd lost their children. They were asked to give a Christmas message to their missing children.

"Johnny, if you're still out there and if you're alive and you're getting this message, I'll help you in any way I possibly can. I still live in West Des Moines. I've divorced your father. My name and address are listed in the phone book, so you can find me. Contact me and I'll help you." Noreen flew home.

In March 1997 in the middle of the night, someone knocked continuously on Noreen's door. Noreen got up. Living alone, she wouldn't normally have opened the door at that time. The peephole revealed two young men in the doorway with the hall lights illuminating the face of a man resembling Johnny. "Who's there?"

"It's me, mom. It's Johnny."

Overwhelmed by emotion, she opened the door and let them in. "You're gonna have to have a safe place to stay," Noreen said, thinking Johnny was back for good. "Let me call someone who can come here tonight and give us some legal advice and help."

"I can't stay. You don't understand. It's not safe. You wouldn't be safe if I stayed here. They'll kill me." Johnny said he'd been abducted into a high-level pornography and prostitution ring that was also involved in drug running. They catered to people across the country at the top of politics from senators all the way to the White House. In shock, Noreen listened as Johnny said he wanted her to get his story out in the hope of making arrests happen, so that he and the other kids could be free to safely reunite with their families.

Johnny said that a few years ago, he and another boy had stolen a car and escaped from the kidnappers, who stored the kids across the country in safe houses. He'd sought sanctuary on an Indian reservation, which he considered safe from the authorities because reservations are classified as a sovereign state. But he was tracked down and brought back into the ring.

Johnny said that it was too dangerous for him to stay. He said goodbye.

After they left, Noreen ran outside in a daze and saw them disappear into the night on foot. She never saw Johnny again.

The witness who'd come forward, Paul, who said he'd helped to lure Johnny into the car, had been involved in the Franklin paedophile network. It had been run by Larry King – a personal friend of Bush – and Craig Spence, a lobbyist, CIA asset and blackmail artist.

A rising star in the Republican Party, King had operated in Franklin, where he was the vice chairman for finance of the National Black Republican Council. King had campaigned for Bush to become president and had hosted a $100,000 gala for Bush at the 1998 Republican Convention in New Orleans. He also had an appetite for sex with boys. He'd operated a well-tuned pornography and prostitution ring, using kids from foster homes and Boys Town: a Catholic orphanage for troubled boys.

Craig Spence threw sex and drug parties at his home, which had been bugged by the CIA to facilitate blackmail. While Bush was president, Spence took call boys on midnight tours of the White House. Some of the children King flew around the country ended up in Spence's home in Washington DC, where orgies were filmed.

The first victim to speak out was Eulice Washington, a sixteen-year-old who'd been placed in a foster home run by one of Larry King's cousins, where children were whipped and beaten. She'd arrived at age eight, and had eventually been transferred to a different foster home. She told her new foster mother that her adopted father at the previous foster home had molested her. She passed a polygraph, but her adopted father was never prosecuted.

In March 1986, Eulice told a Boys Town youth worker that Larry King had flown her and other kids from Boys Town to orgies in New York and Chicago. She added that she had seen Bush at one of the orgies. The FBI was informed, but no action was ever taken. A social worker investigating the abuse at Eulice's previous foster home was threatened by the FBI.

In 1988, the Omaha police started investigating King and a photographer for child pornography. They gathered evidence, but the investigation was shut down.

A fifteen-year-old victim in a psychiatric hospital told the staff that she had been in a prostitution and pornography ring since age nine. She told Omaha police about Larry King's involvement. The police report said that the victim had been credible, but she was never interviewed again and no investigation happened.

On July 20, 1988, a supervisor of the Nebraska foster care system reported the existence of a child exploitation ring to the Attorney General. The investigator assigned to the case didn't interview any victims.

On November 4, 1988 – four days before Bush was elected

president – federal agents raided Larry King's Franklin Credit Union, from which King had allegedly embezzled $39.4 million. Researchers have speculated that Bush was getting rid of King because his paedophile ring was attracting too much attention.

Senator Schmit, who'd drafted a resolution to form the Franklin Committee to investigate the failure of King's credit union, received a call warning him not to investigate because it would "reach to the highest levels of the Republican Party." Disregarding the warning, the committee uncovered accounts of child trafficking and abuse that had occurred without the authorities acting even though they knew about it.

After receiving more threats, Schmit said, "I've been told to leave it alone or my kids were going to be orphans."

A group of Nebraskans who'd heard about children such as Johnny getting snatched from the streets formed Concerned Parents. At one of their meetings, a woman stood up and said, "I think George Bush is involved in this child-abuse case and that is why all these people have been dying."

An ex-CIA employee, a psychologist in Omaha, came to the attention of Concerned Parents, after he claimed that rumours of Bush engaging in paedophilia were rampant when Bush was running the CIA.

The Franklin Committee assigned Gary Caradori – an ace private investigator with a background in the military and the police – to investigate the allegations of paedophilia. From the outset, his efforts were blocked. Witnesses and victims were too fearful to talk to him. FBI agents were waiting at places he went to as if they knew his movements in advance. A phone-company employee confirmed Caradori's phones had been tapped.

Caradori learned that Larry King had been taking almost weekly chartered flights across the country without listing the names of the kids accompanying him.

Over time, Caradori found four victims willing to go on the record. He videotaped them describing their abuse at the hands of prominent people. Their statements all matched up. Caradori took the tapes to the Franklin Committee, who didn't know what to do with them because of their mistrust of the state and federal authorities who'd previously failed to act on the earliest victims' testimonies. In December, 1989, the Franklin Committee sent twenty-one hours of videotaped testimony to the Nebraska attorney general and Nebraska's US attorney, forcing the state and federal authorities to act.

A grand jury was formed to investigate the allegations the same week that President Bush arrived in Omaha for the Nebraska governor's fundraiser. King had purchased a ticket for the fundraiser, but the Secret Service whisked him off to an Omaha federal courthouse, where he appeared on February 7, 1990. The magistrate ordered King to undergo an immediate mental-health evaluation at the US Medical Center for Federal Prisoners in Springfield, Missouri. Federal marshals escorted King to Springfield, where a US District Court judge assigned him to a psychiatric hospital, safely away from the grand-jury investigation into his paedophile ring.

Over a year, despite obstacles placed in his way by the authorities and the media, Caradori gathered more evidence and testimonies about child-sex crimes. He was tipped-off about a plot to implicate him in scripting the allegations that would have led to his arrest. He wrote to a lawyer that the paedophile ring reached "to the highest levels of the United States."

As the case revolved around child pornography, Caradori set about obtaining some as evidence. He tracked down one of King's pornographers. He called a *Washington Times* reporter from a payphone to say that he was on the verge of acquiring photos. He also told another person "we got them by the shorthairs." Five sources claimed that Caradori had obtained pictures.

The next day, July 11, at approximately 2 am, his single-engine plane crashed in a cornfield, killing Caradori and his eight-year-old son. According to the National Transportation Safety Board, his plane had broken up in flight, but no mechanism by which it had happened was ever discovered.

Caradori had been working closely with Paul Rodriguez, a reporter for the *Washington Times*, whose first article on the subject was titled, "Homosexual prostitution inquiry ensnares VIPs with Reagan, Bush 'Call Boys' took midnight tour of White House." The next story was titled, "Power Broker Served Drugs, Sex At Parties Bugged For Blackmail."

Six victims, including Eulice Washington, agreed to testify to the Franklin Committee and the police. Despite receiving threats, Eulice maintained her story, including that she had seen Bush at a paedophilic orgy in Chicago in 1984. FBI intimidation saw off two of the witnesses, who recanted their testimony.

With Caradori out of the way, a special prosecutor presented evidence and witnesses in such a way that the state grand jury concluded that the child-sex allegations were a "carefully crafted hoax." The grand jury concluded that no children had been trafficked across state lines for immoral purposes. Two of the brave victims who'd testified about the sexually horrific things that had happened to them at the hands of the paedophile ring were charged by the state with perjury, and told they were facing hundreds of years of imprisonment if convicted. Eulice Washington wasn't charged. The media backed up the grand-jury verdicts and called the Franklin Committee a disgrace. Even Larry King's partner in crime, Spence, was exonerated of all of his crimes.

One of the victims, twenty-one-year-old Alicia Owen, was told that she was facing over three-hundred years in prison. If she was convicted, the paedophile ring would be protected. Before the trial, her brother died in strange circumstances. The vast resources of the state were used against her in the longest trial in Nebraska history. After deliberating for three days, the jurors found her guilty. She was sentenced to between nine and fifteen years. She spent the first two in solitary confinement. All of the members of the judicial system who'd facilitated the cover-up were promoted. Some became judges.

The Bush administration's FBI and Secret Service helped to suppress any exposure of the Franklin paedophile network.

Author Roger Stone believes that was coordinated from the top. The end result was that the victims ended up in prison, not the perpetrators.

Throughout his years in politics, Bush feigned having a heart, while protecting associates engaged in paedophilia. Someone willing to stoop to that level would have had no twinge of conscience when it came to ordering the assassination of Barry Seal.

CHAPTER 45

War on Drugs and CIA Drug Trafficking

Throughout the 1980s, the Reagan-Bush administration launched an expansion of the War on Drugs. The "Just say no" campaign was funded largely by tobacco, alcohol and pharmaceutical companies. The government claimed that the war was necessary to take down drug lords such as Pablo Escobar, but its burden fell mostly on hundreds of thousands of non-violent marijuana users, many of whom were SWAT-team raided and dragged off to jail.

Reagan's wife, Nancy, was a leading spokesperson: "If you're a casual drug user, you're an accomplice to murder." The campaign, in combination with sensational headlines about rabid black crack users murdering white people, prostituting themselves for a pittance and giving birth to malnourished alien-like babies, caused public opinion about drugs to swing in favour of the zero-tolerance policies that filled prisons with non-violent drug users from the poorest neighbourhoods. Private prisons and all of the industries that grew up around them became a massive source of profit for the politicians taking contributions from them.

In 1982, Ronald Regan created the South Florida Task Force, headed by Bush. It combined elements of the FBI, army and Navy to fight traffickers who weren't working with the CIA. The media published images of soldiers, surveillance planes and helicopter gunships off the coast of Florida, waging war with Pablo's smugglers. As drug seizures rose, Reagan and Bush posed for photos amid tons of confiscated cocaine, and proclaimed their success in the War on Drugs. They never mentioned that the price of cocaine in America was falling despite the gunboats, a sure sign that the supply into America was increasing. Even DEA agents complained that the War on Drugs was just a handover of money to the military.

In 1983, a program called Drug Abuse Resistance Education (DARE) started in American schools. Students were encouraged to let the police know about their friends' and families' drug habits, so they could swiftly be incarcerated. The Reagan-Bush administration doubled the federal prison population. Young offenders and non-violent drug users were sent to Special Alternative Incarceration boot camps to have their rebellious attitudes demolished. They often emerged traumatised and more inclined to take drugs.

Simultaneously, the Reagan-Bush administration quietly instructed American universities to destroy all of the research into marijuana undertaken between 1966 and 1976, which could have benefited people with a range of ailments, including cancer patients at risk of death because they couldn't eat, and children born with rare conditions who had hundreds of seizures a week and were at risk of entering comas and dying.

The federal government used planes to illegally spray marijuana fields in Kentucky, Georgia and Tennessee with the toxic weed-killer Paraquat, risking the lives of marijuana smokers. Banned in several European countries, Paraquat is highly toxic to animals and has serious and irreversible delayed effects if absorbed. As little as one teaspoonful of the active ingredient is fatal. Death occurs up to thirty days after ingestion. It's also toxic if absorbed through the skin, and can cause nose bleeding if inhaled. No antidote for poisoning exists although it is recommended that hospitalisation is sought without delay. The government was able to use it by classifying it as having low acute toxicity when sprayed.

Reagan's Drugs Czar, Carlton Turner, said that kids deserved to die as a punishment for smoking poisoned weed, to teach them a lesson. Two years later, he called for the death penalty for all drug users. On one occasion, the DEA had been ordered to spray Paraquat on a marijuana plantation in Georgia, but the Forest Service had miscalculated the location. The Paraquat ended up on a corn crop. Drugs Czar Turner was a co-owner of a patent, along with the University of Mississippi, on a chemical test that detected the presence of Paraquat on crops. Although he stood to earn royalties from the patent, he denied any conflict of interest.

Extending the War on Drugs into Colombia included dropping chemical poisons on peasants and their crops. Many had to leave the little pieces of land they owned, and they were reduced to begging. Their land often ended up in the hands of the wealthy and foreign corporations.

By 1986, officials in Florida acknowledged that the amount of drugs entering the US had skyrocketed. The Government Accounting Office stated that cocaine imports had doubled in one year.

In the summer of 1989, the Commissioner of US Customs resigned because he believed that the only real battles were being fought against minorities and the downtrodden, while those in authority were protecting the government's monopoly in the trade. "The War on Drugs is a war of words," he said.

While the international narcotics trade thrived, Reagan declared the War on Drugs to be one of his best achievements. But in 1989, the Iran-Contra scandal revealed that the US government – via the CIA – had been trafficking in hard drugs for military weapons. During the investigation, the increasingly frail and senile Reagan feigned ignorance and most people believed him. Throughout Reagan's term, ex-CIA-director Bush had really been calling the shots.

On September 5, 1989, President Bush outlined his strategy for eradicating drug use. He asked Congress for $7.9 billion, 70 percent for law enforcement, including $1.6 billion for prisons. "This scourge will stop." His focus was on reducing demand, meaning arresting more drug users, rather than prevention, education and medical treatment. He increased the repressive measures against marijuana users. "Our nation has zero tolerance for casual drug use… You do drugs, you will be caught, and when you're caught, you will be punished. Some think there won't be room for them in jail. We'll make room."

The story of Keith Jackson illustrates Bush's duplicity in the War on Drugs. On September 5, 1989, President Bush appeared on TV. "This is the first time since taking the oath of office that I've felt an issue was so important, so threatening, that it warranted talking directly with you, the American people. All of us agree that the gravest domestic threat facing our nation today is drugs. Drugs have strained our faith in our system of justice. Our courts, our prisons, our legal system, are stretched to breaking point. The social costs of drugs are mounting. In short, drugs are sapping our strength as a nation. Turn on the evening news or pick up the morning paper and you'll see what some Americans know just by stepping out their front door: Our most serious problem today is cocaine, and in particular, crack..." Reaching to his side, Bush produced a bag labelled EVIDENCE with chalky rocks in it. "This is crack cocaine seized a few days ago by Drug Enforcement agents in a park just across the street from the White House. It could easily have been heroin or PCP. It's as innocent-looking as candy, but it's turning our cities into battle zones and it's murdering our children. Let there be no mistake: this stuff is poison. Some used to call drugs harmless recreation; they're not. Drugs are a real and terribly dangerous threat to our neighbourhoods, our friends and our families..."

Bush's claim aroused suspicion in Michael Isikoff, an NBC correspondent, who doubted that crack was being sold in Lafayette Square, an urban park north of the White House. Through contacts at the DEA, Isikoff learned the truth. Bush's speech writers had decided that a prop would enhance the president's rhetoric, so they wrote the Lafayette Square crack story into the script before it had happened. After Bush approved the idea, the DEA was told to make a drug purchase near the White House in order to fit the script.

The assignment ended up with Special Agent Sam Gaye, who was asked by his boss, "Can you make a drug buy around 1600 Pennsylvania Avenue? Can you call any defendants you've been buying from?" In court, Gaye testified, "I had twenty-four hours to buy three ounces of crack."

Using informers, Gaye set up a purchase, which fell through after the dealer didn't show up in the park. During the second attempt, the agent's body microphone malfunctioned, and the cameraman about to film the transaction was assaulted by a homeless person.

Finally, an informant contacted an amenable low-level dealer, Keith Jackson, an eighteen-year-old high-school student who lived across town. Gaye asked Keith to meet him in the park.

"Where's Lafayette Park?" Keith said.

"It's across the street from the White House."

"Where the fuck is the White House?" Keith said.

"We had to manipulate him to get him down there," said William McMullan, assistant special agent in charge of the DEA's Washington field office. "It wasn't easy."

When the DEA video tape was played in court, the jury laughed. It showed Gaye waiting on Pennsylvania Avenue with the White House and tourists behind him. Before Jackson and an informant arrived by car, an irate woman sprung up from below the camera's vision, and yelling was heard as an altercation unfolded.

"There was this lady," Gaye said, "who got up off the ground and said, 'Don't take my photo! Don't take my photo!'"

For the White House transaction, as well as three earlier sales, Keith ended up facing ten years to life without parole even though he had no previous convictions. The first trial was a mistrial, but on retrial he was convicted of three counts with two being dropped, including the Lafayette Park sale. The judge sentenced him to ten years due to the mandatory minimums for selling crack near a school, but suggested that he seek clemency, which was never granted.

A teenager had been sacrificed to improve Bush's ratings.

After the fall of the Berlin Wall in 1989 and with the Soviet Union contracting, the US was rapidly running out of Communists to fight. Bush needed enemies to maintain his popularity at the voting booths and to keep the war machine in business. Pablo was ideal.

In November 1990, Bush signed a bill that coerced the states into suspending the driver's licences and revoking government permits and benefits (including college loans) of those convicted of drug crimes. He advocated the heavy use of forfeiture or confiscation of property that the government believed to be drug related. It was primarily used to take cars and currency, and the money was recycled back into the state and federal government. These laws operated under presumed guilt, which did not require a trial or even a conviction.

By 1992, there were more people in federal prisons for drug charges than there were for all crimes in 1980, with the burden overwhelmingly falling on black people. Twice as many people were arrested for possession than supplying. Chief Justice of the Supreme Court, William Rehnquist, said there were too many arrests. New York City jails filled to breaking point, and jail boats had to be opened. Bush's policies did nothing to stop people from buying and selling drugs.

That Bush was simultaneously waging a War on Drugs while facilitating their importation via the CIA is hard for some people to swallow. But it must be probed further to understand Bush's ability to deceive.

In 1985, Retired US Navy Lieutenant Commander Al Martin had dinner with George HW Bush, Jeb Bush and a CIA veteran Felix Rodriguez, who'd taken $10 million from the Medellín Cartel for Nicaraguan rebels involved in trafficking cocaine. Over food, George HW Bush boasted that he operated on the Big Lie principle, whereby big lies would be believed because the public couldn't conceive that their leader was capable of bending the truth that far, such as a president railing against drugs while overseeing drug trafficking worth billions.

Anyone who tried to blow the whistle on Bush's phoney War on Drugs ended up paying a price. Former DEA agent Cele Castillo wrote *Powderburns: Cocaine, Contras & the Drug War* (1998), in which he detailed a meeting with Bush. Assigned to El Salvador in 1986 to investigate a pilot who stored his plane at the Ilopango airbase, Castillo had discovered that the Nicaraguan rebels were smuggling cocaine to the US, using the same pilots, planes and hangers as the CIA and NSC (National Security Council), under the direction of Bush's frontman Oliver North. At Ilopango, he often saw Bush's buddy, Felix Rodriguez, whom Castillo described as an American terrorist. Bewildered, he told his bosses about the cocaine smuggling. They instructed him to use the word "alleged" in his reports instead of stating things as factual.

Castillo reported that a CIA agent was requesting a US Visa for a Nicaraguan-rebel drug smuggler who was flying cocaine from Costa Rica to anti-Castro Cubans in Miami. The cocaine in Costa Rica was picked up from the ranch of an American, John Hull, who, by the admission of the CIA's station chief in Costa Rica, was working with the CIA on military supply and other operations on behalf of the Nicaraguan rebels, and was being paid $110,000 a month by Oliver North.

After Castillo blew the whistle, Vice President Bush met him briefly during a visit to Guatemala City on January 14, 1986, at a cocktail party at the ambassador's residence. Protected by a retinue of Secret Service agents, Bush was talking to embassy personnel and Guatemalan dignitaries. Bush approached Castillo and read the tag on his lapel, which identified him as a member of the US embassy. Shaking hands, Bush asked what he did.

"I'm a DEA agent assigned to Guatemala."

"Well, what do you do?"

"There's some funny things going on with the Contras in El Salvador."

Without uttering a response, Bush smiled and walked away. Castillo realised that Bush was in on the drug trafficking.

Following the party at the ambassador's house, the US Ambassador to El Salvador sent a back-channel cable to the State Department. A few days later, the DEA closed down Castillo's investigation. The reports he'd filed disappeared into what Castillo called a black hole at DEA headquarters. In February 1987,

DEA investigators found "no credible information" to indicate that traffickers were part of any political organisation, including the Nicaraguan rebels and the government of Nicaragua. Castillo received so much harassment that he ended up quitting the DEA in 1990.

Presidential candidate and billionaire Ross Perot hired Bo Gritz, a Green Beret who'd earned multiple medals for bravery, to find American POWs imprisoned in Asia decades after the Vietnam War. While on his mission, Gritz came across General Khun Sa, a Burmese drug lord who offered to identify US government officials he claimed had been trafficking in heroin for over twenty years. Having uncovered CIA drug trafficking in Asia, Perot and Gritz were shocked.

Perot requested a meeting with Bush, so that he could present his evidence. Bush told Perot to go to the proper authorities and refused to help any further.

Here are extracts from a letter Gritz wrote to Bush:

Sir:

Why does it seem that you are saying "YES" to illegal narcotics in America?

I turned over video tapes to your NSC staff assistant, Tom Harvey, January 1987, wherein General KHUN SA, overlord of Asia's "Golden Triangle" offered to stop 900 tons of heroin/opium from entering the free world in 1987. Harvey told me, "...there is no interest here in doing that."

Unfortunately, Khun Sa knew nothing about US POWs. He did, however, offer to trade his nation's poppy dependence for a legitimate economy.

Instead of receiving an "Atta Boy" for bringing back video tape showing Khun Sa's offer to stop 900 tons of illegal narcotics and expose dirty USG officials, Scott was jailed and I was threatened. I was told that if I didn't "erase and forget" all that we had discovered, I would, "hurt the government." Further, I was promised a prison sentence of "15 years."

I returned to Burma with two other American witnesses, Lance Trimmer, a private detective from San Francisco, and Barry Flynn from Boston. Gen Khun Sa identified some of those in government service he says were dealing in heroin and arms sales. We video-taped this second interview and I turned copies over in June 1987, to the Chairman of the Select Committee on Intelligence; Chairman of the House on Foreign Affairs Task Force on Narcotics Control; Co-Chairman, Senate Narcotics Committee; Senator Harry Reid, NV; Representative James Bilbray, NV; and other Congressional members. Mister Richard Armitage, Assistant Secretary of Defense for International Security Affairs, is one of those USG officials implicated by Khun Sa. Nothing was done with this evidence that indicated that anyone of authority, including yourself, had intended to do anything more than protect Mr Armitage. I was charged with "Misuse of Passport." Seems that it is alright for Oliver North and Robert MacFarlane to go into Iran on Irish Passports to negotiate an illegal arms deal that neither you nor anyone else admits condoning, but I can't use a passport that brings back drug information against your friends.

Lance Trimmer and I submitted a "Citizen Complaint of Wrongdoing by Federal Officers" to Attorney General Edwin Meese, III on 17 September 1987. Continuous private and Legislative inquiries to date indicate that the Attorney General's Office has "lost" the document. Congressional requests to the Government Accounting Office have resulted in additional government snares and stalls.

January 20, 1988, I talked before your Breakfast Club in Houston, Texas. A distinguished group of approximately 125 associates of yours, including the Chief Justice of the Texas Supreme Court, expressed assurance that you are a righteous man. Almost all of them raised their hand when I asked how many of them know you personally. If you are a man with good intent, I pray you will do more than respond to this letter. I ask that you seriously look into the possibility that political appointees close to you are guilty of by-passing our Constitutional process, and for purposes of promoting illegal covert operations, conspired in the trafficking of narcotics and arms.

Please answer why a respected American Citizen like Mister H Ross Perot can bring you a pile of evidence of wrongdoing by Armitage and others, and you, according to *TIME magazine* (May 4, page 18), not only offer him no support, but have your Secretary of Defense, Frank Carlucci tell Mr. Perot to "stop pursuing Mr Armitage." Why Sir, will you not look into affidavits gathered by The Christic Institute (Washington, D.C.), which testify that Armitage not only trafficked in heroin, but did so under the guise of an officer charged with bringing home our POWs. If the charges are true, Armitage, who is still responsible for POW recovery as your Assistant Secretary of Defense ISA, has every reason not to want these heroes returned to us alive. Clearly, follow-on investigations would illuminate the collective crimes of Armitage and others.

...in May 1987, Gen Khun Sa, in his jungle headquarters, named Richard Armitage as a key connection in a ring of heroin trafficking mobsters and USG officials. A US agent I have known for many years stopped by my home last month en route to his next overseas assignment. He remarked that he had worked for those CIA chiefs named by Khun Sa, and that by his own personal knowledge, he knew what Khun Sa said was true. He was surprised it had taken so long to surface.

I am a registered Republican. I voted for you twice. I will not do so again. If you have any love or loyalty in your heart for this nation; if you have not completely sold out, then do something positive to determine the truth of these most serious allegations. You were Director of the CIA in 1975, during a time Khun Sa says Armitage and CIA officials were trafficking in heroin. As Director of Intelligence you were responsible to the American people for the activities of your assistant – even as you should know what some of these same people are doing who are close to you now as our Vice President because I feel these "parallel government" types will only be promoted by you, giving them more reason to bury our POWs.

Parting shot Mr Vice President: On 28 January 1988, General Khun Sa tendered an offer to turn over to me one metric ton (2,200 pounds) of heroin. He says this is a good faith gesture to the American people that he is serious about stopping all drugs coming from the infamous Golden Triangle. If you and Nancy Reagan are really serious about saying "NO" to drugs, why not test Gen Khun Sa? I challenge you to allow me in the company of agents of your choice to arrange to receive this token offer worth over $4 billion on the streets of New York City. It will represent the largest "legal" seizure of heroin on record. You can personally torch it, dump it in the ocean, or turn it into legal medication; as I understand there is a great shortage of legal opiates available to our doctors. I think Gen Khun Sa's offer is most interesting. If you say "YES" then the ever increasing flow of heroin from Southeast Asia (600 tons—'86, 900 tons—'87, 1200 tons—'88) may dry up – not good for business in the parallel government and super CIA circles Oliver North mentioned. If you say "NO" to Khun Sa, you are showing colors not fit for a man who would be President.

Respecting Your Office,

James "Bo" Gritz, Concerned American, Box 472 HCR-31 Sandy Valley, NV 89019, Tel: (702) 723-5266

Further investigation of the CIA drug trafficking led Ross Perot to Mena and Bush's involvement.

"When you look into the [Vietnam POW] cover-up," Perot said, "you find government officials in the drug trade who can't break themselves of the habit. What I have found is a snake pit [CIA drug trafficking] without a bottom. They will do anything to keep this covered up."

Unable to get Bush to acknowledge the trafficking, Perot ran against Bush in the 1992 election.

Chip Tatum was a CIA deep-cover agent for twenty-five

years. Like Barry, he flew cocaine into Arkansas for the CIA. Realising he was expendable, Chip filed away documents and conversations he'd recorded that would incriminate the CIA and government officials such as George HW Bush and Bill Clinton. When he refused to surrender the documents to the CIA, he was imprisoned for embezzlement and so was his wife. In jail, he broke the leg of a debt collector working for the Mexican Mafia, who subsequently put a hit out on him. Realising that if he died, the documents would be released, the CIA secured his release.

Chip Tatum stated that Bush was so terrified of Perot becoming president and prosecuting Bush for drug crimes that Bush made plans to assassinate him. When Perot ran again in 1996, Tatum wrote him a letter:

Dear Mr Perot:

As you prepare your part for the 1996 election, there is a matter of grave importance of which you should be aware.

In 1992, as the commander of a Black Operations Unit called Pegasus, I was ordered to neutralize you. Our unit was directed by President George Bush. It was determined, at some point, that the party you formed was counter to the American system of democracy. In his attempt to justify your neutralization, Mr Bush expressed not only his concerns of the existence of your party and the threat which you posed to free America, but also the positions of other US and world leaders.

I had been associated with Pegasus since its creation in 1985. The original mission of our unit was to align world leaders and financiers with the United States. I was personally responsible for the neutralization of one Mossad agent, an army Chief of Staff of a foreign government, a rebel leader and the president of a foreign government.

However, all of these missions were directed toward enemies of the United States as determined by our President. And because of this, I did not hesitate to successfully neutralize these enemies.

The order to neutralize you, however, went against all that I believed in. It was obvious to me that his order was predicated on a desire to remain as President rather than a matter of enemy alignment. I refused the order. I further advised the President and others that if you or members of your organization or family were threatened or harmed in any way, I would cause information, which includes certain documents, to be disseminated from their six locations in various areas of the world, to various media and political destinations. I walked away from Special Operations that day with the knowledge that you don't just quit! I felt, however, that the time capsules protected my interests.

In September of 1994, I received a telephone call demanding the information "or else!" It was obvious from the day that I walked out of Pegasus that to turn this information over would be terminal. In the spring of 1995, I was arrested by the FBI for wire fraud. Although innocent of the allegations, I found it necessary to plead guilty in an attempt to tarnish my credibility. It was my opinion, as I expressed it to [Felix] Rodriguez when he called and threatened me, that if I were of questionable credibility, the documents, if ever made public, may not stand on their merits.

With this arrest, I seized upon the opportunity to effect this theory. I have since been indicted on a second fraud charge, this time involving my wife. I will not allow this prosecution of my family. I have notified the authorities that I intend to put my case to a jury. While awaiting the trial, I wrote a book involving my first experience in the Special Operations arena. Since then, I have found that the US Marshals have instructed the Hillsborough County jail to hold me, regardless of the outcome of the instant trial charge.

The new charge is treason. For over twenty years I have dedicated my skills, time, and health to my country. I have been shot, tortured, and beaten, fighting to protect our right to form and run our government as determined by the Constitution. I am not aware of an active Pegasus unit. I had assumed it was disbanded with the new President... Someone had to orchestrate this. So, be aware and alert!

Good luck and good fortune in 1996.

In 1996, Perot's strategy to take votes from Bush worked, and Bill Clinton won – a president involving in drug trafficking was replaced by another involved in trafficking.

On YouTube, Chip Tatum stated that Bush had direct knowledge of the drug operation coming out of Central and South America. Tatum saw Bush at a drugs camp, standing by a cocaine press. Thanks to YouTube, the testimonies of numerous US pilots who flew drugs into America for the CIA are available: Google Beau Abbott, Tosh Plumlee or Terry Reed.

In April 1989, Senator John Kerry's Subcommittee on Terrorism Narcotics and International Operations released its report, "Drugs, Law Enforcement and Foreign Policy." It included diary entries from Bush's frontman Oliver North. In July 1984, North wrote that he wanted "aircraft to go to Bolivia to pick up paste, want aircraft to pick up 1,500 kilos." On July 12, 1985, he wrote, "$14 million to finance [arms] Supermarket came from drugs."

While others took the fall for trafficking, the DEA never investigated North. Even though he'd kept his hands clean by not actually flying the drugs himself, he was guilty of conspiracy under statutes passed by Congress in 1953, concerning anyone committing any act, no matter how small, in the furtherance of a crime. The DEA had stood down, even though North had used international traffickers on the DEA's most wanted list.

One example in the Kerry Report was the airline SETCO, described as "the principal company used by the Contras in Honduras to transport supplies and personnel," in 1986. As early as 1983, US Customs had told the DEA that the owner of the airline was Juan Matta Ballesteros, one of the biggest cocaine traffickers in the world. By 1980, the DEA was aware that Matta and his co-conspirators were estimated to be trafficking one-third of the cocaine used in America. Oliver North had obtained funding from the State Department for Matta's SETCO and three other airlines, all established and run by traffickers. The DEA's response was to close their office in Honduras and to have their officials lie to the public. The difficulty of this deceit was compounded after Matta and his accomplices conspired to kidnap, torture and murder a DEA agent in Mexico in 1985. As they'd all been contributing drug money and weapons to the Nicaraguan rebels, Matta wasn't arrested until 1988, as part of a strategy for Bush's run for the presidency.

Born into a CIA family, Mike Ruppert rose up the ranks as an LA police officer. After witnessing huge CIA shipments of cocaine into California, he blew the whistle and was forced to quit amid death threats. After the journalist Gary Webb detailed the CIA cocaine trafficking that Bush had overseen, people were so outraged that the CIA director appeared at a town-hall meeting at a high school in LA – an epicentre of the crack epidemic that CIA cocaine had helped to fuel. Mike Ruppert decided to attend.

A Congresswoman approached the microphone. "It's not up to us to prove the CIA was involved in drug trafficking in South Central Los Angeles. Rather, it's up to them to prove they were not."

As CIA director Deutch got up to speak, the crowd booed and jeered. "I'm going to be brief," he said. "I want to make four points, and only four points. First, the people of the CIA and I understand the tremendous horror that drugs have been to Americans, what drugs do to families and communities, and the way drugs kill babies. We understand how ravaging drugs are in this country. CIA employees and I share your anger at the injustice and lack of compassion that drug victims encounter."

"He sounds just like Clinton!" someone yelled.

"During the past two years," Deutch said, "while I have been director of Central Intelligence, our case officers' intelligence operations have directly worked to capture all of the Cali Cartel drug lords. We have seriously disrupted the flow of coca paste between the growing areas of Peru and Bolivia to the cocaine processing facilities in Colombia. We have seized huge amounts of heroin grown in the poppy fields of Southwest Asia. Our purpose is to stop drugs from coming into the US. So my second point is that the CIA is fighting against drugs." The audience grumbled.

"Our activities are secret. Accordingly, there's not a lot of public understanding of what we do. I understand that people are suspicious of the CIA, and in the course of recruiting agents to break up those groups that bring drugs into the US, our case officers, our men and women deal with bad people, very bad people, sometimes at great risk to their lives. These are criminals with which we must deal, if we are going to stop drugs from coming to the country. They frequently lie about their relationships with us for their own purpose. So it is hard for members of the public to know what is true and what is not true…

"Now we all know that the US government and the CIA supported the Contras [Nicaraguan rebels] in their efforts to overthrow the Sandinista government in Nicaragua in the mid-80s. It is alleged that the CIA also helped the Contras raise money for arms by introducing crack cocaine into California. It is an appalling charge that goes to the heart of this country. It is a charge that cannot go unanswered," Deutch said, pounding on the table.

"It says that the CIA, an agency of the United States government founded to protect Americans, helped introduce drugs and poison into our children and helped kill their future. No one who heads a government agency – not myself or anyone else – can let such an allegation stand. I will get to the bottom of it and I will let you know the results of what I have found.

"I've ordered an independent investigation of these charges. The third point I want to make to you is to explain the nature of the investigation. I've ordered the CIA Inspector General to undertake a full investigation." The crowd yelled their discontent so loudly that Deutch had to wait a minute before continuing. "Let me tell you why he's the right official to do the job. First, the IG is established by law of Congress to be independent, to carry out activities, to look for fraud and crimes within the CIA. Secondly, the inspector general has access to all CIA records and documents, no matter how secret. Third, the IG has the authority to interview the right people. Fourth, he is able to cooperate with other government departments. For example, the Department of Justice, the DEA, the Department of Defense, all of which had operations on-going in Nicaragua at the time. Finally, the IG has a good track record of being a whistle-blower on past misdeeds of the CIA. For example, just last month he uncovered that some CIA employees were misusing credit cards and they are now in jail."

"What about Guatemala? What about those murders?" a heckler yelled, referring to CIA-sponsored military regimes in Guatemala murdering thousands of civilians.

"Most importantly, when this investigation is complete, I intend to make the results public, so that any person can judge the adequacy of the investigation. Anyone in the public who has a wish to look at the report will be able to do so. I want to stress that I am not the only person in the CIA who wants any American to believe that the CIA was responsible for this kind of disgusting charge. Finally, I want to say to you that as of today, we have no evidence of conspiracy by the CIA to engage in encouraging drug traffickers in Nicaragua or elsewhere in Latin America during this or any other period."

A question came from a graduate student of the Tuskegee Institute in Alabama: "I'd like to know how this incident differs from what happened at my school, where, for forty years, the government denied inflicting syphilis on African-American men?"

Deutch conceded that what had happened at Tuskegee was terrible. "Let me say something else. There was no one who came forward forty years ago and said they were going to investigate."

"Where I live there are no jobs for the children and our kids are just seen as commodities," a woman said. "They are being cycled through the prisons. They come back to the street and are marked and scarred for the rest of their life. You, the President and everybody else should be highly upset. You should be saying, how did this cancer get here?"

A man stood up. "And now we are supposed to trust the CIA to investigate itself?"

Deutch tried to quell the malcontents by overemphasising the Inspector General's independence, which incensed the crowd.

"Why don't you turn it over to an independent counsel? Someone who has the power to issue subpoenas. It would have more credibility."

Deutch responded that no independent counsel was possible because no criminal complaint had been filed.

It was Mike Ruppert's turn to speak. For years, he'd been waiting for such an opportunity. The rowdy audience hushed as Mike said, "I will tell you, director Deutch, as a former Los Angeles Police narcotics detective, that your agency has dealt drugs throughout this country for a long time."

There was a standing ovation. The audience went wild. It took a few minutes to calm everybody down.

"Director Deutch, I will refer you to three specific agency operations known as Amadeus, Pegasus and Watchtower. I have Watchtower documents heavily redacted by the Agency [CIA]. I was personally exposed to CIA operations and recruited by CIA personnel who attempted to recruit me in the late 70s to become involved in protecting Agency drug operations in this country. I have been trying to get this out for eighteen years, and I have the evidence. My question for you is very specific, sir. If in the course of the IG's [CIA Inspector General's] investigations... you come across evidence of severely criminal activity, and it's classified, will you use that classification to hide the criminal activity or will you tell the American people the truth?"

There was more applause and cheering as Deutch wrung his hands and clasped them together as if praying.

"If you have information," Deutch said, "about CIA illegal activity in drugs, you should immediately bring that information to wherever you want, but let me suggest three places: the Los Angeles Police Department–"

"No! No!" the crowd yelled.

"It is your choice: the Los Angeles Police Department, the Inspector General or the office of one of your congresspersons..."

The audience started chanting, "He told you!"

"If this information turns up wrongdoing," Deutch said, growing exasperated, "we will bring the people to justice and make them accountable."

"For the record..." Mike said, "I did bring this information out eighteen years ago and I got shot at and forced out of LAPD because of it." Mike finished to massive applause.

"My question to you is," a spectator said to Deutch, "if you know all this stuff that the Agency has done historically, then why should we believe you today, when you say certainly this could never happen in Los Angeles, when the CIA's done this stuff all over the world?"

"I didn't come here thinking everyone was going to believe me," Deutch said. "I came here for a much simpler task. I came here to stand up on my legs and tell you I was going to investigate these horrible allegations. All you can do is listen to what I have to say and wait to see the results."

"But how can we know how many documents have been shredded and how can we be certain that more documents won't be shredded?"

"I don't know that anybody has found any lost documents in the operational files," Deutch said. "I know of nobody who has found any gaps in sequences, any missing files, any missing papers for any period of that time. That may come up."

"Hey, do you know Walter Pincus?" a man asked, referring to a journalist who spied on American students abroad for the CIA.

"Yes," Deutch said. "Why?"

"Is he an asset of the CIA?"

As if he'd had enough, Deutch clasped his head and shook it.

The crowd vented on the lady who'd invited Deutch to the meeting. "I don't know why this lady is saluting Deutch's courage for coming here today, when everybody knows this building has got hundreds of pigs in it. There's pigs behind those curtains.

There's pigs on the roof. We're not going to get no ghetto justice today." The crowd murmured its approval.

A man stood and pointed at Deutch. "To see you coming in this community today in this way is nothing more than a public-relations move for the white people of this country. So you are going to come into this community today and insult us, and tell us you're going to investigate yourself. You've got to be crazy."

Refusing to take any more questions, Deutch concluded with, "You know, I've learned how important it is for our government and our agency to get on top of this problem and stop it. I came today to try and describe the approach and have left with a better appreciation of what is on your mind."

Immediately, the media tried to spin the meeting in a way favourable to the CIA. Via satellite, Ted Koppel of *Nightline* interviewed members of the audience, trying to extract a positive testimony, only to find himself rebuffed by questions such as, "You come down here and talk about solutions. We have kids that are dying. We have hospitals for babies born drug addicted. When are you guys going to come down and bring cameras to our neighbourhood?"

"I'm not sure that anybody even thought that was why Director Deutch came there today," Koppel said. "He's come here because a lot of you are in anguish. A lot of you are angry. A lot of you are frustrated by what you believe to be the CIA's involvement in bringing drugs to South Central LA. Now, I want to hear from someone who thought it did some good."

"Well, I am glad Mr Deutch was here today," said Marcine Shaw, the mayor pro tem of Compton. "I'm glad Congresswoman Macdonald had him here because that's what it took to get your cameras here, Mr Koppel."

Koppel shook his head. "Yes, but that's not the question." Koppel finished his broadcast with, "If any suspicions were put to rest or minds changed, there was no evidence of it in South Central this evening."

Originally, Pablo Escobar was in bed with the CIA through the Medellín Cartel's contributions to the Nicaraguan rebels. Traffickers who made such payments to the CIA were allowed to operate. Testifying as a US government witness at the Noriega trial, the Medellín Cartel's Carlos Lehder admitted contributing millions to the Nicaraguan rebels.

The CIA had helped to overthrow the government of Bolivia in 1980, and put cocaine traffickers in charge – detailed in my book, *We Are Being Lied To: The War on Drugs*. In the name of fighting Communism, the CIA had put Klaus Barbi – a Nazi war criminal responsible for the deaths of up to 14,000 people – in charge of the coup in Bolivia. His Argentine death squad had massacred numerous civilians.

After the coup, the CIA-backed Bolivian government exported raw coca. One of its customers was the Medellín Cartel. As the anti-Communist cause was being advanced, the CIA protected this activity by obstructing investigations by other law-enforcement agencies. In doing so, it created a secure route for coca paste to go from Bolivia to Colombia. In Medellín, the Bolivian paste was processed and distributed to the US.

The Argentine intelligence services made a fortune from selling Bolivian paste. Some of the money was laundered in Miami and recycled into other anti-Communist causes, which included buying massive amounts of weapons from US manufacturers, which Bush represented, along with banking interests. That's how Bush used drug money to finance the Nicaraguan rebels.

Prompted by the journalism of Gary Webb, the CIA and Justice Department investigations confirmed that the Nicaraguan rebels had been involved in the cocaine trade throughout the 1980s. The CIA had been aware of it, and they'd steered other agencies, such as DEA investigators, away from the truth.

Despite Bush holding Pablo accountable for nearly all of the cocaine entering America, CIA-protected cocaine wasn't only coming from Colombia. Pablo was used as a smokescreen for cocaine coming from various routes originating in South

America. In El Salvador, the military were involved. Honduras was a major transiting point. Anti-Castro Cubans active in Costa Rica sent boatloads of cocaine to Miami. As usual, the CIA stopped all of the investigations into these areas. The mainstream media avoided it. Long after Pablo's demise, the tangled roots of this infrastructure keep the cocaine flowing to this day.

PART 3

THE VERDICT

CHAPTER 46

Verdict

Pablo Escobar ordered approximately 4,000 deaths, but he was an amateur in the murder leagues in comparison to George HW Bush, whose proclivity for taking America to war and to drop bombs on impoverished populations caused well over 100,000 deaths and the poisoning of hundreds of thousands of US troops and personnel. Backed up by presidential pomp and circumstance, video-casts of precision bombing and an ability to write off the mass murder of civilians as collateral damage, Bush committed murder with panache. With God and the media on his side, he acted out his capacity for violence and never suffered any consequences.

The analysis of Bush's character suggests that someone who initiated wars for personal gain, protected political paedophiles and was the head of the CIA would easily have ordered the elimination of Barry Seal, who had threatened Bush in various ways.

To reach a verdict, it's necessary to go beyond a character analysis. It's time to examine the clues that arose in the aftermath of the murder.

After shooting Barry Seal, Quintero Cruz sprinted to the getaway car and handed his MAC-10 to Cumbamba, who was wearing green surgical trousers. Speeding away, the Buick almost hit a bystander. Roughly a quarter of a mile away, the car was abandoned – with its engine still running and the MAC-10 inside – at a children's activity centre parking lot. The Colombians dashed to a red Cadillac. Two sheriff's deputies providing security at a bingo game noticed the Colombians laughing as they switched cars.

Hunting for the killers, FBI agents poured into the airport. Some checked hotels for Colombian names.

At 7:30 pm, two of the Colombians checked out of the New Orleans Hilton. At New Orleans International Airport, they abandoned the red Cadillac shortly after 8:36 pm.

At 8:45 pm, two FBI agents grew suspicious of a nervous sweaty man at an Eastern Airlines ticket counter attempting to get a direct flight to Miami. When questioned, Cumbamba claimed to be a lost traveller and provided a passport for Miguel Velez. With no probable cause or description, the agents released him. He said he intended to return to his hotel and get a taxi to another airport. Fifteen minutes later, descriptions of the hit men were broadcast. The FBI realised that Velez was one of them. Agents found out that he had taken a taxi.

But for a deer running onto a highway, Cumbamba might have escaped. At 2:20 am, in Meridian, Mississippi, the police spotted a broken-down taxi that had collided with a deer. They pulled over and questioned the passenger in green trousers. Upon finding $3,270 and the keys to the red getaway car on Cumbamba, they arrested him. Cumbamba had made the mistake of changing his green surgical trousers for another pair of green trousers. Upset with losing his fare, the taxi driver couldn't understand why the police were so concerned about a dead deer.

Vasquez had made a few errors, too. He'd used his true identity, including his American Express card, to hire the getaway car. He managed to ensconce himself in a friend's house in Algiers, New Orleans, unaware that his friend was an FBI informant. The next day, the FBI captured him with $860 in cash and $9,800 in cashier's checks. Quintero Cruz suffered a similar fate, busted in a safe house in Marrero, Louisiana with $3,127.

It seems that the Colombians were meant to be captured quickly, so that the case could be closed.

Cumbamba's lawyer, Richard Sharpstein, told author Daniel Hopsiker that representing Cumbamba was one of the most amazing experiences of his life. Sharpstein said that the three

Colombians who'd been arrested all told their lawyers the same thing: after they'd arrived in America, their mission to assassinate Barry Seal was directed by an anonymous gringo, a US military officer, who they figured out was Oliver North. After they'd rendezvoused together in America, they received instructions over the phone from a man who insisted on remaining anonymous, but identified himself as an American military officer. They'd been put in touch with the officer through Rafa.

Numerous sources confirmed to Hopsiker that Oliver North was running assassinations from his White House office. North had also drawn up contingency plans, including implementing martial law if the drug-trafficking facilitated by the CIA were ever exposed to the public.

The official story is that a three-man hit team assassinated Barry Seal. Yet six Colombians were arrested fleeing the scene. A seventh, Rafa was charged in absentia for organising the hit, but was shot to death at his antique car dealership in Colombia, thus eliminating the contact between the arrestees and Oliver North.

The eighth co-conspirator was the supplier of the MAC-10, Jose Coutin. He owned Broadway Boutique, which stocked ladies' clothes in the front of the shop and military supplies in the back. Being a CIA asset, an FBI informant and a weapons supplier for the Nicaraguan rebels, Coutin wasn't charged with the hit even though he was guilty of conspiracy to commit murder by supplying the MAC-10. Coutin testified against the three Colombians. When asked about his connections to the CIA and the Nicaraguan rebels, he lost his cool on the stand.

Three of the six Colombians originally arrested included Rafa's brother, John Cordona who was busted at a safe house; Eliberto Sanchez, who was caught at New Orleans International Airport; and Jose Renteria, who was arrested at Miami Airport about to board a plane. Sanchez and Cordona were deported without any charges being filed.

Renteria had picked up the weapons from Coutin and delivered them to the three Colombians. On the basis that he wasn't at the murder scene, Renteria's trial was severed from the trial of the three Colombians, which Cumbamba's lawyer, Sharpstein, found highly suspicious. Sharpstein said that Renteria had offered to cooperate, but the federal government was not keen on that happening. According to witness testimony, Renteria had photographed the murder scene. At New Orleans Airport, an FBI agent had confiscated his camera and exposed the film inside. In record time, Renteria received a plea bargain for minor charges and was deported, to avoid, according to Sharpstein, his testimony ever being heard.

The trial of the three was structured to create an official version of events that precluded any involvement of George HW Bush's proxy Oliver North. As the residents of Baton Rouge had heard so much about Barry Seal, the trial was moved to Lake Charles, Louisiana, an oil-refinery town near the Texas border, 170 miles away from the tainted jury pool. Hoping to boost its local economy, Lake Charles had launched a campaign to host the trial.

The trial started on April 6, 1987, over a year after Barry's death. With none of the Colombians willing to cooperate against their co-defendants, the prosecutor sought the death penalty for all three.

Protected by federal marshals, Max Mermelstein – whose half-hearted attempt to assassinate Barry Seal on behalf the Medellín Cartel had failed – was handed a MAC-10 by the prosecutor, while in the witness box.

"Mr Mermelstein, would you look at these two exhibits before you mark State's 14 [the MAC-10] and State's 15 [a silencer for the MAC-10], please?" said the prosecutor, a short no-nonsense woman with dark hair. "Have you ever seen previously either Exhibit 14 or 15?"

"Yes, I have," said Max, overweight with grey hair and a beard, wearing a colourful shirt and a blue blazer. With the three Colombians gazing at him, he spoke slowly and with little emotion.

"Would you tell the jury the circumstances under which you first saw that?"

"Sometime in April or May of 1984, they were brought to my residence," Max said.

"By whom were they brought?"

"By Rafael Cardona," Max said, referring to Rafa, a link to Oliver North who was silenced by assassination.

"And why did he have that weapon with him?"

"To show me what he had just gotten..."

"Was anything done with that weapon when it got to your residence?"

"He showed me the weapon and told me he wanted to test-fire it by the pool." Max admitted organising the logistics for thirty-eight 450-kilo air-shipments of cocaine, and for being responsible for 50,000 kilos of cocaine entering America. As well as providing compelling testimony, Max identified Cumbamba.

"How much cash did you arrange to be taken out of the United States?" said Sharpstein, the tanned and well-dressed Miami lawyer defending the Colombians.

"Approximately three-hundred million."

The jury gasped.

"You yourself arranged for approximately $300 million in illegal money to be taken out of the country?"

"That is correct, sir."

Addressing the jury, ten women and two men, Sharpstein said, "Max Mermelstein is a man who would make Barry Seal look like a midget... [Max was] another Barry Seal, a clone, maybe even worse than Seal..."

Physical evidence presented by the prosecutor included the fingerprints of the three Colombians found in the murder vehicle, chemical evidence on Cumbamba's hand indicating that he'd handled a recently fired weapon, and car keys found in Cumbamba's pocket. A car salesman described selling the murder vehicle to Vasquez for $6,500. Two witnesses placed Quintero Cruz at the murder scene. It took five weeks and 118 witnesses for the prosecution's case to be presented.

"Why did they use a machine gun instead of walking up to Barry Seal and shooting him?" the prosecutor said, brandishing the MAC-10. "Because this weapon was used to teach a lesson – gangland style – to deter other snitches."

Sharpstein called no witnesses. He attacked Barry Seal's character. "The man was too complex. The man had many sides, not just two sides, right and wrong. Adler Barry Seal was a drug smuggler. He was a soldier of fortune. He was a mercenary. He was a man who would do what benefited Barry Seal. He was a man who understood the system… He always found a back door out and he always used it to benefit Barry Seal. He put bullets in his own head. I tell you the tale of Barry Seal will point in the direction of that because he himself is responsible for where he is."

After deliberating for thirty minutes, the jury found the three Colombians guilty with a penalty of life imprisonment.

After the trial, when asked why Barry was murdered, Sharpstein recounted the various times that Barry had telephoned George HW Bush for help. Barry had been moved to the halfway house and stripped of carrying weapons just one week after he had asked Bush to get the tax authorities off his back. Although Cumbamba had pulled the trigger, the Colombians, according to Sharpstein, had received orders from government officials who wanted him dead.

Sharpstein's conclusion was backed up by Red Hall, a CIA electronics expert. Hall told author Hopsiker that the CIA had a lot to do with it, and that Oliver North had directed the assassins. Hall added that North had previously tried to eliminate Barry much earlier by blowing the whistle on Barry's sting operation while Barry was in Nicaragua.

Ex-CIA deep-cover agent Chip Tatum told Hopsiker that Oliver North's role in the death of Barry Seal wasn't exactly the secret of the century.

The night Barry died, federal agents swarmed the state police headquarters at Baton Rouge, and demanded all of the evidence from the homicide detectives in charge of preserving it. They physically seized Barry's belongings from the boot of his Cadillac, including files on important people that he had kept as leverage.

By law, the state police should have prevented the FBI from confiscating the evidence. A lawyer for one of the Colombian hit men stated that the state police would have had to draw their guns on the federal agents to prevent them from taking the evidence. Some of the things accounted for in the trunk were never returned. Barry was known to have kept three boxes of precious documents, including the encrypted numbers of Swiss bank accounts, where senior politicians stashed money. One account under the encrypted code KPFBMMBODB with over $10 million belonged to the Secretary of Defense, Caspar Weinberger, who'd allegedly received kickbacks on drugs and arms sales.

On March 16, 1986, four months after Barry's death, Ronald Reagan appeared on TV, hoping to gain support for his request for $100 million in aid for the Nicaraguan rebels. Brandishing one of the grainy photos Barry had snapped during the Nicaraguan sting, Reagan said, "I know every American parent concerned about the drug problem will be outraged to learn that top Nicaraguan government officials are deeply involved in drug trafficking. There is no crime to which the Sandinistas will not stoop. This is an outlaw regime."

The War on Drugs is about spending money, but in this case, the public wasn't swayed. Even the DEA knew that Reagan had lied. The DEA stated that it had no information implicating "the Minister of Interior or other Nicaraguan officials."

The Nicaraguan rebels were allowed to finance their war through the importation of cocaine to America with the help of the CIA. Business continued as usual after Barry's death. Weapons out and drugs in. Even though Barry couldn't talk from the grave, the Fat Lady almost revealed all.

On October 5th, 1986, the Fat Lady was shot down over Nicaragua. After Barry's death, she had reverted to the CIA's

Southern Air Transport and had continued to smuggle weapons illegally to the Nicaraguan rebels.

Only one crew member survived, Eugene Hasenfus. The fatalities included the pilot who'd replaced Emile Camp at Mena, Bill Cooper, and Wallace Sawyer Jr, who was in possession of a notebook with the names of thirty-four CIA operatives and a card with a number on its back, pertaining to a Swiss bank account with a balance of $12 million – profits from arms sales. Other records on-board linked the Fat Lady to Barry and Area 51: a CIA base in Nevada and a nuclear weapons facility.

Under interrogation by the Nicaraguans, Hasenfus revealed details about the operation. He identified two of his commanders as Ramon Medina and Max Gomez [Felix Rodriguez], both heavy hitters in the CIA and close friends of George HW Bush. Hasenfus identified the operation's safe house in El Salvador, from which telephone records showed numerous calls to Oliver North at the White House (202-395-3345), to Southern Air Transport and to the Stanford Technology Trading Corp, a Virginia front run by retired Air Force General Richard Secord, who was involved in US assistance to Southeast Asian heroin operations during the Vietnam War.

In response to the downing of the Fat Lady, Oliver North embarked on a document- shredding binge that lasted for three days. Among the names shredded was Barry Seal's. Plenty of incriminating documents survived. Investigators found over 500 references to drugs in North's notebooks.

The co-conspirators in Barry's death allowed the media to run with stories of illegal arms shipments, but stories of CIA drug trafficking were off-limits. Due to the CIA's relationships with the media, the strategy worked.

"After the Hasenfus plane was shot down, you couldn't find a soul around Mena," said William Holmes, an Arkansas gun manufacturer, who'd supplied Barry and the CIA.

But business quickly resumed. In early 1987, an Arkansas state police investigator wrote, "New activity at the [Mena] airport," involving C-130s and an Australian company linked to the CIA. Under oath, the investigator said that two FBI agents warned him that the CIA had something going on at the Mena airport involving Southern Air Transport, and they didn't want him to screw it up.

In 1991, an IRS investigative memorandum stated that "the CIA still has ongoing operations out of the Mena, AR airport... and that one of the operations at the airport is laundering money."

In 1985, when confronted with accusations of participating in activity at Mena, the CIA blamed Mena on "a rogue DEA operation." The DEA's response was "no comment."

A few weeks before Barry's death, state authorities were monitoring a cocaine shipment on one of Barry's boats, Captain Wonderful. When they tried to get on board, they were prevented by DEA and CIA agents.

The same day that Barry was killed, three senior members of the Medellín Cartel were assassinated: Pablo Ochilla, Pablo Carrera and a brother-in-law of Jorge Ochoa. Author Hopsicker believes that these murders and Barry's were parts of a co-ordinated black op and that all along the CIA had been using the war against the Medellín Cartel as cover, while they worked with the Cali Cartel. Hopsicker goes so far as to claim that the CIA, with Barry's help, had created the Medellín Cartel by encouraging the different factions to work together, a claim that was backed up by Paul Etzel, a Colombian accountant who interpreted for Barry during the Panamanian meeting with Pablo Escobar. Journalist Alexander Cockburn has claimed that in the beginning, the Medellín Cartel was working with the CIA. After the demise of the Medellín Cartel, cocaine continued to pour into America on planes used in CIA covert operations.

None of Barry's fleet of planes, including the Fat Lady, were seized following his assassination because they were still being used in black ops.

In August, 1987, two teenagers, Kevin Ives and Don Henry, witnessed a CIA drug drop at Mena and were killed. Their bodies were put on a railroad track. The medical expert appointed by Bill Clinton ruled that they'd gotten stoned on marijuana, fallen asleep side-by-side and were run over by a train. All of the family's attempts to get to the truth were blocked. I detail their story and Linda Ives struggle to get justice for her son in the third part of this trilogy: *We Are Being Lied To: The War on Drugs*.

A decade later, journalist Gary Webb exposed the CIA drug trafficking in the 1980s, which had helped to spawn the crack epidemic. The story caused a sensation, but the propaganda machine responded quickly. Hounded out of his job, Webb eventually committed suicide by shooting himself in the head – twice. Webb's revelations forced the CIA to announce that it was investigating itself. In a 1998 CIA Inspector General's report, the CIA admitted "briefing" Vice President Bush on how it had lied to Congress about cocaine trafficking by its agents.

The CIA continues to deny that it facilitated the arms-for-cocaine trafficking performed by Barry Seal. Authors and journalists investigating the paper trail of federal aircraft registrations and outfittings have discovered that many of the aircraft that Barry used were previously owned by Air America, a CIA proprietary company. The transportation service that Barry provided was part of a government operation that expanded way beyond Colombia and Nicaragua to include the provision of arms to Bolivia, Argentina, Peru and Brazil, an area known as the Southern Tier. The multi millions that were made financed black ops, and was used to pay off politicians such as Bill Clinton who played along with the CIA. Mena was a part of a network of rural airports in states such as Arizona, Alabama, Florida, Louisiana, Mississippi and Kentucky used by the CIA; all afforded the same protection – under the guise of national security – from conventional law enforcement.

Two law enforcement officials investigating Mena documented the crimes they'd discovered in a thirty-five volume 3,000-page Arkansas State Police archive. Not only were they never asked to testify, their investigation and careers were destroyed.

One wrote in his diary on November 17, 1987, "Should a cop cross over the line and dare to investigate the rich and powerful, he might well prepare himself to become the victim of his own government... The cops are all afraid to tell what they know for fear that they will lose their jobs."

After 1987, nine more investigations into Mena were suppressed. In December 1988, a US Senate subcommittee report stated that a Mena investigation had been dropped even though there was enough evidence "sufficient for an indictment on money laundering charges," because "the prosecution might have revealed national security information, even though all the crimes which were the focus of the investigation occurred before Seal became a federal informant [in 1984]."

In 1996, one of Barry's former associates testified that Barry's flights had been provided CIA security, including the installation of highly classified encoding devices that thwarted air defence and surveillance.

After Barry's death, Terry Reed continued to work for the CIA in Mexico, where he witnessed first-hand the CIA's involvement in drugs. He attempted to quit the business, so the CIA tried to assassinate him. With his family, he went on the run. Arrested on bogus charges, he and his wife ended up in prison and were ruined financially. By saddling him with a criminal record, the feds destroyed Terry's whistle-blower potential – all documented in his book, *Compromised: Clinton, Bush and the CIA.*

In 1991, a month before announcing his candidacy for president, Bill Clinton made his only statement as governor about the crimes of Mena. Continuing the cover-up, he claimed that the state had done all it possibly could have to investigate allegations about drugs and weapons smuggling through Mena airport. "I've always felt we never got the whole story there, and obviously if the story was that the DEA was using Barry Seal as a drug informant... then they ought to come out and say that because he's dead." The state police had conducted a "very vigorous" investigation several years ago, and the enquiry had raised questions "that involved linkages to the federal government." A file had been turned over to the US attorney, who convened a grand jury that returned no indictments, which was not the state's fault.

He blamed Barry's murder on inadequate security. "[The Seal case] raised all kinds of questions about whether he had any links to the CIA and if he was involved with the Contras... and if that backed into the Iran-Contra deal."

The next day, the *Gazette* reported: "CLINTON: STATE DID ALL IT COULD IN MENA CASE."

It is the verdict of this book that George HW Bush sanctioned the hit on Barry Seal in response to threats by an increasingly desperate Barry to expose the drugs side of the operation. Barry also antagonised Bush by claiming that he had evidence that Bush's sons had been caught in a drug sting operation – an allegation that still remains unproved.

According to Hopsicker, there was a persistent rumour that Barry had organised a DEA sting on the Bush brothers because George HW Bush wasn't helping him. With the Bush brothers ensnared by videotape evidence, Barry supposedly posed as a saviour by using his influence to make their problem go away. Now they owed Barry a favour, but just in case they didn't follow through, Barry had kept a copy of the videotape. It had been in one of the boxes of the precious documents in his car that had been confiscated by the FBI, who arrived ten minutes after Barry's death.

A lawman told Hopsicker that he'd found a drilling rig moored in Mexican waters that served as a safe harbour for drug smuggling. A sting operation had been set up at a Florida airport, but cancelled at the last minute by someone high up after it was discovered that the Bush Brothers – George W and Jeb – were flying in on a King Air the lawman was tracking.

In *Blue Thunder*, authors Burdick and Mitchell quote an imprisoned drug smuggler called Teagle, who claimed that Jeb Bush and Donald Aronow – who built speedboats for George HW Bush – had been partners in a cocaine-trafficking operation, and they owed Colombians $2.5 million. In his car on February 2, 1987, Aronow was assassinated.

After his death, Barry became a fall guy for the orchestrators of the Mena activity. The importation of tons of cocaine on CIA planes was blamed on a renegade smuggler. Those in charge of Mena had the most to gain from Barry's death. So who was running things? Certainly not Bill Clinton, who, as a mere governor, could only provide legal and police protection for the bigger players. Under the provisions of Executive Order 12333 and National Security Decision Directives Number 2 and Number 3, George HW Bush was in charge of all intelligence operations, including Mena.

Barry died with George HW Bush's telephone number in his possession. Their relationship had soured after Bush reneged on what Barry had perceived as their agreement. Barry had worked diligently for Bush at Mena in the expectation of Bush using his power to squash any unforeseen legal difficulties. But by mid-1985, Barry was more valuable to Bush as a scapegoat. When Bush failed to provide protection, Barry must have realised – based on the pattern of his deceased associates, including Lee Harvey Oswald, David Ferrie and Emile Camp – that his end was near.

Barry had spearheaded Mena for Bush, but, after his death, the smuggling flights continued, proving not only that Barry hadn't been a rogue smuggler, but also that he was no longer needed to keep the operation going. Any doubts as to whom Barry was working for were laid to rest by the IRS in a posthumous tax assessment, which cited his "CIA-DEA employment," and claimed that Barry owed $86 million in back taxes on earnings from Mena in 1982 and 1983.

Killers sometimes keep trophies of their crimes. After Barry's death, his 1982 Beechcraft King Air 200 (FAA registration number N6308F and Serial Number BB-1014) ended up becoming one of George W Bush's favourite methods of transportation.

On March 30, 1985, Chip Tatum took notes while conversing with Oliver North as they inspected cocaine factories at villages on Nicaragua's border with Honduras. North said that they were making so much money from drugs and arms that they'd be able to retire after a year if they could keep the Arkansas hicks in line. He was referring to Clinton and his cronies stealing cash that Barry had been assigned to launder through Arkansas. He said Bush was so concerned about the missing money that he was going to have Jeb Bush arrange something out of Colombia, which Chip later understood to be the assassination of Barry, whom they also suspected of stealing money.

Rather than help Barry, Bush had him killed. All Mafia dons have underlings who carry out their orders, so that there is no trail of evidence linking directly to them. Oliver North performed this function for Bush. With the threat from the Medellín Cartel, North's work was easy and he had the perfect smokescreen.

"All the federal government had to do to kill Barry Seal was to do nothing. Then let mischief work its will," said Barry's Baton Rouge lawyer.

But just in case mischief didn't work, George HW Bush and Oliver North helped it along.

In Baton Rouge, Barry was buried in a sky-blue casket with a Snickers bar, his telephone pager and a bunch of twenty-five cent coins. He had written his own epitaph in his personal Bible which was etched onto his grave marker and read at the funeral: "A rebel adventurer the likes of whom in previous days made America great."

GET A FREE BOOK

Sign Up For My Newsletter At:

http://shaunattwood.com/newsletter-subscribe/

MY SOCIAL-MEDIA LINKS

Email: attwood.shaun@hotmail.co.uk
Blog: Jon's Jail Journal
Website: shaunattwood.com
Twitter: @shaunattwood
YouTube: Shaun Attwood
LinkedIn: Shaun Attwood
Goodreads: Shaun Attwood
Facebook pages: Shaun Attwood, Jon's Jail Journal, T-Bone Appreciation Society

I welcome feedback on any of my books.
Thank you for the Amazon reviews!

MY BOOKS

English Shaun Trilogy

Party Time
Hard Time
Prison Time

War on Drugs Trilogy

Pablo Escobar: Beyond Narcos
American Made: Who Killed Barry Seal? Pablo Escobar or George HW Bush
We Are Being Lied To: The War on Drugs (Expected 2017)

Life Lessons

Making a Murderer: The Framing of Avery and Dassey by Kratz and Other Parasites (Expected 2017)

Two Tonys (Expected 2017)
T-Bone (Expected 2020)

REFERENCES

Bowden, Mark. *Killing Pablo*. Atlantic Books, 2001.

Bowen, Russell. *The Immaculate Deception*. America West Publishers, 1991.

Cockburn, Leslie. *Out of Control*. Bloomsbury, 1988.

Cockburn and Clair. *Whiteout*. Verso, 1998.

Escobar, Roberto. *Escobar*. Hodder & Stoughton, 2009.

Grillo, Joan. *El Narco*. Bloomsbury, 2012.

Gugliotta and Leen. *Kings of Cocaine*. Harper and Row, 1989.

Hari, Johann. *Chasing the Scream*. Bloomsbury, 2015.

Hopsicker, Daniel. *Barry and the Boys*. MadCow Press, 2001.

Leveritt, Mara. *The Boys on the Tracks*. Bird Call Press, 2007.

Levine, Michael. *The Big White Lie*. Thunder's Mouth Press, 1993.

Marquez, Gabriel Garcia. *News of a Kidnapping*. Penguin, 1996.

Marrs, Jim. *Rule By Secrecy*. Perennial, 2000.

Massing, Michael. *The Fix*. Simon & Schuster, 1998.

McCoy, Alfred. *The Politics of Heroin in Southeast Asia*. Harper and Row, 1972.

Morris, Roger. *Partners in Power*. Henry Holt, 1996.

Noriega, Manuel. *The Memoirs of Manuel Noriega*. Random House, 1997.

North, Oliver. *Under Fire*. Harper Collins, 1991.

Paley, Dawn. *Drug War Capitalism*. AK Press, 2014.

Porter, Bruce. *Blow*. St Martin's Press, 1993.

Reed, Terry. *Compromised*. Clandestine Publishing, 1995.

Ross, Rick. *Freeway Rick Ross*. Freeway Studios, 2014.

Ruppert, Michael. *Crossing the Rubicon*. New Society Publishers, 2004.

Saviano, Roberto. *Zero Zero Zero*. Penguin Random House UK, 2013.

Schou, Nick. *Kill the Messenger*. Nation Books, 2006.

Shannon, Elaine. *Desperados*. Penguin, 1988.

Stich, Rodney. *Drugging America* 2nd Ed. Silverpeak, 2006.

Stone, Roger. *The Clinton's War on Women*. Skyhorse, 2015.

Stone, Roger. *Jeb and the Bush Crime Family*. Skyhorse, 2016.

Streatfield, Dominic. *Cocaine*. Virgin Publishing, 2001.

Sutton, Antony. *Wall Street and the Rise of Hitler.* Clairview, 2010.

Tarpley and Chaitkin. *George Bush*. Progressive Press, 2004.

Valentine, Douglas. *The Strength of the Pack.* Trine Day LLC, 2009.

SHAUN ATTWOOD'S TRUE-LIFE JAIL EXPERIENCE

HARD TIME 2ND EDITION CHAPTER 1

Sleep deprived and scanning for danger, I enter a dark cell on the second floor of the maximum-security Madison Street jail in Phoenix, Arizona, where guards and gang members are murdering prisoners. Behind me, the metal door slams heavily. Light slants into the cell through oblong gaps in the door, illuminating a prisoner cocooned in a white sheet, snoring lightly on the top bunk about two thirds of the way up the back wall. Relieved there is no immediate threat, I place my mattress on the grimy floor. Desperate to rest, I notice movement on the cement-block walls. *Am I hallucinating?* I blink several times. The walls appear to ripple. Stepping closer, I see the walls are alive with insects. I flinch. So many are swarming, I wonder if they're a colony of ants on the move. To get a better look, I put my eyes right up to them. They are mostly the size of almonds and have antennae. American cockroaches. I've seen them in the holding cells downstairs in smaller numbers, but nothing like this. A chill spreads over my body. I back away.

Something alive falls from the ceiling and bounces off the base of my neck. I jump. With my night vision improving, I spot cockroaches weaving in and out of the base of the fluorescent strip light. Every so often one drops onto the concrete and resumes crawling. Examining the bottom bunk, I realise why my cellmate is sleeping at a higher elevation: cockroaches are pouring from gaps in the decrepit wall at the level of my bunk. The area is thick with them. Placing my mattress on the bottom bunk scatters them. I walk towards the toilet, crunching a few under my shower sandals. I urinate and grab the toilet roll. A cockroach darts from the centre of the roll onto my hand, tickling my fingers. My arm jerks as if it has a mind of its own, losing the cockroach and the toilet roll. Using a towel, I wipe the bulk of them off the bottom bunk, stopping only to shake the odd one off my hand. I unroll my mattress. They begin to regroup and inhabit my mattress. My adrenaline is pumping so much, I lose my fatigue.

Nauseated, I sit on a tiny metal stool bolted to the wall. *How will I sleep? How's my cellmate sleeping through the infestation and my arrival?* Copying his technique, I cocoon myself in a sheet and lie down, crushing more cockroaches. The only way they can access me now is through the breathing hole I've left in the sheet by the lower half of my face. Inhaling their strange musty odour, I close my eyes. I can't sleep. I feel them crawling on the sheet around my feet. *Am I imagining things?* Frightened of them infiltrating my breathing hole, I keep opening my eyes. Cramps cause me to rotate onto my other side. Facing the wall, I'm repulsed by so many of them just inches away. I return to my original side.

The sheet traps the heat of the Sonoran Desert to my body, soaking me in sweat. Sweat tickles my body, tricking my mind into thinking the cockroaches are infiltrating and crawling on me. The trapped heat aggravates my bleeding skin infections and bedsores. I want to scratch myself, but I know better. The outer layers of my skin have turned soggy from sweating constantly in this concrete oven. Squirming on the bunk fails to stop the relentless itchiness of my skin. Eventually, I scratch myself. Clumps of moist skin detach under my nails. Every now and then I become so uncomfortable, I have to open my cocoon to waft the heat out, which allows the cockroaches in. It takes hours to drift to sleep. I only manage a few hours. I awake stuck to the soaked sheet, disgusted by the cockroach carcasses compressed against the mattress.

The cockroaches plague my new home until dawn appears at the dots in the metal grid over a begrimed strip of four-inch-thick bullet-proof glass at the top of the back wall – the cell's only source of outdoor light. They disappear into the cracks in the walls, like vampire mist retreating from sunlight. But not all of them. There were so many on the night shift that even their vastly reduced number is too many to dispose of. And they act like they know it. They roam around my feet with attitude, as if to make it clear that I'm trespassing on their turf.

My next set of challenges will arise not from the insect world, but from my neighbours. I'm the new arrival, subject to scrutiny about my charges just like when I'd run into the Aryan Brotherhood prison gang on my first day at the medium-security Towers jail a year ago. I wish my cellmate would wake up, brief me on the mood of the locals and introduce me to the head of the white gang. No such luck. Chow is announced over a speaker system in a crackly robotic voice, but he doesn't stir.

I emerge into the day room for breakfast. Prisoners in black-and-white bee-striped uniforms gather under the metal-grid stairs and tip dead cockroaches into a trash bin from plastic peanut-butter containers they'd set as traps during the night. All eyes are on me in the chow line. Watching who sits where, I hold my head up, put on a solid stare and pretend to be as at home in this environment as the cockroaches. It's all an act. I'm lonely and afraid. I loathe having to explain myself to the head of the white race, who I assume is the toughest murderer. I've been in jail long enough to know that taking my breakfast to my cell will imply that I have something to hide.

The gang punishes criminals with certain charges. The most serious are sex offenders, who are KOS: Kill On Sight. Other charges are punishable by SOS – Smash On Sight – such as drive-by shootings because women and kids sometimes get killed. It's called convict justice. Gang members are constantly looking for people to beat up because that's how they earn their reputations and tattoos. The most serious acts of violence earn the highest-ranking tattoos. To be a full gang member requires murder. I've observed the body language and techniques inmates trying to integrate employ. An inmate with a spring in his step and an air of confidence is likely to be accepted. A person who avoids eye contact and fails to introduce himself to the gang is likely to be preyed on. Some of the failed attempts I saw ended up with heads getting cracked against toilets, a sound I've grown familiar with. I've seen prisoners being extracted on stretchers who looked dead – one had yellow fluid leaking from his head. The constant violence gives me nightmares, but the reality is that I put myself in here, so I force myself to accept it as a part of my punishment.

It's time to apply my knowledge. With a self-assured stride, I take my breakfast bag to the table of white inmates covered in neo-Nazi tattoos, allowing them to question me.

"Mind if I sit with you guys?" I ask, glad exhaustion has deepened my voice.

"These seats are taken. But you can stand at the corner of the table."

The man who answered is probably the head of the gang. I size him up. Cropped brown hair. A dangerous glint in Nordic-blue eyes. Tiny pupils that suggest he's on heroin. Weightlifter-type veins bulging from a sturdy neck. Political ink on arms crisscrossed with scars. About the same age as me, thirty-three.

"Thanks. I'm Shaun from England." I volunteer my origin to show I'm different from them but not in a way that might get me smashed.

"I'm Bullet, the head of the whites." He offers me his fist to bump. "Where you roll in from, wood?"

Addressing me as wood is a good sign. It's what white gang members on a friendly basis call each other.

"Towers jail. They increased my bond and re-classified me to maximum security."

"What's your bond at?"

"I've got two $750,000 bonds," I say in a monotone. This is no place to brag about bonds.

"How many people you kill, brother?" His eyes drill into mine, checking whether my body language supports my story. My body language so far is spot on.

"None. I threw rave parties. They got us talking about drugs on wiretaps." Discussing drugs on the phone does not warrant a $1.5 million bond. I know and beat him to his next question. "Here's my charges." I show him my charge sheet, which includes conspiracy and leading a crime syndicate – both from running an Ecstasy ring.

Bullet snatches the paper and scrutinises it. Attempting to pre-empt his verdict, the other whites study his face. On edge, I wait for him to respond. Whatever he says next will determine whether I'll be accepted or victimised.

"Are you some kind of jailhouse attorney?" Bullet asks. "I want someone to read through my case paperwork." During our few minutes of conversation, Bullet has seen through my act and concluded that I'm educated – a possible resource to him.

I appreciate that he'll accept me if I take the time to read his case. "I'm no jailhouse attorney, but I'll look through it and help you however I can."

"Good. I'll stop by your cell later on, wood."

After breakfast, I seal as many of the cracks in the walls as I can with toothpaste. The cell smells minty, but the cockroaches still find their way in. Their day shift appears to be collecting information on the brown paper bags under my bunk, containing a few items of food that I purchased from the commissary; bags that I tied off with rubber bands in the hope of keeping the cockroaches out. Relentlessly, the cockroaches explore the bags for entry points, pausing over and probing the most worn and vulnerable regions. *Will the nightly swarm eat right through the paper?* I read all morning, wondering whether my cellmate has died in his cocoon, his occasional breathing sounds reassuring me.

Bullet stops by late afternoon and drops his case paperwork off. He's been charged with Class 3 felonies and less, not serious crimes, but is facing a double-digit sentence because of his prior convictions and Security Threat Group status in the prison system. The proposed sentencing range seems disproportionate. I'll advise him to reject the plea bargain – on the assumption he already knows to do so, but is just seeking the comfort of a second opinion, like many un-sentenced inmates. When he returns for his paperwork, our conversation disturbs my cellmate – the cocoon shuffles – so we go upstairs to his cell. I tell Bullet what I think. He is excitable, a different man from earlier, his pupils almost non-existent.

"This case ain't shit. But my prosecutor knows I done other shit, all kinds of heavy shit, but can't prove it. I'd do anything to get that sorry bitch off my fucking ass. She's asking for something bad to happen to her. Man, if I ever get bonded out, I'm gonna chop that bitch into pieces. Kill her slowly though. Like to work her over with a blowtorch."

Such talk can get us both charged with conspiring to murder a prosecutor, so I try to steer him elsewhere. "It's crazy how they can catch you doing one thing, yet try to sentence you for all of the things they think you've ever done."

"Done plenty. Shot some dude in the stomach once. Rolled him up in a blanket and threw him in a dumpster."

Discussing past murders is as unsettling as future ones. "So what's all your tattoos mean, Bullet? Like that eagle on your chest?"

"Why you wanna know?" Bullet's eyes probe mine.

My eyes hold their ground. "Just curious."

"It's a war bird. The AB patch."

"AB patch?"

"What the Aryan Brotherhood gives you when you've put enough work in."

"How long does it take to earn a patch?"

"Depends how quickly you put your work in. You have to earn your lightning bolts first."

"Why you got red and black lightning bolts?"

"You get SS bolts for beating someone down or for being an

enforcer for the family. Red lightning bolts for killing someone. I was sent down as a youngster. They gave me steel and told me who to handle and I handled it. You don't ask questions. You just get blood on your steel. Dudes who get these tats without putting work in are told to cover them up or leave the yard."

"What if they refuse?"

"They're held down and we carve the ink off them."

Imagining them carving a chunk of flesh to remove a tattoo, I cringe. He's really enjoying telling me this now. His volatile nature is clear and frightening. *He's accepted me too much. He's trying to impress me before making demands.*

At night, I'm unable to sleep. Cocooned in heat, surrounded by cockroaches, I hear the swamp-cooler vent – a metal grid at the top of a wall – hissing out tepid air. Giving up on sleep, I put my earphones on and tune into National Public Radio. Listening to a Vivaldi violin concerto, I close my eyes and press my tailbone down to straighten my back as if I'm doing a yogic relaxation. The playful allegro thrills me, lifting my spirits, but the wistful adagio provokes sad emotions and tears. I open my eyes and gaze into the gloom. Due to lack of sleep, I start hallucinating and hearing voices over the music whispering threats. I'm at breaking point. Although I have accepted that I committed crimes and deserve to be punished, no one should have to live like this. I'm furious at myself for making the series of reckless decisions that put me in here and for losing absolutely everything. As violins crescendo in my ears, I remember what my life used to be like.

WAR ON DRUGS TRILOGY BOOK 1

PABLO ESCOBAR: BEYOND NARCOS

The mind-blowing true story of Pablo Escobar and the Medellín Cartel beyond their portrayal on Netflix.

Colombian drug lord Pablo Escobar was a devoted family man and a psychopathic killer; a terrible enemy, yet a wonderful friend. While donating millions to the poor, he bombed and tortured his enemies – some had their eyeballs removed with hot spoons. Through ruthless cunning and America's insatiable appetite for cocaine, he became a multi-billionaire, who lived in a $100-million house with its own zoo.

Demolishes the standard good versus evil telling of Pablo's story. The authorities were not hunting Pablo down to stop his cocaine business. They were taking over it.

WAR ON DRUGS TRILOGY
BOOK 3

WE ARE BEING LIED TO: THE WAR ON DRUGS

A collection of harrowing, action-packed and interlinked true stories that demonstrate the devastating consequences of drug prohibition.

PARTY TIME

In *Party Time*, Shaun Attwood arrives in Phoenix, Arizona a penniless business graduate from a small industrial town in England. Within a decade, he becomes a stock-market millionaire.

But he is leading a double life.

After taking his first Ecstasy pill at a rave in Manchester as a shy student, Shaun becomes intoxicated by the party lifestyle that changes his fortune. Making it his personal mission to bring the English rave scene to the Arizona desert, Shaun becomes submerged in a criminal underworld, throwing parties for thousands of ravers and running an Ecstasy ring in competition with the Mafia mass murderer "Sammy The Bull" Gravano.

As greed and excess tear through his life, Shaun experiences eye-watering encounters with Mafia hit men and crystal-meth addicts, extravagant debaucheries with superstar DJs and glitter girls, and ingests enough drugs to kill a herd of elephants. This is his story.

HARD TIME 2ND EDITION

As a teenager in an industrial UK town, Shaun Attwood covets the American Dream. He moves to Arizona with only student credit cards and becomes a millionaire. After throwing Ecstasy parties for thousands of ravers, Shaun bumps heads with Sammy the Bull Gravano, an Italian Mafia mass murderer, who puts a hit out on him.

The dream turns into a nightmare when a SWAT team smashes Shaun's door down. Inside Arizona's deadliest jail, Shaun struggles to survive against an unpredictable backdrop of gang violence and sickening human-rights violations. Over time and bolstered by the love and support of his fiancée and family, he uses incarceration for learning and introspection.

With a tiny pencil sharpened on a cell door, Shaun documents the conditions: dead rats in the food, cockroaches crawling in his ears at night, murders and riots... Smuggled out of maximum-security and posted online, his writing shines the international media spotlight on the plight of the prisoners in Sheriff Joe Arpaio's jail.

Join best-selling author Shaun Attwood on a harrowing voyage into the darkest recesses of human existence in *Hard Time*, the second book from the English Shaun trilogy.

PRISON TIME

Sentenced to 9½ years in Arizona's state prison for distributing Ecstasy, Shaun finds himself living among gang members, sexual predators and drug-crazed psychopaths. After being attacked by a Californian biker in for stabbing a girlfriend, Shaun writes about the prisoners who befriend, protect and inspire him. They include T-Bone, a massive African American ex-Marine who risks his life saving vulnerable inmates from rape, and Two Tonys, an old-school Mafia murderer who left the corpses of his rivals from Arizona to Alaska. They teach Shaun how to turn incarceration to his advantage, and to learn from his mistakes.

Shaun is no stranger to love and lust in the heterosexual world, but the tables are turned on him inside. Sexual advances come at him from all directions, some cleverly disguised, others more sinister – making Shaun question his sexual identity.

Resigned to living alongside violent, mentally-ill and drug-addicted inmates, Shaun immerses himself in psychology and philosophy to try to make sense of his past behaviour, and begins applying what he learns as he adapts to prison life. Encouraged by Two Tonys to explore fiction as well, Shaun reads over 1000 books which, with support from a brilliant psychotherapist, Dr Owen, speed along his personal development. As his ability to deflect daily threats improves, Shaun begins to look forward to his release with optimism and a new love waiting for him. Yet the words of Aristotle from one of Shaun's books will prove prophetic: "We cannot learn without pain."

ABOUT SHAUN ATTWOOD

Shaun Attwood is a former stock-market millionaire and Ecstasy supplier turned public speaker, author and activist, who is banned from America for life. His story was featured worldwide on National Geographic Channel as an episode of Locked Up/ Banged Up Abroad called Raving Arizona (available on YouTube).

Shaun's writing – smuggled out of the jail with the highest death rate in America run by Sheriff Joe Arpaio – attracted international media attention to the human rights violations: murders by guards and gang members, dead rats in the food, cockroach infestations…

While incarcerated, Shaun was forced to reappraise his life. He read over 1,000 books in just under six years. By studying original texts in psychology and philosophy, he sought to better understand himself and his past behaviour. He credits books as being the lifeblood of his rehabilitation.

Shaun now tells his story to schools to put young people off drugs and crime. He campaigns against injustice via his books and blog, Jon's Jail Journal. He has appeared on the BBC, Sky News and TV worldwide to talk about issues affecting prisoners' rights.

CPSIA information can be obtained
at www.ICGtesting.com
Printed in the USA
LVHW080419100721
692359LV00006B/11